COMPUTER LOGIC

Springer

New York
Berlin
Heidelberg
Barcelona
Hong Kong
London
Milan
Paris
Singapore
Tokyo

John Y. Hsu

COMPUTER LOGIC

Design Principles and Applications

With 67 Illustrations

Springer

John Y. Hsu
Department of Computer Science
California Polytechnic State University
San Luis Obispo, CA 93407
USA
jyhsu@calpoly.edu

Library of Congress Cataloging-in-Publication Data
Hsu, John Y.
    Computer logic : design principles and applications / John Y. Hsu.
        p. cm.
    Includes bibliographical references and index.
    ISBN 0-387-95304-3 (alk. paper)
    1. Computer logic.   I. Title.
QA76.9.L63 H758 2002
005.1′01′5113—dc21   2001057679

Printed on acid-free paper.

Production managed by Lesley Poliner; manufacturing supervised by Joseph
Quatela.
Composition by MATRIX Publishing Services, Inc., York, PA.
Printed and bound by Hamilton Printing Co., Rensselaer, NY.
Printed in the United States of America.

9 8 7 6 5 4 3 2 1

ISBN 0-387-95304-3   SPIN 10839029

Springer-Verlag New York Berlin Heidelberg
A member of BertelsmanSpringer Science+Business Media GmbH

Dedicated to the memory of my parents,
James and Margaret Hsu,
and to my late classmate at the Electrical Engineering Department
of National Taiwan University, Bob Chen, who encouraged me
to study computers forty years ago.

Contents

Preface

Motive for Writing This Book

My first two computer books were written in reverse order as technical depth is concerned. However, my job is not done unless I write a book on computer logic. As any good teacher might say, it is often the lack of basic knowledge that keeps readers from understanding more advanced books. For this reason, I have attempted in this volume to write the basics about computer logic, flash memory, semiconductor processes, noise, logic simulations, and Verilog. It is imperative to acquire knowledge of computer logic prior to learning computer architecture or programming. Just like practicing marshal arts, learning computers is a step-by-step process and there is no shortcut. This book is written for those who wish to pursue a career in computing or to design logic.

Who Should Read This Book

This book emphasizes computer logic, including theories, design principles, implementations, and applications. Readers should know binary number systems, number conversions, Boolean algebra, combinational logic circuits, semiconductor memories, and sequential circuits before learning the detailed functions of a central processing unit (CPU) in a digital computer. If desired, a reader can take a programming language course concurrently.

The intended audience of this book includes:

- Undergraduate students of computer science. (The selected topics in this book can be covered in 30 to 45 hours of lectures.)
- Undergraduate students of computer engineering and electrical engineering.
- Professionals in the electronics industry.

After learning about logic circuits and semiconductor memories, a reader can go on to study more about computer architectures, software system design, and computer networks.

Organization of This Book

This book is divided into five chapters that primarily cover number systems, Boolean algebra, transistors, combinational logic circuits, and sequential logic circuits. A brief description of each chapter follows.

The first chapter covers the history of computing devices, various number systems, positional notation, binary numbers, hexadecimal numbers, number conversions, signed numbers, biased numbers, and external codes.

Chapter 2 focuses on Boolean algebra, basic laws, basic theorems, the dual theorem, the DeMorgan theorem, exclusive OR theorems, the parity theorem, algebraic simplifications, Karnaugh maps, don't cares, and logic implementations.

Chapter 3 is devoted to the practical design aspects of electronic circuits. Because many transistors are placed on an integrated circuit (IC) chip nowadays, it is vital to acquire some basic knowledge about electronics. Some important topics include semiconductor processes, scale of integration, bipolar transistors, unipolar transistors, and logic circuits. Circuit design examples are provided, such as inverters, NAND gates, NOR gates, and EOR gates. Copper interconnect technology, signal waveforms, timing delays, noise, reliability, and compatibility are also discussed.

Chapter 4 mainly covers combinational logic circuits. The design of logic gates, decoders, encoders, multiplexers, binary adders, comparators, multiplication trees, programmable logic arrays, semiconductor memories, and others are discussed. The design principles of a programmable logic array and nonvolatile flash memory are also explained.

Chapter 5, the last chapter, provides the functional descriptions of flip-flops, sequential logic circuits, and specific applied integrated circuits. Some of the topics covered in this chapter include the characteristic equations of a flip-flop, registers, shift registers, binary counters, decade counters, switch-tail counters, finite state machines, state transition diagrams, and excitation tables. Furthermore, we introduce Hardware Description Language (HDL), logic simulation software tools, and Verilog.

Sources and References

The acronyms and abbreviations, logic symbols and equations, references, and index are presented at the end of the book. All references are sorted in alphabetical order and each is formatted in square brackets according to the following rules:

1. A reference name for a book or article has the first four letters of the author's last name appended by the last two digits of the year the document was published. A full article name is enclosed in double quotes with page numbers placed in parentheses at the end of the notation.
2. A standard or product is noted by a proprietary name with or without a model number.
3. To differentiate between distinct notes, it is sometimes necessary to add a suffix to note numbers (such as a, b, c).

Acknowledgments

This book, in part or whole, was reviewed by many wonderful individuals. My students Diller Ryan, Zetri Prasetyo, Kurt Voelker, Francis Shaw, and Delora Sowle all offered helpful advice on the presentation of the text. I salute all the reviewers who helped me shape the manuscript to its final form. Some of their names and affiliations are: Alan Beverly (Ziatech-Intel), Wesley Chu (UCLA), Fred Depiero (Cal Poly), Lin-Shan Lee (National Taiwan University), Miroslaw Malek (Humboldt University, Germany), C. Ramamoorthy (UC, Berkeley), Linda Vanasupa (Cal Poly), Changyu Wu (IBM), and Xuelung Zhu (Tsinghua University, Bejing). The wonderful assistance of Wayne Yuhasz and his project team at Springer-Verlag deserves recognition. Finally, I wish to thank my ole taiTai, Sheryl Lyn, for her looking, thinking, and cooking.

John Y. Hsu
San Luis Obipso

CHAPTER 1

Introduction

1.1 Prolog

In the history of computing, mechanical devices were invented before electronic devices. In 1642 in France, Blaise Pascal invented a gear-driven machine named "Pascalene"; it was the first calculator to perform arithmetic [Comp96]. In 1833, the Englishman Charles Babbage created the Analytical engine, which was used to calculate and print mathematical tables. In fact, Babbage conceived the idea of a stored-program computer in which all the numbers and instructions were entered before a computation could begin. In 1889, the Electric Tabulating Machine was invented by Herman Hollerith in the United States; it was the very first data-processing machine, and it was used to tabulate the 1890 census.

A digital computer is an electronic machine that is used for computations and information retrieval. In 1946, the first electronic computer, ENAIC, was implemented by J. P. Echkert and J. Mauchly at the Moore School of the University of Pennsylvania. This machine contained 18,000 vacuum tubes and weighed 30 tons. Although ENAIC could perform fast mathematical computations, it had to pause for each instruction to be entered in real time by its human operators. Later, John von Neumann revised the stored-program concept that was first introduced by Babbage. Neumann, Arthur Burks, and Herman Goldstine published the report, "Preliminary discussion of the logical design of an electronic computing instrument" [Burk46].

A simplified block diagram of a digital computer is shown in Figure 1.1. A computer has three major hardware components. The first component is the CPU (central processing unit), whose function is to process data. The second component is the central memory, or memory, whose function is to store all the information or data during computation. The third component is the I/O (input/output) controller. An I/O controller operates very much like a small processing unit whose function is to control and communicate with I/O devices, including keyboard, monitor, mouse, hard disk, floppy disk, and printer.

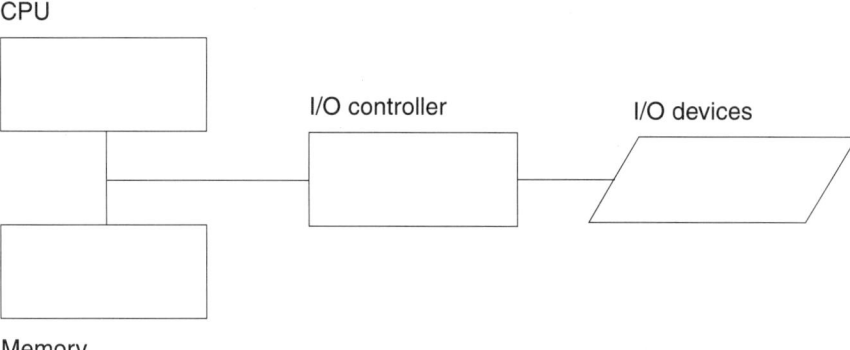

Figure 1.1. Simplified block diagram of a digital computer.

The central memory is also called the internal memory; it is very fast. In contrast, a removable or non-removable disk is considered external memory and is also called an intermediate storage device. Many wires are used to connect two hardware components. The wires may be etched on a PC (printed circuit) board or bundled together in a cable. While the CPU is in operation, it constantly interacts with the central memory by varying the voltage levels on the wires. The wires connected to the memory are called the memory bus. The voltage signals on the memory bus, high or low, collectively tell the memory module what to do. The voltage on each wire has only two levels, and each signal received by the memory module has two possible levels. For example, a high voltage 5 v. (volt) may represent a signal one and a low voltage (0 v.) a signal zero. The CPU places digital signals on the wires or bus in the form of combinations of ones and zeros.

Interestingly, all the hardware components in a computer use logic circuits in dealing with ones and zeros. The logic circuits may be complicated, but the basic design principles are simple and intuitive. This chapter is intended to introduce the digital concept; positional notation; binary and hexadecimal numbers; conversions; unsigned, signed, and biased integers; binary coded decimals; external code, and digitizing. Subsequent chapters will cover the design of logic circuits in more detail.

1.2 Digital Concept

A digital computer uses two electronic voltage levels to represent a bit (binary digit). It is possible for us to use 3.3 v. to represent one and 0 v. to represent zero. As a matter of fact, a mechanical switch in Figure

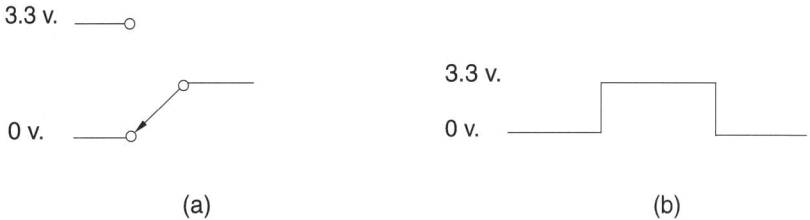

Figure 1.2. Digital concept: (a) binary switch and (b) low-high-low digital signal.

1.2(a) can be used to store one bit. If the switch position is down, its output is 0 v., that is, ground voltage. If the switch position is up, its output is 3.3 v. If we hold down the switch for a while, flip the switch up for a while, and then put it back down, its output is a pulse that starts with a low voltage, followed by a high voltage, and then a low voltage, as depicted in Figure 1.2(b). The time duration of a low-high-low pulse signal indicates the speed of the switch. In practice, we can implement this switch by electronic circuits that operate at a much higher switching speed.

1.3   Number Systems

We can use our fingers to count a decimal number between one and ten, provided the digit starts with one. Because in a computer all information and data of various types are represented in binary, we must discuss some notations that can be used to represent the bits.

1.3.1   POSITIONAL NOTATION

The *positional notation* is developed to represent a positive number of a given base in our society. Let B be a positive integer; any integer A may be written in a positional notation as shown here:

$$A = C_n * B^n + C_{n-1} * B^{n-1} + \ldots + C_1 * B^1 + C_0 * B^0 = \sum_{i=0}^{n} C_i * B^i$$

where C_i is the coefficient of the ith term under the condition such that $0 \leq C_i < B$. All the symbols can be typed on a computer keyboard as defined here:

1. The symbol * indicates multiply.
2. The symbol + means add.

3. The symbol $\leq$ indicates less than or equal to.
4. The symbol $>$ indicates greater than.

The positive integer B is referred to as the *base* or *radix*. The same set of coefficients may represent a different value if the base is different. In positional notation, note that A and B are the names of two integers. We compute a positive integer A of any base B in decimal as a reference point for number conversions. To generalize the concept, any positive integer of base B may be written in an abbreviated positional notation as follows:

$$C_{j-1} \ldots C_0 {}_B$$

In this notation, C_0 is the least significant digit and C_j is the leading nonzero digit. If the base B is omitted from the notation, the default base is 10, that is, decimal. In such a system, each coefficient is a decimal digit. A binary system uses base 2, so each coefficient is a bit. A hex (hexadecimal) system uses base 16, so each coefficient is a hex digit.

1.3.2 DECIMAL NUMBERS

Our society uses a decimal system, that is, base 10, so the decimal number 1111 has a value as computed here:

$$1111 = 1 * 10^3 + 1 * 10^2 + 1 * 10^1 + 1 * 10^0$$
$$= 1 * 1000 + 1 * 100 + 1 * 10 + 1$$

Here, each coefficient or decimal digit carries a weight. The rightmost digit carries a weight of 1, that is, 10^0, where the symbol ^ is an exponential operator for easy keyboard input. The second digit from the right has a weight of 10 (10^1), the third digit has a weight of 100 (10^2), and the fourth digit has a weight of 1000 (10^3). We call the number one thousand, one hundred, eleven. Our society has evolved to use the base 10 system because we can represent a decimal number using our 10 fingers. When a logic circuit is concerned, the base 2 system is not only elegant, it's also easier to implement.

1.3.3 BINARY NUMBERS

The number 1111 in binary has a different value, as computed here:

$$1111_2 = 1 * 2^3 + 1 * 2^2 + 1 * 2^1 + 1 * 2^0$$
$$= 8 + 4 + 2 + 1 = 15$$

As we can see, the 4-bit 1111 represents a positive integer, that is, unsigned 15. If we add two 4-bit unsigned integers 7 and 8, the sum would be unsigned 15, as shown here:

$$
\begin{array}{r}
0111 \\
1000 \\
+)\underline{} \\
1111
\end{array}
$$

Each 4-bit number is a string of ones and zeros, and the sum is another string of ones and zeros. A *bit string* is an ordered sequence of ones and zeros whose length determines the number of combinations. Even though the 2-bit strings may look the same, they may represent different information, as determined by how to use them. Because binary numbers start with zero, computers use zeros to index and our society uses ones to index. The logic circuits in a computer can be used to process or store bits. For example, a 16-bit adder can add any two 16-bit numbers to generate a sum.

1.3.4 HEXADECIMAL NUMBERS

In a hex number system, we use 16 different symbols to represent the hex digits. Because we use the 10 decimal digits to represent the first 10 hex digits, we need 6 more symbols. One convenient answer is to use the first six letters: A, B, C, D, E, F. Therefore, hex number A is 10, B is 11, C is 12, D is 13, E is 14, and F is 15. Because 16 means hexadecimal, it is common to replace base 16 with x (hex). Hence, 1111_{16} can be written as 1111_x; its value is computed here:

$$
\begin{aligned}
1111_{16} &= 1 * 16^3 + 1 * 16^2 + 1 * 16^1 + 1 * 16^0 \\
&= 4096 + 256 + 16 + 1 = 4369
\end{aligned}
$$

In hex, 1111 is counted as four thousand, three hundred, sixty nine in decimal. Let us use 4 bits to represent an unsigned integer. Because each bit can be one or zero, the total number of combinations is 16 (2^4). The 4-bit number has a decimal value that ranges from 0 to 15. We use 4-bit 0 to represent 0. To represent 1, we add 1 to 0000 and obtain 0001. To represent 2, we add 1 to 0001 to obtain 0010. In the arithmetic operation, each bit cannot be more than 1, so the sum bit is 0 and a carry bit is added to the next bit. Given four bits, we list all 16 numbers in bases 10, 2, and 16 in Table 1.1.

If a binary number is too long it may be hard to visualize. To solve this problem, the binary number can be displayed in hexadecimal with each hex digit representing 4 bits in a compact manner. In the next sec-

Table 1.1. First 16 numbers of bases 10, 2, and 16.

Decimal	Binary	Hexadecimal
0	0000	0
1	0001	1
2	0010	2
3	0011	3
4	0100	4
5	0101	5
6	0110	6
7	0111	7
8	1000	8
9	1001	9
10	1010	A
11	1011	B
12	1100	C
13	1101	D
14	1110	E
15	1111	F

tion, we will study how to convert an unsigned integer from decimal to binary or hex.

1.4   Number Conversions

If we know the positional notation, we can convert a positive integer A into a number of any base B. One method of conversion is the divide algorithm:

Given a base as B and a number as N;
REPEAT
Dividing N by B, we obtain a quotient and a remainder;
The remainder is collected as the next digit of base B counting from the rightmost end;
Set N to the value of the quotient;
UNTIL the number named N is zero;

This algorithm is further explained in the following. Recall that the positive integer A of base B can be represented as

$$A = C_j * B^j + C_{j-1} * B^{j-1} + \ldots + C_0 * B_0$$

The positive integer A has a decimal value as reference, even if it is written in binary or any other base. Our challenge is to convert A to a number of any base B and to determine the coefficients in its new positional notation. If the integer A is written in decimal, we can easily perform the arithmetic divide operations in decimal. Thus, dividing A by B, we obtain both the quotient and the remainder, as follows:

$$Q1 = C_j * B^{j-1} + C_{j-1} * B^{j-2} + \ldots + C_1$$
$$R1 = C_0$$

where $Q1$ is the quotient and $R1$ is the remainder, that is, C_0. Dividing the quotient $Q1$ again by B, we obtain the quotient $Q2$ and the remainder $R2$ or C_1. We repeat this process until the quotient is 0, and we collect all the remainders, or coefficients, and lay them from right to left in sequential order as follows:

$$C_j\ C_{j-1} \ldots C_2\ C_1\ C_{0\ B}$$

1.4.1 DECIMAL TO BINARY

In the following, we convert 1111_{10} to a 16-bit binary number:

2	1111	$1 = C_0$
2	555	$1 = C_1$
2	277	$1 = C_2$
2	138	$0 = C_3$
2	69	$1 = C_4$
2	34	$0 = C_5$
2	17	$1 = C_6$
2	8	$0 = C_7$
2	4	$0 = C_8$
2	2	$0 = C_9$
2	1	$1 = C_{10}$
	0	

After the division is completed, we collect the remainders:

$$1111_{10} = 0000\ 0100\ 0101\ 0111_2$$
$$= 0\ 4\ 5\ 7_x$$

The spaces inserted between the digits are for clarification only. The hex number on the second line can be obtained by the same divide algorithm using base 16. That is, divide 16 into the decimal number repeatedly and collect the remainders in hex. Interestingly, we should be able to obtain the hex number from the binary number by inspection. By grouping four bits from right to left and evaluating its value, we can write down the hex digit directly. When computer information is concerned, a string of ones and zeros on paper is hard to read. As an alternative, we often write the number in hex. That is, from each hex digit we can picture the four bits it represents.

1.4.2 BINARY TO HEX

The mathematics to convert a binary number to hex is explained as follows. Given 16 bits, an unsigned integer A can be represented by the following positional notation:

$$A = C_{15} * 2^{15} + C_{15-1} * 2^{15-1} + \ldots + C_1 * 2^1 + C_0$$

Each bit C_i in the notation can be 1 or 0. Dividing A by 2^4, we obtain a remainder and a quotient as shown here:

$$R1 = C_3 * 2^3 + C_2 * 2^2 + C_1 * 2^1 + C_0$$
$$Q1 = C_{15} * 2^{11} + C_{14} * 2^{10} + \ldots + C_5 * 2^1 + C_4$$

The remainder $R1$ has the rightmost four terms in the positional notation. Dividing the quotient $Q1$ by 2^4 again, we obtain a remainder and a quotient as shown here:

$$R2 = C_7 * 2^3 + C_6 * 2^2 + C_5 * 2^1 + C_4$$
$$Q2 = C_{15} * 2^7 + C_{14} * 2^6 + \ldots + C_9 * 2^1 + C_8$$

Henceforth, in a given bit string we can group each four bits from the right. Evaluating the value of the 4-bit positional notation in the group, we obtain a hex digit. Thus, a 16-bit number has four groups, and each group has four bits:

$$C_{15}C_{14}C_{13}C_{12} \quad C_{11}C_{10}C_9C_8 \quad C_7C_6C_5C_4 \quad C_3C_2C_1C_0$$

Evaluating the 4-bit positional notation within each group, we obtain the four hex digits of base 2^4 as follows:

$$(C_{15} * 2^3 + C_{14} * 2^2 + C_{13} * 2^1 + C_{12}) \, (\ldots) \, (\ldots)$$
$$(C_3 * 2^3 \, C_2 * 2^2 + C_1 * 2^1 + C_0)$$

We try one more example, to convert 145_{10} to binary and then to hex:

$$
\begin{array}{r|l}
2 & 145 \\ \hline
2 & 72 \\ \hline
2 & 36 \\ \hline
2 & 18 \\ \hline
2 & 9 \\ \hline
2 & 4 \\ \hline
2 & 2 \\ \hline
 & 1 \\ \hline
 & 0
\end{array}
\qquad
\begin{array}{l}
1 = C_0 \\
0 = C_1 \\
0 = C_2 \\
0 = C_3 \\
1 = C_4 \\
0 = C_5 \\
0 = C_6 \\
1 = C_7
\end{array}
$$

Therefore, we have

$$
\begin{aligned}
145 &= 1001\ 0001_2 \\
    &= 91_x
\end{aligned}
$$

1.4.3   HEX TO BINARY

In practice, we often convert a decimal number to hex and then to binary. Converting the decimal number 145 to hex is easy. Dividing 145 by 16, we obtain a remainder of 1 and a quotient of 9. Because the quotient 9 is smaller than 16, we quit here because 9 is the next remainder. Hence, the decimal 145 is 91 in hex. Each hex digit represents four bits, so 9 means 1001 and 1 means 0001. We conclude that 91 in hex is equal to 1001 0001 in binary.

1.5   Unsigned Integers Vs. Signed Integers

Assume that we use n bits to represent a binary number. Each bit can be either a 1 or a 0, so we obtain a total of 2^n combinations. If the bit string is treated as an unsigned integer, then its value is always positive, ranging from 0 to (2^{n-1}). Take 4 bits as an example; the unsigned integer has a positive value from 0 to 15. However, if we treat the bit string as a signed integer, we change the definition so that a positive signed integer must start with a sign bit 0. That is, the msb (most significant bit) indicates the sign of an integer.

1.5.1   POSITIVE INTEGERS

If a bit string is treated as an unsigned integer, it always has a positive value regardless of its sign. However, if the bit string is treated as a signed integer, only a leading bit zero indicates a positive integer. Therefore, after the sign bit zero we place a sequence of bits whose positional notation determines its value. In other words, in order to represent a signed integer, we divide all the bit pattern combinations into two halves. The first half consists of positive integers with a sign bit 0, and the second half consists of negative integers with a sign bit 1.

1.5.2 NEGATIVE INTEGERS

In a computer, a negative integer is represented by twos complement notation that can be obtained in two logical steps as follows:

1. Flip each bit in the positive integer including the sign, to obtain its so-called ones complement form.
2. Add one to this form to obtain its so-called twos complement form.

We may not think the twos complement notation is intuitive, but machines like it. We came up with this great idea after two generations of computer design.

Definition 1.1. A *negative integer in twos complement notation* means taking the ones complement and adding one to it, as shown here:

---

twos complement = ones complement + 1

Using 4-bit arithmetic, we have a signed integer whose value ranges from -8 to 7. Note that the bit string 1000 represents -8 instead of $+8$. The twos complement notation has two advantages. First, after adding two signed numbers, if there is a carry generated from the most significant bit position, we simply discard the carry. The result is correct as long as it is within the range of what the bit string can represent. Second, it has a unique representation of 0: $+0$ or -0. By complementing all zeros in an integer of 4, 16, or 32 bits and adding 1 to the result, we obtain a bit string of zeros. This means that the signed integer -1 in a computer has all binary ones, regardless of whether the length is 16 bits or 32 bits.

Interestingly, taking the twos complement of a positive integer also means negating the integer. How can we convert a negative integer to positive? By taking its twos complement. Thus, by taking the twos complement of a positive integer, we obtain the negative integer. Similarly, by taking the twos complement of a negative integer, we obtain the positive integer. Logically, we tend to think that we should first subtract 1 from the negative integer and then take its ones complement. However, this is the same as taking its ones complement and adding 1:

---

subtract 1 and take ones complement
= take ones complement and add 1

As shown in Figure 1.3, we take the twos complement of an integer to negate, or change the sign, back and forth. Two examples are used to illustrate the novel concept of twos complement arithmetic. First, let us find the 16-bit representations for +25, −25, +26, and −26. Using the conversion-by-divide algorithm, we first convert each decimal number to binary. If the number is negative, then we take its ones complement and add 1. We have

$$
\begin{array}{rl}
+25 & 0000\ 0000\ 0001\ 1001 \\
     & 1111\ 1111\ 1110\ 0110 \leftarrow \text{ones complement} \\
+) & \underline{\hspace{8cm} 1} \\
-25 & 1111\ 1111\ 1110\ 0111 \leftarrow \text{twos complement} \\
+26 & 0000\ 0000\ 0001\ 1010 \\
     & 1111\ 1111\ 1110\ 0101 \leftarrow \text{ones complement} \\
+) & \underline{\hspace{8cm} 1} \\
-26 & 1111\ 1111\ 1110\ 0110 \leftarrow \text{twos complement}
\end{array}
$$

After we convert a number from binary to hex, we use a 16-bit adder to add two 16-bit signed integers. The arithmetic adder is a logical device composed of many one-bit full adders. Each one-bit full adder can add three input bits and generate two output bits: the sum bit and the carry bit. All the one-bit full adders are interconnected so that an arithmetic sum is generated for the two integers given as input. All the arithmetic additions are performed in three bases: decimal, binary, and hex.

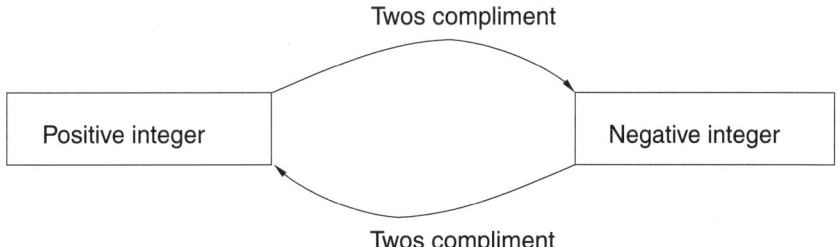

Figure 1.3. Taking twos complement means negate.

EXAMPLE 1.1: 26 − 26 = 0

	Decimal	Binary	Hex
	+26	0000 0000 0001 1010	001A
+)	−26	1111 1111 1110 0110	FFE6
	0	1 0000 0000 0000 0000	0000
		Carry discarded	

EXAMPLE 1.2: 25 − 26 = −1

	Decimal	Binary	Hex
	+25	0000 0000 0001 1001	0019
+)	−26	1111 1111 1110 0110	FFE6
	−1	1111 1111 1111 1111	FFFF

Easily negating a number is essential in computer design. Can we negate an integer easily using twos complement notation? The answer is yes. By using twos complement notation, the CPU can use one add cycle to subtract a signed integer from another signed integer via the adder. This is made possible because a one-bit full adder is placed at the lsb (least significant bit) position. This one-bit full adder has a Cin (Carry In) input that can be tied to 0 or 1. We can use the arithmetic adder to subtract B from A, where A and B are two signed integers, either positive or negative. The trick is to feed A to one input of the adder and the ones complement of B to the other input. At the same time, the Cin bit is turned on, so effectively the twos complement of B is added to A. In the case that A is 0, $-B$ becomes the negated output. If there is an end-around-carry generated, we simply discard the carry.

Serial Algorithm for Generating Twos Complement

A logic circuit may be designed to convert a binary number to its twos complement form, assuming that the bit stream arrives in a serial manner starting from the lsb. As each bit arrives, we can convert the bit right away based on the following algorithm:

```
loop1:
   IF the leading bit is 0,
   THEN DO;
      Copy bit 0 down;
      Goto loop1; ENDDO;
   ELSE copy bit 1 down; ENDIF;
loop2:
   REPEAT
   Complement all the subsequent bits arrived;
   UNTIL the entire bit string is received;
```

Table 1.2. Negating hex numbers.

16-bit number in hex	Twos complement in hex
1234	EDCC
FFFF	0001
00FF	FF01
0190	FE70

This algorithm converts a binary number serially starting from the lsb. Henceforth, search from right to left, bit by bit. If the trailing bit is 0, we copy it down. We copy all the trailing zeros until we encounter the first bit that is not 0. Then, we copy the first bit 1 down and complement the rest of the bits. Interestingly, this method works both ways, from positive to negative and vice versa.

Based on the same principle, we apply this method to negate a number written in hex. As we search from the rightmost digit to the left, we copy any hex digit 0, until we encounter the first hex digit that is not zero. Then we subtract its nonzero value from 16 and write the answer. We subtract the remaining digits, one by one, from 15 and write the answer until all the digits are converted. Some examples of hex number conversion are listed in Table 1.2.

In Table 1.2, the first row shows 1234 on the left-hand side and FDCC on the right. Because the rightmost digit is not 0, the sum of the two digits $(4 + C)$ is 16. For the rest of digits, the sum of each pair of digits is 15. The fourth row shows a number with a trailing 0. Therefore, we copy 0 until the first nonzero digit, 9, is encountered. We subtract 9 from 16 and write the answer, 7. By subtracting each of the rest digits from 15, we write E (15-1), then F (15-0) in that sequence.

To negate a 32-bit number, we also take its twos complement and add 1 to it. Thus, given 32 bits, we divide all the signed integers into two groups: the positive number group with a sign bit 0 and the negative number group with a sign bit 1. The most positive integer is $(2^{31} - 1)$, and the most negative integer in twos complement is -2^{31}.

Meaning of Sign Bit

By performing a direct subtraction on paper, we can also obtain the difference of two given numbers. Using 4-bit arithmetic, if the minuend is 0 and the subtrahend is 1, the difference is -1, as shown here:

```
  1 {borrow}
    0  0  0  0    {minuend}
  - 0  0  0  1    {subtrahend}
  ─────────────
    1  1  1  1    {difference}
```

This operation merely illustrates the direct subtraction concept and is not used by the CPU internally. The top row is the *minuend*, the second row is the *subtrahend*, and the third row is the *difference*. As we can see, the minuend is smaller than the subtrahend. Therefore, in concept we need to borrow a bit from the far left side of the minuend, and this borrow bit carries a weight of 16 (2^4). After subtracting 1 from 16, we obtain the difference as a bit string (1 1 1 1). Interestingly, this bit string represents the signed -1 or the unsigned 15. As shown here, by subtracting 7 from -1, we obtain -8 with no borrow:

$$
\begin{array}{r}
0 \ \{\text{no borrow}\} \\
1 \quad 1 \quad 1 \quad 1 \quad \{\text{minuend}\} \\
- \ 0 \quad 1 \quad 1 \quad 1 \quad \{\text{subtrahend}\} \\
\hline
1 \quad 0 \quad 0 \quad 0 \quad \{\text{difference}\}
\end{array}
$$

Let us examine the subtract operation from the viewpoint of encoding. In general, *encoding* means how to construct bits for a piece of information. Our thinking goes like this. If the minuend is 0, it can be decomposed as the sum of -8 and $+8$. Subtracting 1 from $+8$, we obtain 7 as represented by the lower three bits (1 1 1) in the difference. The -8 is left as the sign bit in the difference. That is, a sign bit 1 carries a negative weight in twos complement notation. The exact value of this weight is determined by the sign bit position in the positional notation. If 4 bits are given, the sign bit carries a weight of -8 (-2^3). We conclude the following two important points:

1. The sign bit carries a negative weight, and each bit to its right carries a positive weight.
2. The weight value of each bit is determined by its bit position in the positional notation.

In the following, we show two negative integers as extreme cases in 4-bit arithmetic:

1. The value of -1 is:

$$
\begin{aligned}
(1\ 1\ 1\ 1) &= -2^3 + 2^2 + 2^1 + 2^0 \\
&= -8 + 4 + 2 + 1 \\
&= -8 + 7 \\
&= -1
\end{aligned}
$$

2. By subtracting 7 from -1, we obtain -8:

$$
\begin{aligned}
(1\ 0\ 0\ 0) &= -2^3 + 0 * 2^2 + 0 * 2^1 + 0 * 2^0 \\
&= -8 + 0 + 0 + 0 \\
&= -8
\end{aligned}
$$

1.5.3   BIASED INTEGERS

A biased integer is obtained by adding a positive integer with a fixed value to a signed integer. Recall that -1 in a computer has all ones, regardless of the length of the bits. Let us use 4-bit arithmetic and say binary 1111 in twos complement notation represents -1. By adding a bias to all 4-bit signed numbers, we obtain a set of 4-bit biased numbers. If the bias is 7, that is, 0111 in binary, we obtain the biased signed integer in excess of 7. Thus, if the integer is positive, we add 7 to it. If the integer is negative, we also add 7 to it. To illustrate this concept, we show all 4-bit biased integers in excess of 7 in Table 1.3.

From Table 1.3, we see that the 4-bit 0000 $(-7 + 7)$ represents -7 and the 4-bit 0111 represents 0. In addition, the largest 4-bit 1111 $(8 + 7)$ is chosen to represent $+8$ instead of -8. In other words, we rearrange all the bit patterns from -7 to $+8$ so that all biased numbers are sorted in ascending order. This enables easy comparisons between two biased signed integers. The logic circuit compares two biased integers from left to right, bit by bit. If the leading two bits are equal, the next two bits must be compared. This process is repeated until the two bits differ. The integer with a bit 0 is smaller than the integer with a bit 1. If

Table 1.3. Four-bit biased integers.

Unsigned decimal	Binary	Integer in excess of 7
15	1111	+8
14	1110	+7
13	1101	+6
12	1100	+5
11	1011	+4
10	1010	+3
9	1001	+2
8	1000	+1
7	0111	0
6	0110	−1
5	0101	−2
4	0100	−3
3	0011	−4
2	0010	−5
1	0001	−6
0	0000	−7

all four bits are the same, then the two biased integers are equal. In essence, we turn the signed compare problem into an unsigned compare problem so that a simpler logic circuit is required. Other data representations in a computer can be decomposed into various fields, and each field is a bit string. As an example, a biased integer is used to represent the exponent part of a floating-point number [Hsu01].

1.5.4 BINARY CODED DECIMALS

For banking applications, an integer can be represented in the form of BCD (binary coded decimal) digits. There are two formats to construct a BCD digit: the packed format and the unpacked format. A packed BCD digit occupies 4 bits, and an unpacked BCD digit occupies 8 bits. A packed BCD number consists of many 4-bit fields. The leftmost 4-bit field is the sign, and the rest of the 4-bit fields are decimal digits. Usually, a sign of 4-bit zeros (0 in hex) means positive, and a sign of 4-bit ones (F in hex) means negative. In contrast, an unpacked BCD number consists of many 8-bit bytes. The leftmost 8-bit byte is the sign, and the rest of the 8-bit bytes are decimal digits. That is, an 8-bit sign is followed by many 8-bit BCD digits, and each byte is padded with 4 leading zeros. In the following, we discuss the representations of some 64-bit packed BCD numbers and 128-bit unpacked BCD numbers. Each number has a sign and 15 decimal digits.

EXAMPLE 1.3:

```
Decimal value        = +000  0000  0000  0000
Packed BCD in hex    = 0000  0000  0000  0000
Unpacked BCD in hex = 0000  0000  0000  0000  0000  0000
                      0000  0000
```

The given number is a positive 15-digit 0. In the packed format, a 4-bit sign 0 is followed by 15 BCD zero digits. The spaces inserted between digit groups here are for clarification. In the unpacked format, an 8-bit sign 0 is followed by 15 8-bit zero digits.

EXAMPLE 1.4:

```
Decimal value        = +200  0001  0000  0099
Packed BCD in hex    = 0200  0001  0000  0099
Unpacked BCD in hex = 0002  0000  0000  0001  0000  0000
                      0000  0909
```

In this example, a decimal point is assumed to exist before the last two digits. Therefore, the last two digits represent a monetary value in dimes and cents, so the number represents a monetary asset of two trillion, one million, and 99 cents.

EXAMPLE 1.5:

Decimal value $= -200$ 0001 0000 0099
Packed BCD in hex $= f200$ 0001 0000 0099
Unpacked BCD in hex $= 0f02$ 0000 0000 0001 0000 0000
0000 0909

Like the previous example, a decimal point is assumed to exist before the last two digits. In the packed format, the sign field has 4 ones. In the unpacked format, the sign field has 4 leading zeros followed by 4 ones. In either case, the given number represents a monetary debt of two trillion, one million, and 99 cents.

When packed BCD numbers are used in a computation, accuracy is guaranteed down to the cent level, a requirement in financial transactions. If a check is to be issued, a printer cannot accept a packed BCD number and print it. In order to print a packed BCD number, we need to do two more things. First, we convert a packed BCD number to an unpacked form. Second, we add a bias of 30 in hex to each unpacked BCD digit in order to make an external code. A laser printer understands the external code, as introduced in the following section.

1.6 External Code

Fundamentally, a computer deals with binary digits. The various internal data representations are designed for processing, and the external data representations are for transmission purpose from one computer to another. Interestingly, a printer often uses a small computer to control printing. Therefore, when one computer sends information to a printer, the information on the line, or bus, is in encoded form, known as external code. The terms *external code* and *external data* are synonymous. A popular external code is ASCII (American Standard Code for Information Interchange); it uses 7 bits to encode external data, such as English letters, digits, and control information. Where global communications are concerned, it is necessary to develop a longer external code that can cover all the international languages.

1.6.1   ASCII

The basic addressable unit in memory is a byte of 8 bits. The rightmost bit is the lsb, and the leftmost bit is the leading bit, which is also the msb. When a 7-bit ASCII code is stored in one byte, bit 7 (b7) is padded with 0, as shown in Figure 1.4(a).

All the ASCII characters are divided into two sets. The first set, as shown in Table 1.4, contains control codes with values between 00 and 1F in hex, so this set is not printable. In each set of three columns, the left-hand side shows the encoded value in decimal and hex and the right column shows the character name. The second set in Table 1.5 is printable, except for SP (Space) and DEL (Delete).

1.6.2   UNICODE

Unicode (Universal Code) is a new international standard that uses 16-bit encoding, as shown in Figure 1.4(b) [Unicode]. The default length is 2 bytes. The high-order byte is on the left and the low-order byte is on the right. In 1991, the Unicode Consortium was formed as a non-profit organization whose purpose is to promote a standard for global

Table 1.4. The encoding of ASCII control characters.

Dec	Hex	Name	Dec	Hex	Name
0	00	NUL (Null)	16	10	DLE (Data Link Escape)
1	01	SOH (Start Header)	17	11	DC1 (Device Control 1)
2	02	STX (Start Text)	18	12	DC2 (Device Control 2)
3	03	ETX (End Text)	19	13	DC3 (Device Control 3)
4	04	EOT (End Transmission)	20	14	DC4 (Device Control 4)
5	05	ENQ (Enquire)	21	15	NAK (Negative Ack)
6	06	ACK (Acknowledge)	22	16	SYN (Synchronize)
7	07	BEL (Bell)	23	17	ETB (End Trans. Block)
8	08	BS (Back Space)	24	18	CAN (Cancel)
9	09	HT (Horizontal Tab)	25	19	EM (End of Medium)
10	0A	LF (Line Feed)	26	1A	SUB (Substitute)
11	0B	VT (Vertical Tab)	27	1B	ESC (Escape)
12	0C	FF (Form Feed)	28	1C	FS (File Separator)
13	0D	CR (Carriage Return)	29	1D	GS (Group Separator)
14	0E	SO (Shift Out)	30	1E	RS (Record Separator)
15	0F	SI (Shift In)	31	1F	US (Unit Separator)

Table 1.5. The encoding of printable ASCII characters.

Dec	Hex	Name	Dec	Hex	Name	Dec	Hex	Name
32	20	SP	64	40	@	96	60	'
33	21	!	65	41	A	97	61	a
34	22	"	66	42	B	98	62	b
35	23	#	67	43	C	99	63	c
36	24	$	68	44	D	100	64	d
37	25	%	69	45	E	101	65	e
38	26	&	70	46	F	102	66	f
39	27	'	71	47	G	103	67	g
40	28	(	72	48	H	104	68	h
41	29	)	73	49	I	105	69	i
42	2A	*	74	4A	J	106	6A	j
43	2B	+	75	4B	K	107	6B	k
44	2C	,	76	4C	L	108	6C	l
45	2D	−	77	4D	M	109	6D	m
46	2E	.	78	4E	N	110	6E	n
47	2F	/	79	4F	O	111	6F	o
48	30	0	80	50	P	112	70	p
49	31	1	81	51	Q	113	71	q
50	32	2	82	52	R	114	72	r
51	33	3	83	53	S	115	73	s
52	34	4	84	54	T	116	74	t
53	35	5	85	55	U	117	75	u
54	36	6	86	56	V	118	76	v
55	37	7	87	57	W	119	77	w
56	38	8	88	58	X	120	78	x
57	39	9	89	59	Y	121	79	y
58	3A	:	90	5A	Z	122	7A	z
59	3B	;	91	5B	[	123	7B	{
60	3C	<	92	5C	\	124	7C	|
61	3D	=	93	5D	]	125	7D	}
62	3E	>	94	5E	^	126	7E	~
63	3F	?	95	5F	_	127	7F	DEL

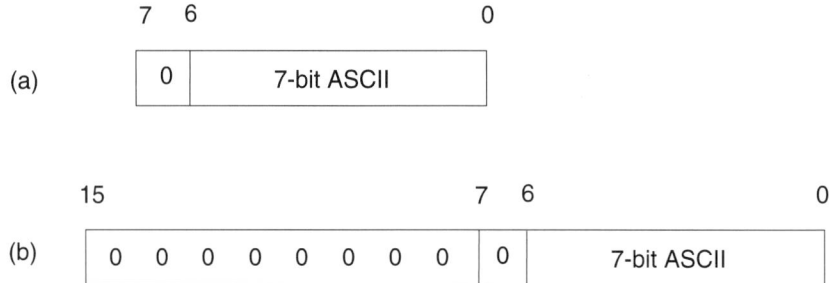

Figure 1.4. External codes: (a) 7-bit ASCII in a byte and (b) the same ASCII in 16-bit Unicode.

commerce [wwwa]. Even the default length of 16 bits is long enough to cover more than 65,000 characters that include all the European alphabetic scripts, Middle Eastern scripts, and Asian scripts. The leading bits on the right byte define a subset. For example, the Han subset alone contains 27,484 ideographic characters defined by China, Japan, Korea, Taiwan, Vietnam, and Singapore. This encoding scheme assigns each character a unique numeric value and a name in a simple and efficient way. How can we represent an ASCII character in Unicode? Very easily. After padding the high-order byte with zeros, we place a leading bit 0 followed by the 7-bit ASCII in the low-order byte. With vision, the 16-bit Unicode can also be extended to 24 bits as an option. As a result of this consideration, the Unicode can cover every known character on earth, including historic scripts.

1.7 Digitizing Concept

In system design, *digitizing* is an important concept that means to convert an analog voltage signal into bit strings. An analog signal may vary with time on a continuous basis. For example, during a telephone conversation, our voice is first converted by electronic circuits into an analog voltage signal. Next, the voice voltage can be digitized into a bit string. The basic idea is to take a sample of the amplitude of the analog signal at fixed time intervals. The voltage amplitude of each sample is then converted by an A-D (analog-to-digital) circuit into a bit string [Lenk97]. This bit string is nothing but an unsigned integer representing the amplitude of a voice sample. Each voice sample in bit string form may be transmitted from one computer to another. In fact, we often digitize an analog signal into an 8-bit unsigned integer, as shown in Figure 1.5. The amplitude of a voice signal being sampled at the leftmost instant is 32 in hex (i.e., 0011 0010 in binary).

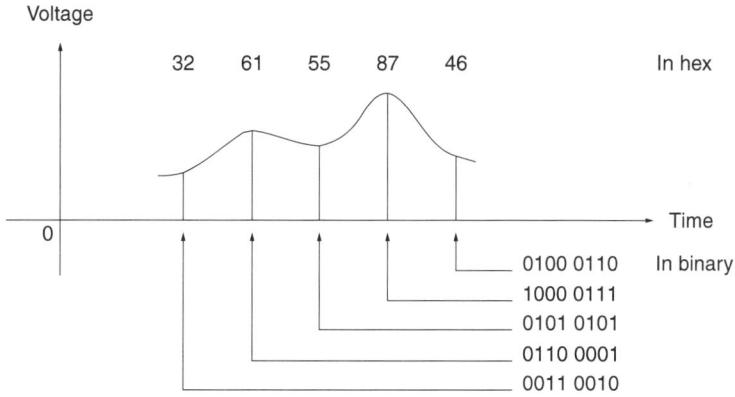

Figure 1.5. Digitized signals.

Subsequent amplitudes of the sampled voice signal are 61, 55, 87, and 46 in hex. For voice signals, the sampling period is 125 μs (10^{-6} second).

A computer can transmit, receive, and process such bit strings. When the bit strings reach the destination, another computer separates and delivers the bit strings to different destination stations. Each destination station then uses a D-A (digital-to-analog) circuit to construct the analog signal back to voice. The accuracy of the restored voice depends on the number of bits representing the sampled signal and the fixed time interval of sampling.

In this century, we live in an exciting world with digital data, voice, and video, and the digital signals are transmitted, received, and processed by computers. In a digital computer, logic circuits are designed to process and store bits. In order to fully understand computer logic, it is important to study the next chapter on Boolean algebra.

1.8   Summary Points

1. A digital computer has three major components: CPU, memory, and I/O controller.
2. Computers use the base 2 number system, so a digital signal has two voltage levels. That is, all information is represented by strings of bits.
3. A decimal number system means that the base is 10.
4. If the base is 16, the number system is hex.
5. A hex digit represents the encoding of four bits.

6. The divide algorithm converts a positive integer from one base to another.
7. To negate an integer means to its take twos complement.
8. Adding a bias 7 to a 4-bit signed integer, we obtain a biased integer from -7 to $+8$.
9. All the biased integers can be thought of as the unsigned numbers sorted in ascending order.
10. A packed BCD digit has 4 bits; an unpacked BCD digit has 8 bits.
11. Digitizing means that we use an A-D converter to change an analog signal to digital.
12. A D-A converter converts a digital signal to analog.
13. All the hardware components in computers use logic circuits of some sort.
14. The internal data are for processing; the external data are for transmission.
15. An ASCII character has 7 bits; a Unicode character has 16 bits.
16. An even parity bit is often appended to a code for single error detection.

Problems

1.1 What are the three major hardware components in a digital computer?
1.2 Is it correct to say that two integers can be added by the CPU but not the memory?
1.3 Given 16 bits, convert the following positive decimal numbers to binary and hex.

   1. 99   2. 100   3. 255   4. 1023

1.4 Convert the following 16-bit unsigned binary numbers to hex and decimal:

   1. 0111 1111 1111 1111   2. 1000 0000 0000 0000
   3. 0001 0001 0001 0001   4. 1110 1110 1110 1110

1.5 Convert each of the following 4-digit hex numbers to 16-bit binary numbers:

   1. CDEF   2. 1234   3. 00FF   4. FF00

1.6 Find the ones complement of the four numbers in Problem 1.5.

1.7 For each of the four numbers given in Problem 1.3, write its twos complement in hex notation. When we negate each signed integer, we can complement first and add 1, or we can subtract 1 first and then complement. Do we obtain the same result? (If your answer is no, you have probably made an error somewhere.)

1.8 Given 4 bits, write all the signed integers from -8 to 7 in binary.

1.9 What are the 16-bit binary and hex representations of the following negative integers in decimal?

    1. -99 2. -100 3. -255 4. -1023

1.10 For an 8-bit signed integer, if the sign bit is 1, what negative weight does it carry?

1.11 Use the serial convert algorithm to negate the following 8-bit binary integers:

    1. 0000 0001   2. 1111 1111
    3. 0111 1111   4. 1000 0001

1.12 Why do we need to construct a 4-bit signed integer in excess of 7?

1.13 What are the 16-bit representations in packed BCD format of the following three-digit numbers? Write each packed number in binary and hex.

    1. $+99$ 2. -101 3. $+219$ 4. -123

1.14 What are the 32-bit representations in unpacked BCD format of the following three-digit numbers? Write each unpacked number in binary and hex.

    1. $+999$ 2. -555 3. $+219$ 4. -123

1.15 An unpacked BCD digit 0 has a total of 8 zeros. In order to convert an unpacked 0 to an ASCII '0', what is the bias to be added to it? Write the bias in hex and in decimal. After we study logic operations in the next chapter, verify that the arithmetic add operation can be replaced by a logical OR operation.

1.16 An ASCII '0' is 30 in hex, so what should be ASCII '9'?

1.17 Write the hex number representation for each of the following ASCII characters:

    1. 'A'   2. 'a'   3. 'Z'   5. 'z'

1.18 In order to print a 4-bit number in hex, we add the bias to the digit. This works fine with all the digits from 0 to 9, but not for digits from A to F. By adding 07 more to 3A in hex, do we obtain the ASCII 'A'?

1.19 What is the difference between 7-bit ASCII 'A' and 16-bit Unicode 'A'?

1.20 When a group of packed BCD digits is transmitted from one device to another, we may use a 5-bit encoding scheme. That means that each 4-bit BCD code is translated into a 5-bit code such that the code has two bits on and three bits off. This is known as the 2-out-of-5 code. The purpose of using this code is to achieve single error detection capability. In other words, if one bit is flipped during transmission, the number of ones in the code is no longer 2, so the receiving station can detect this error condition. In Table 1.6, the 5-bit code is sorted in ascending order, and each line represents a packed 4-bit BCD digit.

Table 1.6. The 2-out-of-5 code.

Decimal digit	2-out-of-5
0	00011
1	00101
2	00110
3	01001
4	01010
5	01100
6	10001
7	10010
8	10100
9	11000

How many ways can we choose 2 out of 5? What is the decimal value of the 5-bit code assigned to each packed BCD digit?

1.21 The 2-out-of-5 code works fine for 4 bits. In practice, we can append an even parity bit at the leftmost end to achieve the same error detection capability. An even parity bit is an extra bit appended to the code so that the total number of ones in the code is always an even number. If any bit is flipped during transmission, the total number of ones is no longer an even number, so the receiving device can detect this error condition. Recall that in algebra zero is considered an even number. In Table 1.7, an even P (Parity) bit is appended to the left of the packed 4-bit BCD digit.

Table 1.7. The even parity bit.

Decimal digit	4-bit BCD with even parity bit
0	0 0000
1	1 0001
2	1 0010
3	0 0011
4	1 0100
5	0 0101
6	0 0110
7	1 0111
8	1 1000
9	0 1001

What is the decimal value of the 5-bit code assigned to each packed BCD digit in Table 1.7?

CHAPTER 2

Boolean Algebra

Boolean algebra was invented by George Boole (1815–64), the eldest son of a shoemaker. He was born in Lincoln, England, on November 2, 1815, and died of pneumonia on December 8, 1864. At an early age, Boole was determined to teach himself Latin, Greek, French, German, and Italian. In 1854, he published his masterpiece, "An Investigation of the Laws of Thoughts, on Which are Founded the Mathematical Theories of Logic and Probability." This paper collected basic laws and theorems that deal with logic. More than 100 years later the algebra he developed has become the theoretical backbone of logic design in digital computers.

A Boolean or logical function has one of two values: true or false. In mathematics, a true value means 1 and a false value means 0. In electronics, when positive logic convention is used, a true value means a high voltage, say 3.3 *V*. and a false value means a low voltage, say close to 0 *V*. Boolean algebra allows us to simplify a logic function of various inputs. The term *Boolean* also means logical or switching, and *Boolean function*, *Boolean equation*, and *Boolean expression* are used interchangeably. In logic design, we use the term *Boolean function* or *equation*, but in programming we usually use *Boolean expression*. In logic design, a Boolean function is implemented by a gate or circuit. Interestingly, one function can be expressed in many different forms and each form generates the correct output function, true or false. Our goal is to minimize a Boolean function to simplify the logic circuit and reduce cost. However, minimization is not the only design goal; there are many other considerations, including circuit delays, circuit simplicity, power assumption, and intuitiveness of design.

2.1   *Boolean Constant Vs. Boolean Variable*

In a logic circuit, a Boolean constant cannot change its value; a Boolean variable can. Therefore, we have the following definitions:

1. A *Boolean constant* can assume one of two values, 1 or 0, and is not subject to change.
2. A *Boolean variable* can assume one of two values, 1 or 0, which may change.

Both Boolean constants and Boolean variables are used as input conditions in logic design and programming languages. In logic design, a Boolean constant 1 means that the input wire is tied to +3.3 V. and a Boolean constant 0 means that an input wire is tied to 0 V. We say that the input value is *hardwired*, or not subject to change. In contrast, a Boolean variable is usually the output of a logic circuit representing a Boolean function. That is, the output is a function of its inputs, and it may serve as the input to another logic circuit. In fact, a Boolean function can be a constant, a variable, or a combination of them inserted with logical operators in the middle, as explained in the following sections.

As far as theory is concerned, a Boolean function is not different from a Boolean variable. In logic design, a circuit may be complex, but it provides one output, true or false. In a programming or simulation language, a Boolean function is the mathematical representation of a logic circuit. Such a function, after evaluating, generates one single output value, true or false. The output of one function can be used as an input Boolean variable in another function. In the following, we discuss basic Boolean operators and Boolean functions and how to simplify such functions.

2.1.1 Basic Operators

A Boolean operator is a logical operator that can only operate on Boolean constants and variables. A Boolean function is an equation of Boolean variables and operators, so its output is a variable whose value is true or false. Just as algebra has arithmetic operators, Boolean algebra has logical operators. There are many different logical operators; each one can be realized by a logic circuit, or logic gate. From a mathematical viewpoint, the three basic operators are NOT, AND, and OR. Note that any Boolean function can be expanded into an equation of Boolean variables and basic operators. Boolean algebra specifies the operations between Boolean variables and operators.

Engineers, programmers, and mathematicians like to select their own set of symbols to represent the basic logical operators. For example, different programming languages use different symbols to represent the same operator. Nonetheless, the semantics of each logical operator remains the same. To illustrate the point, we list three sets of different symbols in Table 2.1. Each operator comprises one or more characters that can be entered from the keyboard of a PC (personal computer).

Table 2.1. Basic Boolean operators in FORTRAN, Logic Circuit, and C.

FORTRAN	Logic Circuit	C
.NOT. A	\A	!A
A .AND. B	A . B	A && B
A .OR. B	A + B	A || B

2.2 Basic Laws

Given Boolean constants 1 and 0 with three basic operators, the basic laws are as follows:

1. $\backslash(\backslash 1) = 1$ 2. $\backslash(\backslash 0) = 0$
3. $0 + 0 = 0$ 4. $1 . 1 = 1$
5. $0 + 1 = 1$ 6. $1 . 0 = 0$
7. $1 + 0 = 1$ 8. $0 . 1 = 0$
9. $1 + 1 = 1$ 10. $0 . 0 = 0$

Each basic law can be thought of as a definition that is intuitive. In each row, the basic law on the left (odd numbers) is the dual of the law on the right (even numbers). A *truth table* is a table tabulated in such a way that it tells the truth about a Boolean function in that all the input conditions are specified, and for each input combination's corresponding output is also specified. Such a table has two sides: The left-hand side specifies all the input conditions and the right-hand side specifies its output. In other words, each row in the truth table precisely specifies a set of inputs and outputs of a logical function. For the sake of convenience, we can combine many functional outputs in one table so that they share inputs and save space. In Table 2.2, we plot the three basic logic functions for variables A and B. The four input combinations are written on the left-hand side, and each input combination is represented by a 2-bit binary number. For each set of inputs, there is an output on the right-hand side. Thus, we have three outputs, and each one represents one basic logic function.

Table 2.2. Truth table of three basic operators.

Input		Output		
A	B	\A	A . B	A + B
0	0	1	0	0
0	1	1	0	1
1	0	0	0	1
1	1	0	1	1

It is important to know that any logic function can be decomposed into the three basic logic functions, as shown in Table 2.2. The NOT operator complements the variable named A from one state to another regardless of input B. If A is 1, its output is 0. If A is 0, its output is 1. Because the function needs only one variable as input, it is a unary operator. In fact, the NOT function is the only unary operator whose logic equation is

$$f = \backslash A = \overline{A}$$

The first expression on the right-hand side shows the NOT function of A. The second expression on the right-hand side shows that a bar is placed on top of the input variable A. This notation was popular before the advent of PCs and software logic simulations. For nostalgic reasons, many engineers still like to say A bar instead of NOT A.

To illustrate the concept, a mechanical switch may represent a variable called A. There are two possible values for a single variable. If the switch is closed, the variable A is said to be 1, so a high voltage applied on the left-hand side will appear on the right-hand side. If the switch is open, the variable A is said to be 0, so a high voltage applied on the left-hand side will not appear on the right-hand side. Regardless of the position of the switch, we can flip the switch to complement A. In other words, we take the NOT function of A by flipping the switch. There are two other basic logic functions or logic operators, and each requires two input variables. The basic AND function requires two inputs, and the basic OR function also requires two inputs. As shown in Figure 2.1(a), we see two single-pole-double-throw switches that are connected in series to realize the AND function. The inputs A and B provide four conditions, but the only condition in which the switch is closed is when both switches are closed. Logically speaking, if A is 1 AND B is 1, the output of the AND function is 1. For the sake of convenience, engineers often replace the AND operator (.) with a space. In other words, when the period or dot is omitted in a logic expression $(A\ B)$, it means $(A.B)$.

As shown in Figure 2.1(b), we see two single-pole-double-throw switches connected in parallel. If A is 1 OR B is 1, the output of the two-input OR function is 1. When both A and B are 1, the output is also 1. Because of this inclusive condition of two 1s, the OR operator is an inclusive OR. It should be stressed that an inclusive OR function is different from an EOR (Exclusive OR) function in that the latter excludes the input condition of both 1, as explained later.

By definition, the basic AND function has two inputs. If an AND function has three inputs A, B, and C, it is no longer basic because it can be decomposed into two two-input AND functions in a sequence as follows:

$$f = A \cdot B \cdot C$$
$$= (A \cdot B) \cdot C$$

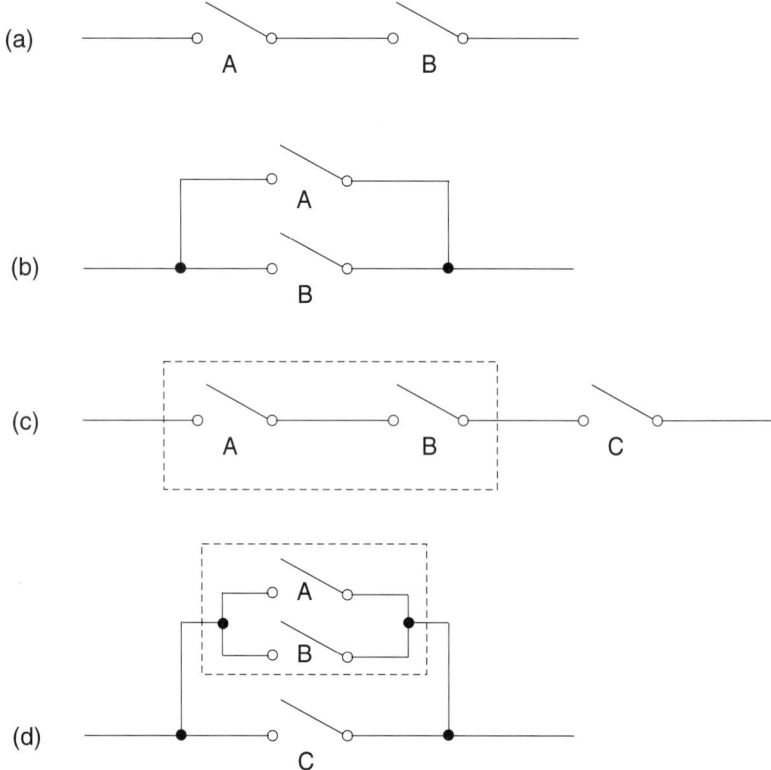

Figure 2.1. Two mechanical switches: (a) serial connection and (b) parallel connection. Three mechanical switches: (c) serial connection and (d) parallel connection.

As shown in Figure 2.1(c), switches A and B are connected in series and the dotted line is used to enclose the switches in a box. The box itself represents a function and is further connected with the switch C in series.

By the same token, if an OR function has three inputs, it is not basic anymore because it can be decomposed into two basic two-input OR functions in a sequence. As shown in Figure 2.1(d), we first connect the two switches A and B in parallel in a dotted box. Next, we connect the dotted box and the switch C in parallel. Mathematically, we show the equation as follows.

$$f = A + B + C$$
$$= (A + B) + C$$

Any Boolean function can be realized or implemented by a logic circuit. Any complicated logic function can be decomposed into the three basic functions—NOT, AND, and OR—in a sequence. In the next chapter, we will discuss transistor circuits and the design of many different

Table 2.3. Operator precedence.

Precedence	Operator
4	(. . .)
3	NOT
2	AND
1	OR

logic functions. As far as programming language is concerned, a Boolean expression may contain many logic variables and operators, and it serves as a logical condition in a control statement. Because many logical operators can exist in a logical expression, some syntactic rules need to be decided, e.g., which operation should be performed first if there is more than one? Therefore, we need to define the precedence for the three basic operators, as shown in Table 2.3.

A priority number between 1 and 4 is assigned to each operator. The larger the number, the higher the priority. In Table 2.3, the pair of parentheses has the highest priority for the purpose of grouping. After what's in the parentheses, we have NOT, AND, and OR in that order:

1. Parentheses can be used to enclose an expression as a group that must be performed or evaluated first.
2. If many operators exist in an expression, the operations are performed in the order of NOT, AND, and OR.
3. If many operators of equal precedence exist in an expression, operations are performed from left to right.

2.3 Basic Theorems

Given three independent variables A, B, and C, we have the following basic theorems:

1. $\backslash(\backslash(A)) = A$
2. $1 . A = A . 1 = A$
3. $0 + A = A + 0 = A$
4. $A . A = A$
5. $A + A = A$
6. $A . \backslash A = 0$
7. $A + \backslash A = 1$
8. $0 . A = A . 0 = 0$
9. $1 + A = A + 1 = 1$
10. $A . B = B . A$
    (communicative law)
11. $A + B = B + A$
12. $A.(B.C) = (A.B).C$
    (associative law)
13. $A+(B+C) = (A+B) + C$
14. $A.(B+C) = A.B+A.C$
    (distributive law)
15. $A + (B.C) = (A+B).(A+C)$

To prove each basic theorem, we must consider all the input combinations. For each set of input conditions, we apply the basic laws to evaluate the left-hand side and the right-hand side and show that the two sides are equal. In other words, we plot the truth table for both sides and show that the two logic functions are identical.

2.3.1   DUAL THEOREM

The basic concept of duality is important. Given two functions $f1$ and $f2$, each function may consist of many variables and basic operators. If their truth tables are identical, the two functions are equal:

$$f1 = f2$$

The dual function (fd) is obtained by interchanging in $f1$,

0 and 1
. and +

but all the variables and the NOT operators in $f1$ remain unchanged. For example, we have the given function f and its dual in the following:

$$f = 0 + A$$
$$\text{fd} = 1 \cdot A$$

Dual Theorem: If two Boolean functions f1 and f2 are equal, then their duals, f1d and f2d are equal.

In the basic theorem (2), the left-hand side ($A = 1 \cdot A$) is true. Hence, in basic theorem (3), the right-hand side ($A = 0 + A$) is also true because they are duals. In the basic theorem (1), by complementing the variable A twice, we obtain A, but it is a dual of itself. For other basic theorems, the right-hand side is a dual of the left-hand side. All the basic theorems are intuitive except (15). The distributive law in (14) is intuitive because the AND operator resembles the arithmetic multiply operator in algebra. Its dual in (15) is also true, but it can hardly be visualized by inspection.

2.3.2   DEMORGAN'S THEOREM

The theorem of Augustus DeMorgan (1806–71), a contemporary of George Boole, is vital to logic design. Given two independent Boolean variables or functions A and B, the DeMorgan theorem consists of two parts:

1. $\backslash(A + B) = \backslash A \cdot \backslash B$
2. $\backslash(A \cdot B) = \backslash A + \backslash B$

The first part allows us to change an OR function to an AND function. The left-hand side of (1) represents a two-input NOR (Not OR) function whose output is low if either of its inputs is high. On the other hand, when both of its inputs are low, its output is high. The second part allows us to change an AND function to an OR function. The left-hand side of (2) is a two-input NAND (Not AND) function whose output is low only if both of its inputs are high. On the other hand, when either of its inputs is low, its output is high. How can we prove De-Morgan's theorem? One easy way is to plot the truth table and show identical outputs for the left- and right-hand sides in Table 2.4.

Another way is to apply the basic theorems and derive the right-hand side from the left-hand side algebraically:

1. $\overline{(A + B)} = \overline{(A\,(\overline{B} + B) + B\,(\overline{A} + A))}$
   $= \overline{(\overline{A}\,B + A\,\overline{B} + A\,B)}$
   $= \overline{A} \cdot \overline{B}$
2. $\overline{(A \cdot B)} = \overline{A}\,\overline{B} + \overline{A}\,B + A\,\overline{B}$
   $= \overline{A}\,(\overline{B} + B) + \overline{B}\,(\overline{A} + A)$
   $= \overline{A} + \overline{B}$

Remember that DeMorgan's theorem can be extended to find the complement of any function, provided we interchange in the function

0 and 1
. and +

and complement all of its variables. Thus, if a function is given as $f(A, B, \ldots , 1, 0, . , +)$, then its complement $\overline{f}$ is $f(\overline{A}, \overline{B}, \ldots , 0, 1, +, .)$.

In electronics, a logic gate can realize the complement (NOT) function of a single variable. Such a gate is called an *inverter*. Although it complements a Boolean expression, it should be stressed that proper parentheses are inserted in the expression so that the order of operations remains the same between any two variables. Let us try a couple more examples.

Table 2.4. Truth table of NOR and NAND operators.

Input		Output			
A	B	$\overline{(A+B)}$	$\overline{A}.\overline{B}$	$\overline{(A.B)}$	$\overline{A}+\overline{B}$
0	0	1	1	1	1
0	1	0	0	1	1
1	0	0	0	1	1
1	1	0	0	0	0

EXAMPLE 2.1.

$$f1 = (\backslash A \ . \ \backslash B) + C$$
$$\backslash f1 = (A + B) \ . \ \backslash C$$

The complement function $\backslash f1$ can be written directly in one step. However, in order to see this, we can apply DeMorgan's theorem to this equation in two steps. First, treat what is grouped in the parentheses as one variable and apply DeMorgan's theorem to expand the group and the variable C. Then apply DeMorgan's theorem again to obtain the final result. The two steps are shown here:

$$\backslash f1 = \backslash (\backslash A \ . \ \backslash B) \ . \ \backslash C$$
$$= (A + B) \ . \ \backslash C$$

EXAMPLE 2.2.

$$f2 = \backslash A1.A2 + \backslash A1.A0 + A1.\backslash A0 + A3.A1$$
$$\backslash f2 = (A1+\backslash A2).(A1+\backslash A0).(\backslash A1+A0).(\backslash A3+\backslash A1)$$

In this example, we can write the complement function $\backslash f2$ directly. We can expand the product terms in four steps and get the same result. We would like to design logic circuits with AND, OR, and NOT gates because they are more intuitive.

2.4   Other Logical Operators

In practice, there are many other logical operators, each of which is implemented by a logic circuit. Thanks to DeMorgan's theorem we can design any logic circuit with only NAND and NOT gates. With two given inputs A and B, algebraically, we show a two-input NAND function as $\backslash (A \ . \ B)$. That means we perform a NOT operation after an AND operation $(A \ . \ B)$. In other words, perform the AND operation in a group and then take the complement of its output. By the same token, we can perform a NOT operation after an OR operation $(A + B)$. Algebraically, this is the two-input NOR function denoted as $\backslash (A + B)$. In other words, perform the OR function in a group and then take the complement of its output. It is equally true that we can design any logic circuit with only NOR and NOT gates.

The EOR operator $\oplus$ is very popular in both hardware and software design. The difference between an Exclusive OR and an Inclusive OR is that when both inputs are 1, the inclusive result is 1, but the exclusive result is 0. That is, given two variables A and B, the EOR function does not contain the complete product term $(A \ B)$ in its equation:

$$A \oplus B = \backslash A \ B + A \ \backslash B$$

Table 2.5. Truth table of EOR and ENOR operators.

Input		Output	
A	B	A $\oplus$ B	A $\odot$ B
0	0	0	1
0	1	1	0
1	0	1	0
1	1	0	1

By complementing the output of an EOR operation, we obtain the ENOR (Exclusive NOR) function. The truth table of EOR and ENOR operators is shown in Table 2.5.

The ENOR function is the complement of EOR, so its output is 1, provided both inputs A and B are alike. For this reason, the $\odot$ operator is also called *coincidence*; its logic equation is shown here:

$$
\begin{aligned}
A \odot B &= \backslash (A \oplus B) \\
&= \backslash (\backslash A\, B + A\, \backslash B) \\
&= A\, B + \backslash A\, \backslash B
\end{aligned}
$$

Interestingly, we have other ways to obtain an ENOR function. In the first line, the NOT function on the right-hand side can be moved to precede all of its inputs A or B. The proof of the following two equations is left as an exercise.

$$
\begin{aligned}
A \odot B &= (\backslash A \oplus B) \\
&= (A \oplus \backslash B)
\end{aligned}
$$

2.4.1 EXCLUSIVE OR THEOREMS

An EOR (Exclusive OR) function can be expanded into a sequence of basic operations. Thus, an EOR operator is not basic, but it works in many applications. One example is to generate and detect error-detecting code in a computer network. It should be mentioned that the terms Exclusive OR, logical sum, and modulo-2 sum are all synonymous. That means that when we have two inputs, the result is 1, provided the two inputs differ. Logical sum also means logical difference in that when two bits are added, no carry is propagated to the next bit. Therefore, the result is 1 so long as the two input bits differ. Because the operation is done on a bitwise basis, EOR also means modulo-2 sum or modulo-2 difference.

EOR = logical sum = logical difference = modulo-2 sum

Each of the two input variables represents a bit. However, an unsigned integer is a bit string, and an EOR logical operation can be performed between two bit strings on a bitwise basis. The symbol $\oplus$ denotes an EOR operator. It can be written as .EOR. in Register Transfer Language (RTL). We show more theorems on EOR operations in Table 2.6.

One way to prove the theorems in Table 2.6 is to plot the truth table and show that the left-hand side is equal to the right-hand side. As an alternative, we can use the basic theorems to prove that the left-hand side is truly equal to the right-hand side. As an example, we prove the EOR theorem (1) as follows:

$$
\begin{aligned}
A \oplus 0 &= A.\backslash 0 + \backslash A.0 \\
&= A.1 + 0 \\
&= A + 0 \\
&= A \qquad \text{Q.E.D.}
\end{aligned}
$$

Next, we describe a theorem that is both interesting and useful.

Theorem 2.1. Given three Boolean variables A, B, and C: If $A \oplus B = C$, then the following two logic equations are true:

1. $B \oplus C = A$
2. $A \oplus C = B$

Proof:

1. $B \oplus C = B \oplus A \oplus B$ (replace C with $A \oplus B$)
   $\qquad\qquad = A \oplus B \oplus B$ (communicative law)
   $\qquad\qquad = A \oplus 1$ (basic theorem)
   $\qquad\qquad = A$ (basic theorem)
2. $A \oplus C = A \oplus A \oplus B$
   $\qquad\qquad = B \oplus 1$
   $\qquad\qquad = B$

Table 2.6. Theorems on Exclusive OR operations.

1. $A \oplus 0 = A$	(no change if A .EOR. 0)
2. $A \oplus 1 = \backslash A$	(complement if A .EOR. 1)
3. $A \oplus A = 0$	(0 if A .EOR. A)
4. $A \oplus \backslash A = 1$	(1 if A .EOR. $\backslash A$.)
5. $(A \oplus B) \oplus B = A \oplus (B \oplus B)$ $\qquad\qquad\qquad = A$ (associative law)	
6. $(A \oplus B) \oplus A = B \oplus (A \oplus A)$ $\qquad\qquad\qquad = B$ (commutative law)	

2.4.2   Parity Theorem

Note that an AND, OR, NAND, or NOR function may have two or more inputs, but an EOR or ENOR function has exactly two inputs. If a function performs a series of EOR operations on its input variables, it is an even parity function. We have two parity bit definitions, as stated next.

Definition 2.1. An *even parity bit* means that the total number of 1s in the inputs, including the parity bit, is an even number.

Definition 2.2. An *odd parity bit* means that the total number of 1s in the inputs, including the parity bit, is an odd number.

A function can generate an even parity bit for its inputs using EOR operators. Assuming we have three input variables X, Y, and Z, one design option is to perform two EOR functions in series. First, perform an EOR function on X and Y to generate the output $f1$. Then perform an EOR function on $f1$ and Z to generate the even parity P:

$$
\begin{aligned}
P &= (X \oplus Y) \oplus Z \\
&= (f1) \oplus Z \\
&= \backslash X \backslash Y Z + \backslash X Y \backslash Z + X \backslash Y \backslash Z + X Y Z \\
&= \{1, 2, 4, 7\}
\end{aligned}
$$

The first and third lines are logically equivalent in the preceding equation. The first line shows two EOR operations performed in series, and the third line shows the conventional NOT-AND-OR operations. A set notation is introduced on the fourth line to represent the same equation. A pair of braces (curly brackets) serves as a symbol to denote the set. By mathematical definition, a *set* is a collection of objects. Each object is a member in the set. In the braces, we see objects separated by commas. In our case, each object is an unsigned number that is used to represent a three-bit complete product. A *complete product* has all the input variables present in either its true form or its complement form. If the variable Z is the least significant bit and the variable X is the most significant bit, the unsigned 1 represents the complete product $(\backslash X \backslash Y Z)$. Similarly, the unsigned 7 represents the complete product $(X Y Z)$. Better yet, we can write hex numbers in the braces, as each number has its bit pattern clearly expressed.

We use set notation for convenience. If any complete product in the set is true, the logic function is true. The set represents the logical equation as a sum of complete products. In this case, the set has four complement products, and this parity equation cannot be further simplified. As an exercise, we will derive the third equation from the first equation algebraically. We can also plot a truth table for the first equation and another truth table for the third equation and show that the two truth tables are identical.

Let us discuss the reasoning behind the equation. The notion is that each complete product has an odd number of true variables in it. If the number of 1s in the input variables is an odd number, one particular product is 1 and so is the parity. That is, the output parity bit makes the total number of 1s an even number. Assume that $X = 1$; $Y = 1$; and $Z = 1$. Obviously, the number of 1s in the complete product is three, an odd number. As seen in the equation, the first three complete products as 0s but the last complete product is 1, so the parity output is 1. In the following, we develop the general parity theorem; its proof is left as an exercise.

Parity Theorem. Given any N input variables, by performing $(N - 1)$ EOR operations on all the input variables one by one in series, we generate an even parity bit output.

2.5   *Algebraic Simplifications*

By applying the basic theorems, we can simplify a Boolean function by inspection. However, it is not always easy to find a reduction because a logic function may be expressed in many different ways. The truth table is unique, however, so we can simplify a function easily from the entries in the table. If reduction is not obvious, we can plot the Karnaugh map (K-map) as an alternative to a truth table. From the K-map, we can group the entries to reduce the function. In the following sections, we will discuss algebraic methods and K-maps.

In practice, algebraic methods are often used to reduce a Boolean function for the sake of convenience. A design problem usually involves many independent variables. As an example, if A, B, and C are true or C, D, and E are true, then the final result is true. That is, the logical function is often an OR function of many cases, and each case is an AND function of many variables.

2.5.1   *PRODUCT TERMS*

Because the AND operator looks like an arithmetic multiply operator in the distributive law, $(A.B)$ is called the *product* of A and B. A product term, or *minterm*, means that several variables or their complement are ANDed together, such as $(\backslash A.B)$, $(\backslash A.C)$, $(A.B.\backslash C)$. A *complete product* has two properties:

1. It is a product where each independent variable has exactly one instance in its true or complement form.
2. The product cannot be further simplified.

Let us try some examples. Given three independent variables A, B, and C, each complete product should have one instance of any variable in its true or complement form. Therefore, complete products include $(\backslash A.\backslash B.C)$, $(A.B.C)$, and $(A.\backslash B.C)$. Products like $(\backslash A.A.B.C)$ and $(B.C)$ are not complete because they can be either simplified or expanded into more terms.

2.5.2 Sum Terms

By the same token, the OR operator looks like the arithmetic add operator in that $A+B$ is the logical sum of A and B. A *complete sum* also has two properties:

1. It is a sum where each independent variable has exactly one instance in its true or complement form.
2. The sum cannot be further simplified.

Given three independent variables A, B, and C, complete sums include $(\backslash A+\backslash B+C)$, $(A+B+C)$, and $(A+\backslash B+C)$.

2.5.3 Sum of Products

If a function is written as a sum of complete products, it is really a truth table in algebraic form. We can realize a function as a sum of simplified products by using the NAO (NOT, AND, OR) gates. In regard to circuit design, a logic equation in the form of SOP (sum of product) is intuitive, because by using an oscilloscope to monitor the inputs and output of a gate, we can find errors. By means of the distributive law, we can also expand a POS (product of sums) into an SOP. Several examples follow.

EXAMPLE 2.3. Expand the following function into a sum of complete products:

$$
\begin{aligned}
f &= \backslash X \,.\, (Y + Z) \\
&= \backslash X.Y + \backslash X.Z \qquad \text{(distributive law)} \\
&= \backslash X.Y.(\,1\,) + \backslash X.Z.(\,1\,) \\
&= \backslash X.Y.(\backslash Z + Z) + \backslash X.Z.(\backslash Y + Y) \\
&= \backslash X.Y.\backslash Z + \backslash X.Y.Z + \backslash X.\backslash Y.Z + \backslash X.Y.Z \\
&= \backslash X.\backslash Y.Z + \backslash X.Y.\backslash Z + \backslash X.Y.Z
\end{aligned}
$$

In the first two lines, we apply the distributive law to expand the equation into a sum of simplified products. Introducing the missing variable for each product term, we obtain the sum of three complete products.

For academic interest, we can use the DeMorgan theorem to complement a function first, simplify, and then complement it back to get the final result. An example illustrating this concept is next.

EXAMPLE 2.4. Simplify the following function into a sum of products:

$$f = (X+Y+Z).(\backslash X+Y+Z).(\backslash X+Y+\backslash Z).(\backslash X+\backslash Y+Z).(\backslash X+\backslash Y+\backslash Z)$$

There are two possible approaches. In the first, we apply the distributive law to expand the equation into 15 product terms. Then, we apply the basic theorems to simplify. The other approach uses three steps.

First, we apply the DeMorgan theorem to find the complement as a sum of five complete products:

$$\backslash f = \backslash X.\backslash Y.\backslash Z + X.\backslash Y.\backslash Z + X.\backslash Y.Z + X.Y.\backslash Z + X.Y.Z$$

We plot Table 2.7 for the given variables X, Y, and Z as input and the function $\backslash f$ as output with five complete product entries. In the second step, we find the function f in the table that has the other three entries. Finally, we write f as a sum of three complete products and apply the basic theorems to simplify it:

$$f = \backslash X.\backslash Y.Z + \backslash X.Y.Z + \backslash X.Y.\backslash Z$$
$$= \backslash X \, Z + \backslash X \, Y$$

In practice, algebraic methods are often used to simplify Boolean functions. From time to time, we rely on an important theorem, stated next.

Theorem of Complete Products. For any Boolean function with a given number of variables, the sum of all its complete products is 1.

Table 2.7. Truth table of the function.

Input			Output	
X	Y	Z	f	\f
0	0	0	0	1
0	0	1	1	0
0	1	0	1	0
0	1	1	1	0
1	0	0	0	1
1	0	1	0	1
1	1	0	0	1
1	1	1	0	1

With one variable, it is a basic theorem such that $(\backslash X + X) = 1$. With two or more variables, we can apply the distributive law to expand the function into a product of all sums. If X represents one of the variables, each sum is in the form of $(\backslash X + X)$. Because each sum is equal to 1, the product of all 1s is 1. From the truth table, we can see that when all the output entries are 1s, the function is 1. Let us try a two-variable example next. With two variables A and B, the sum of all complete products is 1. In the equation, the AND operator (.) is omitted on purpose.

$$\begin{aligned} f &= \backslash A\,\backslash B + \backslash A\,B + A\,\backslash B + A\,B \\ &= (\backslash A + A)\,(\backslash B + B) \\ &= 1 \cdot 1 \\ &= 1 \end{aligned}$$

Note that the dual of this theorem is also its complement, as stated next.

Theorem of Complete Sums. For any Boolean function with a given number of variables, the product of all its complete sums is 0.

The proof is intuitive. Looking at the theorem of complete products, we complement both sides. On the left-hand side, after complementing the sum of all complete products, we obtain a product of all its complete sums. On the right-hand side, after complementing the 1, we obtain a 0.

In the following examples, we tend to simplify more Boolean equations algebraically in order to gain dexterity.

EXAMPLE 2.5. Reduce the following function to a sum of simplified products:

$$f = (\backslash A + \backslash B + C + D)\,(\backslash A + \backslash B + C + D)\,(\backslash A + B + C + D)\,(\backslash A + B + C + \backslash D)$$

By applying the distributive law, we expand the right-hand side of the equation first and then simplify; this approach is tedious. As an alternative, we can apply the DeMorgan theorem forth and back. First, find its complement as an SOP. Second, simplify the product terms using the complement function. Third, complement the simplified SOP to obtain the final answer. The three steps are shown in the following:

$$\begin{aligned} \backslash f &= A\,B\,\backslash C\,\backslash D + A\,B\,\backslash C\,\backslash D + A\,\backslash B\,\backslash C\,\backslash D + A\,\backslash B\,\backslash C\,D \\ &= A\,\backslash C\,(\backslash B\,\backslash D + \backslash B\,D + B\,\backslash D + B\,D) \\ &= A\,\backslash C \\ f &= \backslash A + C \end{aligned}$$

EXAMPLE 2.6. Given four variables W, X, Y, and Z, simplify the given function f as a sum of simplified products:

$$f = X \backslash Y + Z \,(X + Y + W)$$
$$= X \backslash Y + Z \backslash X + Z\, Y + Z\, W \qquad \text{(distributive law)}$$
$$= X \backslash Y \,(\backslash W + W)\,(\backslash Z + Z) + \backslash X\, Z\,(\backslash W + W)\,(\backslash Y + Y) +$$
$$\qquad Y\, Z\,(\backslash X + X)\,(\backslash W + W) + W\, Z\,(\backslash X + X)\,(\backslash Y + Y)$$
$$= \backslash W\, X \backslash Y \backslash Z + \backslash W\, X \backslash Y\, Z + W\, X \backslash Y \backslash Z + W\, X \backslash Y\, Z +$$
$$\qquad \backslash W \backslash X \backslash Y\, Z + \backslash W \backslash X\, Y\, Z + W \backslash X \backslash Y\, Z + W \backslash X\, Y\, Z +$$
$$\qquad \backslash W \backslash X\, Y\, Z + \backslash W\, X\, Y\, Z + W \backslash X\, Y\, Z + W\, X\, Y\, Z +$$
$$\qquad W \backslash X \backslash Y\, Z + W \backslash X\, Y\, Z + W\, X \backslash Y\, Z + W\, X\, Y\, Z$$
$$= X \backslash Y \,(\backslash W + W)\,(\backslash Z + Z) +$$
$$\qquad Z\,(\backslash W \backslash X \backslash Y + \backslash W \backslash X\, Y + \backslash W\, X \backslash Y + \backslash W\, X\, Y +$$
$$\qquad W \backslash X \backslash Y + W \backslash X\, Y + W\, X \backslash Y + W\, X\, Y)$$
$$= X \backslash Y + Z\,(\backslash X + X)\,(\backslash Y + Y)\,(\backslash Z + Z) \qquad \text{(distributive law)}$$
$$= X \backslash Y + Z$$

Two crucial steps in this process need to be explained. First, we use the distributive law to expand the equation into a sum of products. Second, we apply the distributive law again to expand each term into a sum of complete products. Third, we group the complete products to reduce variables. In the next section, we will describe the K-map that allows us to visualize all the possible ways of grouping.

2.6 Karnaugh Maps

A Karnaugh map (K-map) is a tool used to simplify logical equations with up to six variables [Karn53]. A K-map contains the same amount of information as the truth table but it is arranged differently. A K-map has many boxes, and each box has input variables assigned on the left side and on top. If a function is written as the sum of complete products, a 1 is marked in the box that represents the existence of the complete product. The total number of boxes is $2^{\wedge}n$ where $\wedge$ denotes the exponential operator and n is the number of variables in a function.

2.6.1 Two to Four Variables

If n is 2, we have a simple two-variable map. With two variables, the map has four boxes. On the left, we place the labels 0 and 1 for variable A, and on top we place the labels 0 and 1 for variable B. We say that each box or entry represents a complete product. Recall that in each complete product, there must be one instance of a variable in its true form or complement form. The EOR function is specified in Figure 2.2(a). Let us study the meaning of those 0s and 1s in the map:

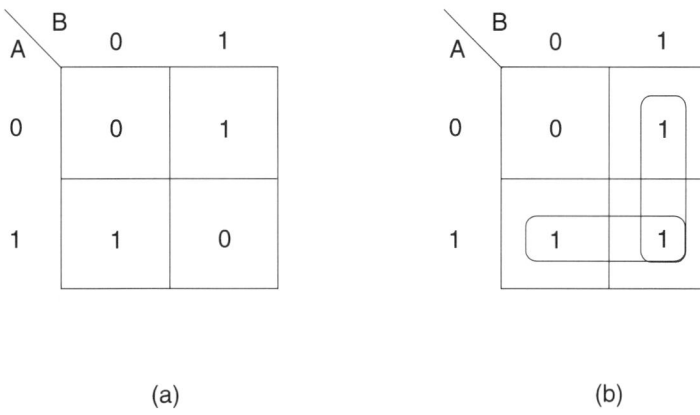

(a)   (b)

Figure 2.2. Two-variable Karnaugh maps: (a) \A B + A \B and (b) A + B.

1. On the left, the variable name A has a label 0 or 1 as an abbreviation for its instance: false or true. A 1 means that when the assigned
   variable is true, its instance in true form is true. A 0 means that when
   the assigned variable is false, its instance in complement form is
   true. Precisely, the label 0 represents the instance of \A and the label 1 represents the instance of A. The label 0 really means that when
   the variable is 0, its complement is 1.
2. On top, the variable B has a label 0 or 1 as an abbreviation for the
   instance of variable. Again, 0 represents \B and 1 represents B.
3. In each box or entry in the map, a marked 1 represents the existence
   of a complete product and a 0 or space means its absence.

In a two-variable map, each complete product is represented by a 1 in
the box at the intersection of the two variables. Recall that the EOR
function can be expanded as (\A B + A \B), so we plot (i.e., mark) a 1
in the upper-right box for \A.B and a 1 in the lower-left box for A.\B.
We can plot a 0 in the boxes of (\A \B) and (A B), or we can leave the
box empty to represent a 0 entry by default. Because the two 1s in the
map are not adjacent, no further simplification is possible.

The OR function (A + B) is plotted in Figure 2.2(b). The variable A
can be expanded into (A.\B + A.B) so that it has two entries in the map.
Similarly, the variable B has two entries (\A.B + A.B). Even though the
entry (A.B) is plotted twice, the end result is 1 because the basic theorem says that any function ORed with itself remains unchanged. In this
case, we have A.B + A.B = A.B. Note that the EOR function has two
complete products and the OR function has three complete products.
From the map of the OR function, we can group the two vertical 1s to
eliminate variable A. We can group the two horizontal 1s to eliminate
variable B. As a result, the simplified form is (A + B).

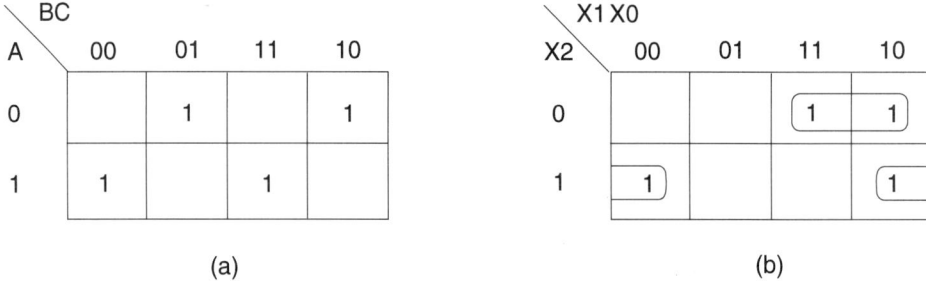

Figure 2.3. The three-variable Karnaugh maps for: (a) $\backslash A \backslash B \, C + \backslash A \, B \backslash C + \backslash A \, B \, C + A \, B \, C$ and (b) $\backslash X2 \, X1 + \backslash X0 \, (X2 + X1)$.

Given three variables A, B, and C, the three-variable map has eight boxes. Vertically, we have 0, 1 for variable A. Horizontally, we have a two-bit number 00, 01, 11, and 10 for variables B and C. With such an arrangement, any adjacent entries differ by one and only one variable. It is important to place the variables 11 after 01 and to follow them by 10. The leftmost column and the rightmost column are also considered adjacent in a wraparound fashion. The upper-left box indicates a complete product term 000, i.e., $(\backslash A \backslash B \backslash C)$.

Let us try to plot a three-variable map for a function. In Figure 2.3(a), we plot the S (sum) output from a one-bit full adder whose logic equation is

$$S = \backslash A \backslash B \, C + \backslash A \, B \backslash C + \backslash A \, B \, C + A \, B \, C$$

where A and B are the two input bits and C is the carry input from the previous stage. Logically, this equation tells us that when the three input bits contain an odd number of 1s, the sum bit is 1. From the map, none of the entries are adjacent, so they cannot be simplified. Note that we leave the box space empty if it contains a 0.

We can often simplify a three-variable equation using the algebraic method. Once in a while, we need a K-map to see whether the function can be simplified. For academic interest, let us simplify the equation:

$$
\begin{aligned}
f &= \backslash X2 \, X1 + \backslash X0 \, (X2 + X1) \\
&= \backslash X2 \, X1 + X2 \backslash X0 + X1 \backslash X0 \\
&= \backslash X2 \, X1 + X2 \backslash X0
\end{aligned}
$$

The algebraic derivation may not be intuitive by inspection. However, after expanding the equation into a sum of products, we plot its K-map, as shown in Figure 2.3(b). It is now obvious that the third term ($X1$ $\backslash X0$) can be eliminated from the equation.

The four-variable map is similar in concept, but it has four by four entries. Let us plot ($\backslash A\ B\ C\ D$) in a four-variable map, as shown in Figure 2.4. The variables A and B are arranged vertically on the left-hand side from top to bottom in the order as 00, 01, 11, 10. The variables C and D are arranged horizontally on top from left to right in the order as 00, 01, 11, 10. If we treat each complete product as a binary number and the variable D is the least significant bit, we can spot the box for each complete product easily as the four variables are sorted from left to right in the order A, B, C, D. The upper-left box represents ($\backslash A$ $\backslash B \backslash C \backslash D$) with a label 0000 whose decimal value is 0. Finding such a complete product, we look for ($\backslash A \backslash B$), i.e., the row with the 00 label on the left-hand side. Looking for ($\backslash C \backslash D$), we find the column with the label 00 on top. Henceforth, the box at this intersection represents this complete product 0. The reason to represent the complete product as a four-bit unsigned integer is for easy inspection. The D bit is the lsb that carries a weight of one ($2^{\wedge}0$). To plot ($\backslash A\ B\ C\ D$), we search for 01 in the row and 11 in the column. Therefore, the entry box is located at the second row, third column. This complete product can be written an unsigned 7 (0111 in binary) for the sake of convenience.

The four basic steps for simplifying a Boolean function are generalized as follows:

1. Expand the function as a sum of simplified products.
2. Expand each product term into a sum of complete products and mark a 1 in the map for each complete product. An empty box is considered the default for a 0 entry. If a 1 is marked in the box more than once, the end result is still a 1.
3. Find the groups in the map by inspection where each group can be further reduced to a simplified product.
4. All the 1s in the map must be covered in any of the groups so that we obtain the final result as a sum of simplified products.

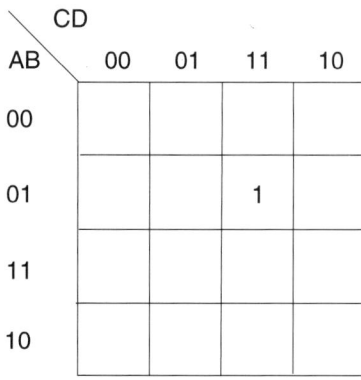

Figure 2.4. A four-variable Karnaugh map for ($\backslash A\ B\ C\ D$).

In a four-variable map, the left column and the right column are considered to be adjacent, and likewise for the top row and the bottom row. We can eliminate one variable by grouping two adjacent 1s horizontally or vertically. We can eliminate two variables by grouping four boxes in the form of a square, a row, a column, or four corners. We can eliminate three variables by grouping eight boxes in a rectangle. All the 1s in the map must be grouped at least once to ensure that the final result covers the product. Let us try more examples.

EXAMPLE 2.7. Simplify the following function:

$$f = A \, B + \backslash A \, B + C \, D + \backslash B$$

Given four variables, A, B, C, and D, the product term $(A \, B)$ really represents four complete products:

$$A \, B = (A \, B).(\backslash C \, \backslash D + \backslash C \, D + C \, \backslash D + C \, D)$$
$$= A \, B \, \backslash C \, \backslash D + A \, B \, \backslash C \, D + A \, B \, C \, \backslash D + A \, B \, C \, D$$

As plotted in Figure 2.5(a), the first product term $(A \, B)$ has four 1s in a row. The second product is plotted in (b), and the third product is in (c).

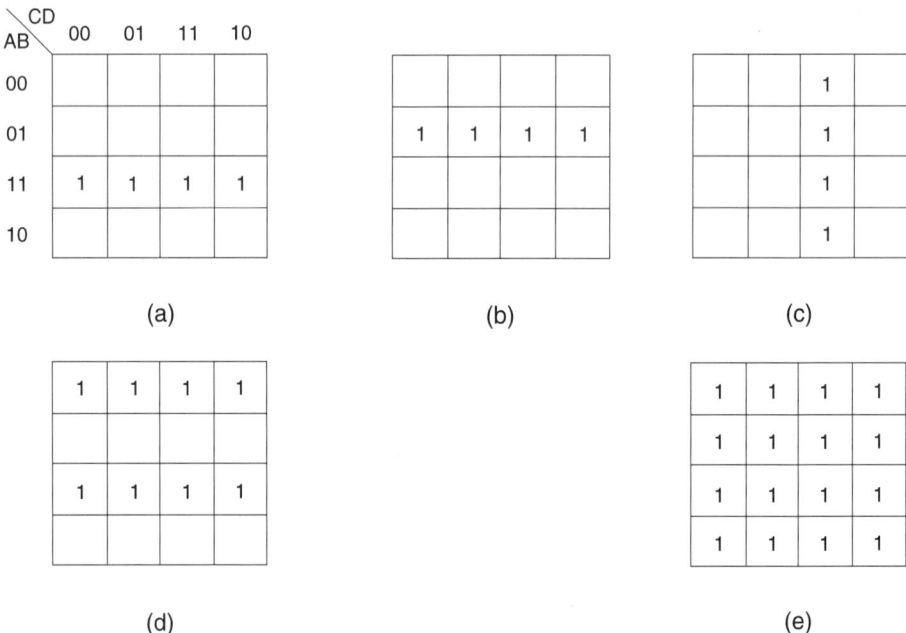

Figure 2.5. The four-variable Karnaugh maps for: (a) $A \, B$, (b) $\backslash A \, B$, (c) $C \, D$, (d) $\backslash B$, and (e) $A \, B + \backslash A \, B + C \, D + \backslash B = 1$.

The fourth product has a total of eight 1s, as shown in Figure 2.5(d). Combining all the entries, we obtain the marked map shown in Figure 2.5(e). Note that each of the two boxes $(\backslash A \backslash B\ C\ D)$ and $(A \backslash B\ C\ D)$ has a total of three 1s marked, but the end result is still a 1. After some practice, we can mark all the entries directly in the map. Because the map is full of 1s, all four variables can be eliminated to reduce the function to 1.

EXAMPLE 2.8. We are given four variables A, B, C, and D. If A is the most significant bit and D is the least significant bit, the function is represented by a set of unsigned decimal integers. Each integer represents a complete product, so we write the sum of complete products first and then simplify:

$$f = \{1,\ 3,\ 6,\ 9,\ 11,\ 14,\ 15\}$$
$$= \backslash A \backslash B \backslash C\ D + \backslash A \backslash B\ C\ D + \backslash A\ B\ C \backslash D +$$
$$A \backslash B \backslash C\ D + A \backslash B\ C\ D + A\ B\ C \backslash D + A\ B\ C\ D$$

The first line shows seven decimal numbers enclosed in a pair of braces. Each number in the set represents a four-bit complete product. Therefore, the unsigned 1 represents $(\backslash A \backslash B \backslash C\ D)$ and the unsigned 15 represents $(A\ B\ C\ D)$. From the K-map in Figure 2.6, the two products $(B \backslash D)$ and $(A \backslash B\ D)$ should be selected. The remaining product term $(A\ B\ C\ D)$ can be grouped in one of two ways. The first option is to group it vertically to obtain $(A.C.D)$. The second option is to group it horizontally to obtain $(A.B.C)$. The simplified equation has the two options enclosed in braces in the following equation. Because either option contains the product $(A.C)$, the real choice may depend on how easy it is to access the signal B or D in a circuit.

$$f = B \backslash D + A \backslash B\ D + \{A\ B\ C \text{ or } A\ C\ D\}$$

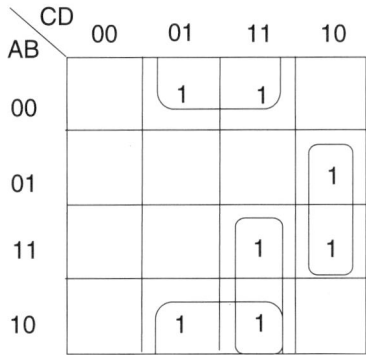

Figure 2.6. A four-variable Karnaugh map for $(\backslash A \backslash B \backslash C\ D + \backslash A \backslash B\ C\ D + \backslash A\ B\ C \backslash D + A \backslash B \backslash C\ D + A \backslash B\ C\ D + A\ B\ C \backslash D + A\ B\ C\ D)$.

2.6.2   DON'T CARES

In practice, the output of a logic circuit is usually fed to another circuit as input. However, certain output conditions in a circuit will never happen. Therefore, those conditions become don't cares to the circuit in the next stage. The term *don't care* means a Boolean product term that does not exist. Each don't care can be selected as an option to simplify the function. Each don't care is marked as a hyphen (-) in the entry of a truth table or Karnaugh map. The following example will illustrate the concept. A decade counter has four outputs constituting a four-bit binary number from 0 to 9. The counter receives input clock pulses, one by one, and counts from 0 to 9 repeatedly. Henceforth, after reaching the count 9 or 1001 in binary, the counter goes back to 0000 instead of 1010. The block diagram of a decade counter is shown in Figure 2.7(a).

The input of the counter is a series of positive pulses. Each pulse starts from a low voltage and goes to a high voltage then back to a low voltage. The four output variables are denoted as C3, C2, C1, C0 where C is the mnemonic for count and C0 is its lsb. While counting is in progress, the voltage level of each output variable may be low or high as a function of time. At any instant, the four counting variables constitute a binary number with a value ranging from 0 to 9. If the t9 signal is used to represent the timing state when the counter reaches count 9, we can decode t9 out using a single AND gate. If no don't cares are chosen, the t9 function is:

$$t9 = C3 \ \backslash C2 \ \backslash C1 \ C0$$

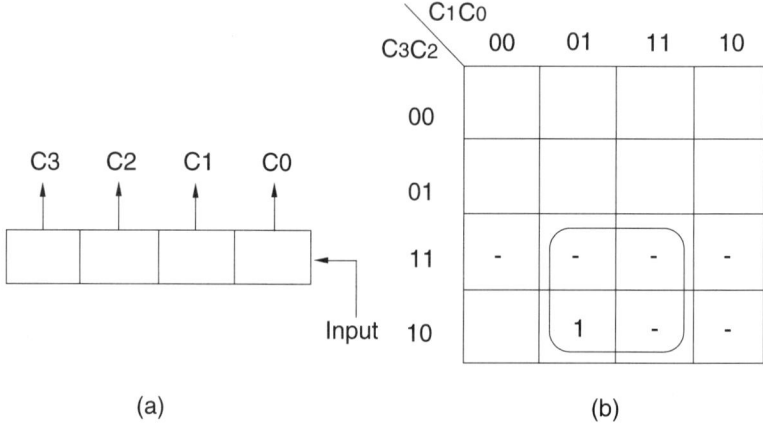

(a)   (b)

Figure 2.7. Decade counter: (a) the block diagram, (b) the truth table for t9, and (c) the Karnaugh map for t9.

Henceforth, a four-input AND gate is needed to implement this function. However, we can use the don't cares among the input conditions to simplify the equation and use a two-input AND gate instead. Because the counter cycles from 0 to 9 repeatedly, a reduced truth table that specifies only 10 states is plotted in Table 2.8.

A full truth table would have 16 entries to cover all the input combinations, but a reduced truth table has fewer entries. A reduced truth table is simple; it only shows those entries of interest. In other words, a reduced truth table does not show don't cares, 0 entries, or combinations of both. In the decade counter, the six timing states from t10 to t15 are don't cares so they are not shown in the table. Remember, a don't care is selected only if it can help simplify a function. The K-map for t9 is shown in Figure 2.7(b); each don't care is a hyphen in the map. As we can see, three of the six don't cares are chosen to simplify t9, so we eliminate both B and C by grouping t9 in a square as follows:

$$t9 = C3 \, \backslash C2 \, \backslash C1 \, C0 + C3 \, \backslash C2 \, C1 \, C0 + C3 \, C2 \, \backslash C1 \, C0 + C3 \, C2 \, C1 \, C0$$
$$= C3 \, C0$$

Using positive logic, the preceding equation says that when the outputs C3 and C0 are high, the timing state t9 is high, that is, it is true.

EXAMPLE 2.9. The timing state t8 from a decade counter is high if the counter reaches count 8, just as t9 indicates count 9. What if we need to decode a new function (t8 + t9)? We plot the K-map in Figure 2.8 for the function t8+9 (t8 + t9), indicating that when the decade counter reaches count 8 or 9, its output should signal high. The function is

Table 2.8. A reduced truth table for a decade counter.

Input				Output
C3	C2	C1	C0	t9
0	0	0	0	0
0	0	0	1	0
0	0	1	0	0
0	0	1	1	0
0	1	0	0	0
0	1	0	1	0
0	1	1	0	0
0	1	1	1	0
1	0	0	0	0
1	0	0	1	1

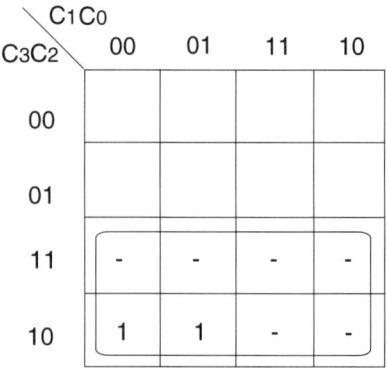

Figure 2.8. The four-variable Karnaugh map for t8+9.

named t8+9, which implies that the timing states t8 or t9. From the K-map, all six don't care are chosen to reduce the function to C3. We can apply the distributive law to single out the C3 variable. As the sum of all the complete products in the parenthesis is 1, the final result is C3:

$$
\begin{aligned}
t8+9 &= t8 + t9 \\
&= C3 \backslash C2 \backslash C1 \backslash C0 + C3 \backslash C2 \backslash C1\ C0 \\
&\quad + C3 \backslash C2\ C1 \backslash C0 + C3 \backslash C2\ C1\ C0 \\
&\quad + C3\ C2 \backslash C1 \backslash C0 + C3\ C2 \backslash C1\ C0 \\
&\quad + C3\ C2\ C1 \backslash C0 + C3\ C2\ C1\ C0 \\
&= C3\ (\backslash C2 \backslash C1 \backslash C0 + \backslash C2 \backslash C1\ C0 + \backslash C2\ C1 \backslash C0 + \backslash C2\ C1\ C0 \\
&\quad + C2 \backslash C1 \backslash C0 + C2 \backslash C1\ C0 + C2\ C1 \backslash C0 + C2\ C1\ C0) \\
&= C3\ (\ 1\ ) \\
&= C3
\end{aligned}
$$

Intuitively, if C3 is high, the counter must be in counting state 8 or 9. The basic theorems pave the theoretical background. The Karnaugh map merely provides an intuitive means, so we can see which products can be simplified.

2.6.3 FIVE TO SIX VARIABLES

Simplifications of equations with up to five or six variables can be achieved by examining a K-map. Assume that we have an equation of five variables V, W, X, Y, and Z, so that the total number of complete products is 32. Let us represent each complete product as a five-bit unsigned number whose decimal value ranges from 0 to 31. Remember that we use two four-variable K-maps to plot the five-bit function. If the variable Z is denoted as the lsb, then the variable V is the msb. First we write the function as a sum of complete products. Next, we divide all the complete products into two groups. The first group has all the numbers from 0 to decimal 15 with its variable V as 0. That is, each complete product has an instance of $\backslash V$ (i.e., NOT V). The second group has all the numbers from decimal 16 to 31 with its variable V as 1. Each product in this group has an instance of V in its true form. After separating the variable V from each complete product in the group, we obtain two groups, and each group has complete products of four variables W, X, Y, and Z.

In the first map, we plot all the complete products with an implied variable $\backslash V$. In the second map, we plot all the complete products with an implied variable V. The plotting of the first map is straightforward because all the numbers range between 0 and 15 without change. The plotting of the second map is done in two steps. First, subtract 16 from each of the remaining numbers because the variable V carries a weight of 16. After that, the difference is a number representing a four-variable entry in the second map. Let us try to plot a five-variable function where all the numbers are in decimal:

$$f(V, W, X, Y, Z) = \{1, 3, 6, 7, 9, 11, 14, 15, 19, 23, 27, 31\}$$

We break f into two functions f1 and f2:

$$
\begin{aligned}
\text{f1} &= \{1, 3, 6, 7, 9, 11, 14, 15\} \\
&= \backslash W \backslash X \backslash Y \, Z + \backslash W \backslash X \, Y \, Z + \backslash W \, X \, Y \backslash Z + \backslash W \, X \, Y \, Z + \\
&\quad W \backslash X \backslash Y \, Z + W \backslash X \, Y \, Z + W \, X \, Y \backslash Z + W \, X \, Y \, Z \\
&\quad \{\text{with } \backslash V \text{ implied}\} \\
\text{f2} &= \{19, 23, 27, 31\} \\
&= \backslash W \backslash X \, Y \, Z + \backslash W \, X \, Y \, Z + W \backslash X \, Y \, Z + W \, X \, Y \, Z \\
&\quad \{\text{with } V \text{ implied}\}
\end{aligned}
$$

In these two equations, a pair of braces again enclose a comment. For f1, the term $\backslash V$ is implied but for f2, the term V is implied. As shown in Figure 2.9(a), the entries in f1 are plotted with the understanding that the variable $\backslash V$ is implied. In other words, $V = 0$ is a necessary condition for any entry in (a) to be true. Similarly, as shown in Figure 2.9(b), the entries in f2 are plotted with the understanding that the variable V is implied. Needless to say, $V = 1$ is a necessary condition for any entry in (b) to be true. As a result of this arrangement, the function f is plotted into two four-variable maps. If any two entries in both maps have identical positions, they are considered adjacent, that is, they differ by one variable. After using the distributive law to group the two entries, we obtain a product with the variable V reduced. The equation after reduction is:

$$f = \backslash V \backslash X \, Z + \backslash V \, X \, Y + Y \, Z$$

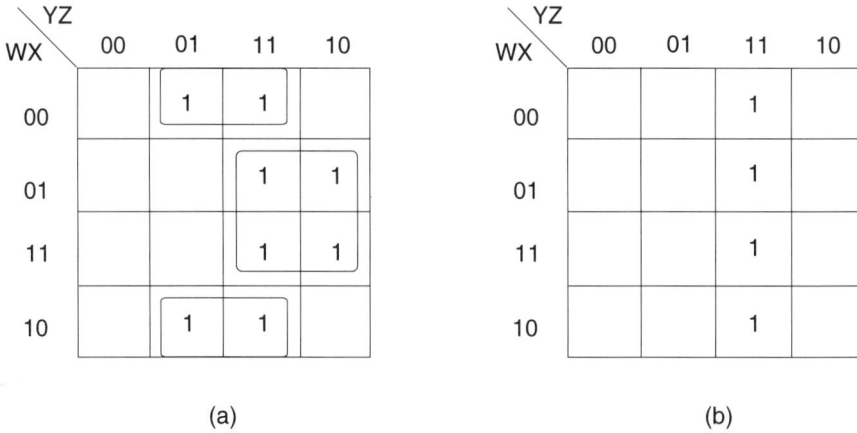

Figure 2.9. The five-variable Karnaugh map: (a) $V = 0$ and (b) $V = 1$.

By looking at Figure 2.9(a), we group products {1, 3} and {9, 11} to obtain ($\backslash V \backslash X Z$). We also group {6, 7, 14, 15} to obtain ($\backslash V X Y$). Because the third column in each map has 1s, we can group eight complete products in the two columns to eliminate V, W, and X. As a result, the reduced product is ($Y Z$).

In practice, a Boolean function may have six or more variables, but often many complete products are don't cares. That is, we can either inspect a truth table or plot a six-variable Karnaugh map. As an example, if an equation has six variables (U, V, W, X, Y, Z), we can write the equation as a sum of many six-bit numbers, and each represents a complete product. Because each variable is a bit, the six-bit K-map is divided into four four-bit K-maps. The crucial idea is to divide all the complete products into four different groups. The first group has $\backslash U \backslash V$ (00) implied, the second group has $\backslash U V$ (01) implied, the third group has $U V$ (11) implied, and the last group has $U \backslash V$ (10) implied. As a consequence, the first group covers numbers from 0 to 15, the second group covers 16 to 31, the third covers 48 to 63, and the last covers 32 to 47.

Each map only covers the complete products of W, X, Y, and Z with different bits assigned to U and V. Two things should be mentioned. First, the six-variable map is arranged as a 4-by-4-by-4 cube, where each cube has four layers and each layer is a four-bit K-map. Second, the four layers are arranged in such a way that any two adjacent layers differ by one bit (i.e., one variable). As shown in Figure 2.10, the 00 map is placed on the upper left, the 01 map on the upper right, the 11 map on the lower right, and the 10 map on the lower left.

In practice, a Boolean function is realized by many logic gates. An inverter provides the NOT function, an AND gate provides the AND function, and an OR gate provides the OR function. There are other types of logic gates, such as NAND, NOR, EOR, and ENOR. We must understand some basic concepts about logic gates, which are discussed in detail in the next chapter. First, each gate has one output, but the number of inputs may be different. An inverter or NOT gate has only one input, and the EOR or ENOR gate has two inputs. For the rest, each gate may have two, three, four, or more inputs. Second, the AND and OR functions are basic from a mathematical viewpoint, but in design the NAND circuit is simpler than an AND. We use a NAND circuit followed by an inverter to make an AND gate.

Let us design an MV (majority vote) circuit to illustrate the concept of a multiple-input gate, such as AND or OR. The six input variables are

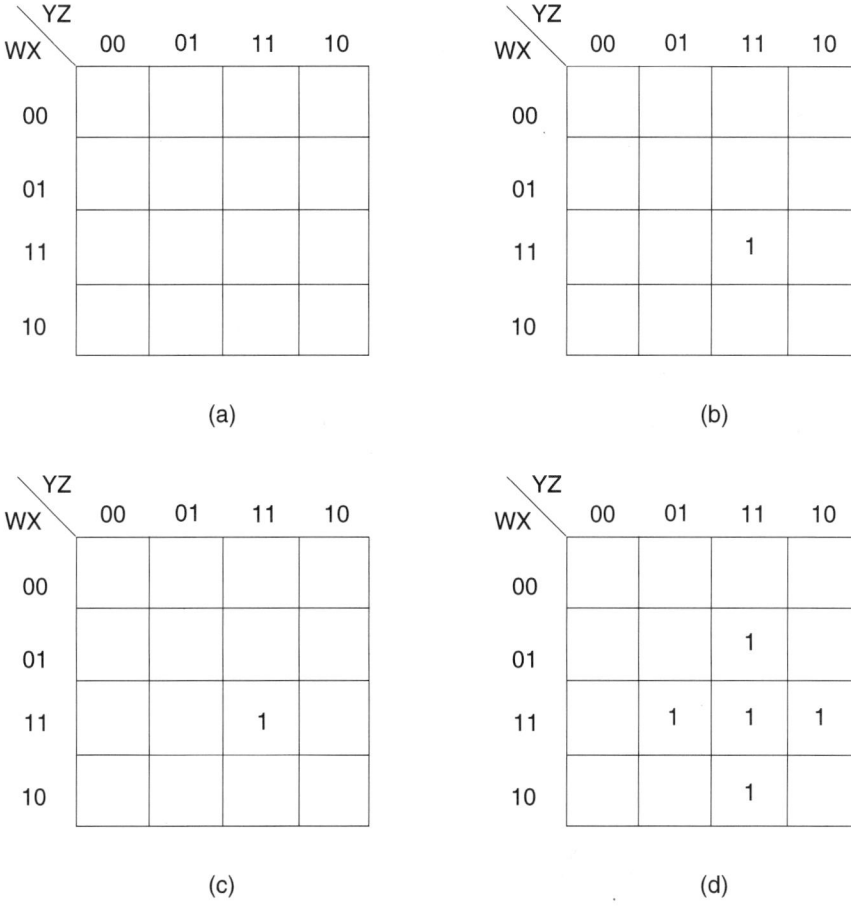

Figure 2.10. The six-variable Karnaugh map: (a) $UV = 00$, (b) $UV = 01$, (c) $UV = 10$, and (d) $UV = 11$.

Table 2.9. Reduced truth table with only the one entries.

Input						Output
U	V	W	X	Y	Z	f
0	1	1	1	1	1	1
1	0	1	1	1	1	1
1	1	0	1	1	1	1
1	1	1	0	1	1	1
1	1	1	1	0	1	1
1	1	1	1	1	0	1
1	1	1	1	1	1	1

designated (U, V, W, X, Y, Z), and one output is designated f (function). The output f is 1 if at least five of the six input variables are 1s. We can use a truth table or a Karnaugh map to simplify the equation and obtain the final result. First, we write down all seven complete products in Table 2.9; this reduced truth table does not show 0 entries.

In the table, the remaining 57 entries are 0s, and there are no don't cares. Obviously, the equation is a sum of seven complete products. If each complete product is treated as an unsigned hex number, the product 3F represents $(U\ V\ W\ X\ Y\ Z)$. By comparing any other product in the table, they differ by only one bit. Thus, by grouping the product 3F with any other product in the table, we reduce the differed bit. After reduction, the final equation has six five-variable products as follows:

$$
\begin{aligned}
f &= \sum (31, 47, 55, 59, 61, 62, 63) \\
&= \{1F, 2F, 37, 3B, 3D, 3E, 3F\} \\
&= (V\ W\ X\ Y\ Z) + (U\ W\ X\ Y\ Z) + (U\ V\ X\ Y\ Z) + \\
&\quad (U\ V\ W\ Y\ Z) + (U\ V\ W\ X\ Z) + (U\ V\ W\ X\ Y)
\end{aligned}
$$

In the first line, we show a different set notation as the decimal numbers are enclosed in a pair of parentheses. The uppercase sigma symbol at the beginning means summation of. Thus, the set notation represents the sum of seven complete products written in decimal. The second line uses a pair of braces to show the set notation. The numbers in the set are written in hexadecimal for easy inspection. The third line is in the form of SOP (sum of products). There are six simplified products in the equation, and the derivation is done in two steps. First, we duplicate the complete product 7F five more times. Next, we OR each instance of 3F with another complete product to reduce the single variable that differs.

As an option, we can use a six-bit K-map to derive the same equation. Figure 2.10 shows 64 (2^6) complete products arranged in four four-variable K-maps from (a) to (d). Seven of the entries are marked as 1s, and each entry represents a six-bit number that has at least five 1s in it. All sixteen entries are 0, as shown in Figure 2.10(a). In Figure 2.10(b), the map has only the entry 1F marked as 1. In Figure 2.10(c), the map has only the entry 2F marked as 1. In Figure 2.10(d), we see five marked entries 37, 3B, 3D, 3E, and 3F. The pivotal entry 3F is grouped with any other adjacent entry to eliminate the differed variable. Interestingly, the entry 3F is adjacent to the entry 1F in Figure 2.10(b), and it is adjacent to 2F in Figure 2.10(c).

The block diagram is shown in Figure 2.11(a); the MV circuit has six input variables and one output variable. We now introduce the concept of multiple input gates. An AND gate with multiple inputs generates a high output if all of its inputs are high. An OR gate with multiple inputs generates a high output if any of its inputs is low. As shown in Figure 2.11(b), the schematic shows six five-input AND gates and one six-input OR gate. A five-input AND gate generates an output if all five inputs are true. The

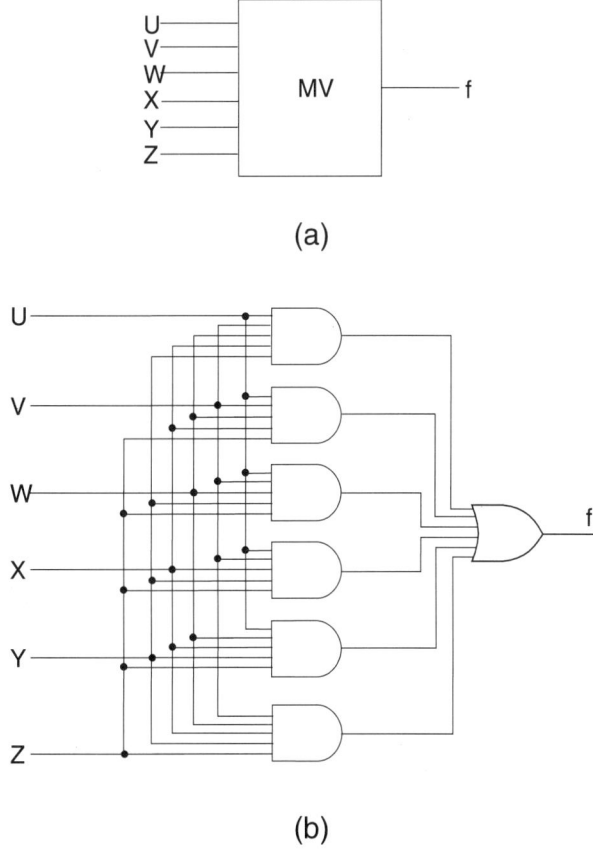

(a)

(b)

Figure 2.11. MV logic circuit: (a) the block diagram and (b) the schematic.

six-input OR gate generates an output 1 if any of its six inputs is true. The output of each AND gate is fed to the OR gate as input. A solid dot at the intersection of two wires indicates a copper connection. We conclude that the output of the OR gate provides the specified function.

In logic design, a reduced truth table is used for simplicity because don't cares and 0 entries are omitted on purpose. In a logic circuit, any voltage change applied to the input does not get reflected instantaneously in its output. Thus, it takes a little bit of time for the voltage to propagate through the logic gate. Propagation delay is a low-level detail, yet it determines the raw speed of a computer. Such topics are left to the next chapter. A logic designer needs to know some basic electronics in the design process.

2.7 Summary Points

1. Boolean algebra is the theoretical backbone of computer design.
2. A Boolean function can be true or false; there is no maybe.
3. Boolean function, logical function, and switching function are all synonymous.
4. The three basic logical operators are NOT, AND, and OR.
5. Other logical operators include NAND, NOR, EOR, and ENOR.
6. Boolean algebra defines the relationships between logical variables and logical operators.
7. The DeMorgan theorem consists of two parts.
   a. $\backslash(A + B) = \backslash A . \backslash B$
   b. $\backslash(A . B) = \backslash A + \backslash B$
   where A and B denote any two Boolean variables or functions.
8. Just as we can design a logic circuit exclusively with NAND and NOT gates, we can design a logic circuit with NOR and NOT gates.
9. EOR, logical sum, logical difference, modulo-2 sum, and modulo-2 difference are all synonymous.
10. Algebraic methods are often used to simplify Boolean functions because they are intuitive.
11. A Karnaugh map can be used to simplify a Boolean function because its graphical representation is intuitive.
12. Any Boolean function written as a sum of complete products is equivalent to a truth table.
13. We can realize a Boolean function as a sum of products by using NAO (NOT, AND, and OR) gates.
14. For any Boolean function with a given number of variables, the sum of all its complete products is 1.
15. For any Boolean function with a given number of variables, the product of all its complete sums is 0.

16. The Karnaugh map, truth table, or sum of complete products of a Boolean function is unique.
17. An even parity function can be realized by a series of EOR (Exclusive Or) operations.
18. An ENOR (Exclusive Nor), also known as the coincidence function, is true if both inputs are the same.
19. The don't cares are the input conditions that never happen.
20. A reduced truth table does not show all the don't cares and 0 entries.

Problems

2.1 Name three basic logical operators from a mathematical point of view.

2.2 Simplify the following functions by inspection:

1. $f = 1 + X$
2. $f = 0 + 1.X$
3. $f = 1.(0 + X)$
4. $f = 1.1.1.X$

2.3 Find the duals of the functions in 2.2.

2.4 Given two variables A and B, the sum of all the complete products is:

$$f = \backslash A\, \backslash B + \backslash A\ B + A\ \backslash B + A\ B$$

Prove that its dual is 0 and its complement is also 0.

2.5 Use the algebraic method to simplify the following functions:

1. $f = X.Y + \backslash X.Y$
2. $f = X + X.Y$
3. $f = \backslash(X.Y + \backslash X.\backslash Y)$
4. $f = \backslash(\backslash X.Y + X.\backslash Y)$

2.6 Use the algebraic method to simplify the following functions:

1. $f = X.\backslash Z + \backslash X.Y + Y.\backslash Z$
2. $f = X.\backslash Y + Z.(\backslash X + Y + W)$
3. $f = X.\backslash Y.\backslash Z + X.\backslash Y.Z + X.Y.Z$
4. $f = X.\backslash Y.\backslash Z + X.\backslash Y.Z + X.Y.\backslash Z + X.Y.Z$

2.7 Use the Karnaugh map method to simplify the functions in 2.6.

2.8 Use the DeMorgan theorem to reduce each of the following two functions into sum of products. Is f1 equal to f2?

1. f1 $= \backslash(A + \backslash A\ B)$
2. f2 $= \backslash(A + B)$

2.9 Use the DeMorgan theorem to simplify the following function:

$$f = \backslash(\backslash(X.\backslash(X.Y).\backslash(Y.\backslash(X.Y))$$

2.10 Assume that we have four independent variables denoted as (W, X, Y, Z). Simplify each of the following functions if possible. First, expand the equation into the sum of complete products, then use the algebraic method or K-map to simplify it.

1. $f = X + \backslash Y + Z$
2. $f = X + \backslash X.Y + \backslash X.\backslash Y.Z$
3. $f = X.\backslash Y + Z.(\backslash X + Y + W)$
4. $f = W.X.Y.Z + W.X.Y.\backslash Z + W.\backslash X.Y.Z + W.\backslash X.Y.\backslash Z$

2.11 Complement each of the functions in 2.11. First, apply the DeMorgan theorem to complement each equation. Second, expand the equation into a sum of complete products. Third, plot its Karnaugh map and simplify.

2.12 Given four variables (W, X, Y, Z), use the set notation of decimal numbers so that 0 means 0000 or ($\backslash W \backslash X \backslash Y \backslash Z$). Find, simplify, and complement the following three functions:

1. $f = \{0, 1, 4, 5\}$
2. $f = \{0, 1, 2, 3, 8, 9, 10 ,11\}$
3. $f = \{1, 2, 3, 5, 6, 7, 13, 14, 15\}$

2.13 Using the set notation of decimal numbers, we have a function of four variables (W, X, Y, Z):

$$f = \{5, 6, 7, 13, 14, 15\}$$

Simplify the function f using the following method:
1. Write down the function f as a sum of complete products and plot its K-map. Collect all the 1 entries in the map and simplify f. Verify that the simplified function is

$$f = X\,Y + X\,Z$$

2. From the same map, we can collect all the 0 entries and simplify $\backslash f$. Apply the DeMorgan theorem to derive the function f.

2.14 Use the algebraic method to expand the following function ($\oplus$ is an EOR operator) and simplify the equation into SOP.

$$f = (X.Y) \oplus (\backslash X.\backslash Y)$$

2.15 Use the algebraic method to prove the following equations:

1. $X \oplus Y \oplus X = Y$ 2. $X \oplus Y \oplus Y = X$

2.16 Use the DeMorgan theorem to prove that an ENOR function can be derived from an EOR function with an inverter (NOT function):

1. $A \odot B = \backslash(A \oplus B)$
2. $A \odot B = (\backslash A \oplus B)$
3. $A \odot B = (A \oplus \backslash B)$

2.17 Given three Boolean variables A, B, and C, the four functions f1, f2, f3, and f4 are logically equivalent. Derive f2 and f3 from f1, then derive f4 from f3 using the DeMorgan theorem.

f1 $= (\backslash A + \backslash B) . C$
f2 $= \backslash A\ C + \backslash B\ C$
f3 $= \backslash A\ \backslash B\ C + \backslash A\ B\ C + A\ \backslash B\ C$
f4 $= (A+B+C)\ (A+\backslash B+C)\ (\backslash A+B+C)\ (\backslash A+\backslash B+C)\ (\backslash A+\backslash B+\backslash C)$

2.18 Given three input variables X, Y, and Z, perform the EOR function on X and Y to generate an output f1. Perform a second EOR function on f1 and Z to generate the even parity bit output for the three inputs:
1. Expand the logic equation for f1 as shown here:

$$\text{f1} = X \oplus Y$$

2. In the following, derive the second line from the first line algebraically. The final logic equation, a sum of four complete products, generates an even parity for the three input bits:

$$\text{f} = \text{f1} \oplus Z$$
$$= \backslash X \backslash Y\ Z + \backslash X\ Y\ \backslash Z + X \backslash Y\ \backslash Z + X\ Y\ Z$$

3. Plot the truth table for the even parity of the three input bits.

2.19 Given four variables ($A\ B\ C\ D$), design a compare function that is true if $A = B$ and $C = D$. Intuitively, we can write down the function as a sum of complete products. Verify that the function can be derived from ENOR and EOR functions as shown here:

$$f = \backslash A\ \backslash B \backslash C \backslash D + \backslash A\ \backslash B\ C\ D + A\ B \backslash C \backslash D + A\ B\ C\ D$$
$$= (A \odot B)\ (C \odot D) \qquad \{\text{ENOR functions}\}$$
$$= (\backslash A \oplus B)\ (\backslash C \oplus D) \qquad \{\text{EOR functions}\}$$

2.20 In three steps, prove the generalized parity theorem as stated here:

> Given N bits denoted as b0, b1, b2, . . . , and bn − 1 as input bits, by performing EOR operations on all the input bits successively, we obtain an even parity bit for the inputs.

> Step 1. Assume $N = 2$, verify the theorem is true.
> Step 2. Assume $N = 3$, verify the theorem is true.
> Step 3. Assume that the theorem is true for N input bits, verify the theorem for $N+1$ input bits is also true.

2.21 Given five variables (V, W, X, Y, Z), each function may use a set notation with decimal numbers enclosed in braces. Write each logic function as a sum of complete products, plot its K-map, and simplify:
1. $f = \{0, 1, 2, 3, 28, 29, 30, 31\}$

Table 2.10. Four-bit Gray code.

\	Input			Output				
A	B	C	D	Gray code				
0	0	0	0	0	0	0	0	{0}
0	0	0	1	0	0	0	1	{1}
0	0	1	0	0	0	1	1	{3}
0	0	1	1	0	0	1	0	{2}
0	1	0	0	0	1	1	0	{6}
0	1	0	1	0	1	1	1	{7}
0	1	1	0	0	1	0	1	{5}
0	1	1	1	0	1	0	0	{4}
1	0	0	0	1	1	0	0	{12}
1	0	0	1	1	1	0	1	{13}
1	0	1	0	1	1	1	1	{15}
1	0	1	1	1	1	1	0	{14}
1	1	0	0	1	0	1	0	{10}
1	1	0	1	1	0	1	1	{11}
1	1	1	0	1	0	0	1	{9}
1	1	1	1	1	0	0	0	{8}

    2. $f = \{0, 2, 5, 8, 10, 16, 18, 21, 24, 26\}$

    3. $f = \{3, 7, 11, 15, 17, 19, 22, 23, 25, 27, 30, 31\}$

2.22 Assume that we have six input variables (U, V, W, X, Y, Z) and one output function f. What is the logical equation to output if at least one of the six inputs is true? *Hint:* Plot a reduced truth table for its complement function and then apply the DeMorgan theorem.

2.23 The even parity function for three variables ($A\ B\ C$) is stated as follows. Use a three-variable Karnaugh map to show that the function cannot be further simplified.

$$P = \backslash A\ \backslash B\ C + \backslash A\ B\ \backslash C + A\ \backslash B\ \backslash C + A\ B\ C$$

2.24 We are given four bits ($A\ B\ C\ D$), where A is the msb and D is the lsb. Any four-bit number has a decimal value ranging from 0 to 15. The four-bit numbers can be mapped into a Gray code sequence, as shown in Table 2.10.

    On the right-hand side, we show the Gray code and its decimal value enclosed in braces. Note that in an adjacent pair, the code and the next code differ by only one bit. The code sequence can be used in counter design so that only one bit changes state at a time. For each code, write its decimal value in the corresponding box of a four-variable K-map. Are you able to draw a continuous line in the map and connect all 16 numbers in sequence?

2.25 Assume that eight coconuts are found on the beach of a southern Pacific island. All the coconuts look the same. One of them weighs 5 pounds, and the other seven weigh 4 pounds each. Use a balance and weigh only twice to locate the 5-pound coconut.

2.26 Form a team to design a two-way switch in a hallway. When the light is off, and you turn on either switch A or B, the light goes on. While the light is on, if you turn off either switch, then the light goes off. What is the Boolean function of the light bulb in terms of the two switches A and B? Build the logic circuit with two single-pole-double-throw switches, a light bulb, and a battery.

CHAPTER 3

Transistor Circuits

3.1 *Introduction*

The terms *logic device* and *logic circuit* are often interchangeable. A logic device or circuit is designed to realize a logic function. In other words, such a device may employ many logic gates, and each gate may employ many transistors. A transistor is a basic element or switch in a logic circuit. The transistor was invented in 1947 by three scientists at Bell Labs: John Bardeen, Walter H. Brattain, and William P. Shockley. What is a transistor? A *transistor* is a current amplifier made of a semiconductor, also called a solid-state material. There are many types of materials used in semiconductors, including Si (silicon), Ge (germanium), and GaAs (gallium arsenide). Silicon is by far the most popular material for semiconductors because silicon-based transistors are reliable, fast, and cheap. However, due to recent developments, GaAs is gathering attention for its ultrahigh speed. Regardless of the material or internal design, a transistor operates like a switch in a logic circuit.

In 1958, two scientists worked independently toward the goal of packing many transistors on one silicon wafer, known as an IC (integrated circuit). One scientist was Jack Kilby at Texas Instruments, and the other one was Bob Noyce at Fairchild Semiconductor. Kilby received the Nobel Prize in 2000 for his work, which made electronic circuits smaller, faster, and cheaper. Bob Noyce (1927–1990) would probably have received the same honor had he lived. This chapter is devoted to the basics of transistor circuits and ICs. Without the rapid development of ICs, PCs (personal computers) would not have become as popular a household commodity.

A very large-scale IC may contain millions of transistors because many logic functions are implemented on a chip the size of a fingernail. That is, many logic circuits can be grouped to make a more complicated logic device on a silicon wafer. There are so many transistors on a chip that the width of a transistor serves as the measuring stick of technical advances. One micron is one-millionth of a meter (10^{-6} m). To get an idea of how small that is, the diameter of a human hair is about 50 microns.

The width of a transistor on a chip is used to represent the technology. That is, a 0.13-micron process implies that a transistor is .13 micron wide. Generally speaking, a CPU (central processing unit) or M (memory) module may have more than a hundred million transistors on the chip. In regard to manufacturing, many new processes were developed; the definition of a semiconductor process follows.

Definition 3.1. A *semiconductor process* consists of many steps to manufacture an IC chip.

From the definition, a semiconductor process is usually a technology that is patented. All the ICs made by the same process belong to one logic family. In each family, the circuit schematic of a logic gate may be different, but the gate symbol is the same. That is, a standard symbol is established for the logic function that is independent of circuit design [IEEE91]. For example, the shape of an AND gate is different from the shape of an OR gate. Looking at a gate symbol, as discussed in the next chapter, we can immediately understand its logic function. How to use the gates is logic design. First, we study the circuit principles to realize a logic function. All the ICs in a family are compatible. Therefore, they can be interconnected to realize a more complicated logic function. Moreover, all the IC chips from different families are compatible as long as their voltages and currents for input and output are compatible. The electronic circuits in some logic families have high speed, but others require less power.

3.2   *Scale of Integration*

How many transistors can be placed on an IC chip? In the 1960s, the answer was about 100. Based on the modified Moore's law, the number of transistors on a chip is doubled about every 18 months. To illustrate the point, we define the scale of integration by the total number of transistors on a chip:

> SSI (small-scale integration)—100 transistors
> MSI (medium-scale integration)—1,000 transistors
> LSI (large-scale integration)—10,000 transistors
> VLSI (very LSI)—1,000,000 transistors
> ULSI (ultra LSI)—100,000,000 transistors or more

A ULSI chip contains more than 100 million transistors. Such a memory chip can store 128 megabits or more. A ULSI chip is characterized by properties, such as high speed, high density, low power, and low cost.

When the transistor gets smaller, less energy is required to switch its state and the wire between two transistors becomes shorter. In all, the switching time can be reduced to the 100-ps (picosecond) range; a picosecond is equal to one-trillionth of a second [Broc00]. It was generally believed that when the 0.13 micron technology was developed, we were approaching the limits of physics. Surprisingly, in 2001 Intel announced that a handful of new silicon transistors are 70 to 80 atoms wide, and the 0.045-micron technology will be ready for commercial production by 2007. Such transistors are capable of switching on and off at 1.5 tHz (trillion Hertz). We say that the Moore's law will hold at least until the end of this decade.

3.3   Bipolar Transistors

How can a transistor act like a switch? First, we need to understand the theory behind a transistor. The bipolar type of transistor was developed before the unipolar type. Bipolar ICs were developed before unipolar ICs. In 1961, RTL (resistor transistor logic) circuits were commercially available, but they were soon superseded by TTL (transistor transistor logic), and ECL (emitter coupled logic; pronounced *echo-l*) [Tred96].

A bipolar transistor is a junction transistor that has three layers. Each layer is properly doped with negative or positive charges. Because of its popularity, we use a silicon-based circuit as an example to describe the design concept. First we define two doped layers as follows:

1. An N-layer is a piece of silicon doped with phosphorus (P) so the material carries free negative electrons.
2. A P-layer is a piece of silicon doped with boron (B) so the material carries free positive holes.

As electron carries a negative charge; a hole carries a positive charge. The term *hole* really means that an electron is missing in the material. The symbol N means a layer that has free negative charges and the symbol P means a layer that has free positive charges. Note that either type of layers is electrically neutral and each bipolar junction transistor has three layers. Based on the combination of three layers, we have two types of bipolar transistors, NPN and PNP, as discussed in the following.

3.3.1   NPN TRANSISTOR

Although the PNP transistor was developed before the NPN transistor, the latter is more popular. The NPN transistor has a physical layout depicted in Figure 3.1(a). As we can see, it has three layers with two junctions. The purpose of the thin P-layer in the middle is to control the

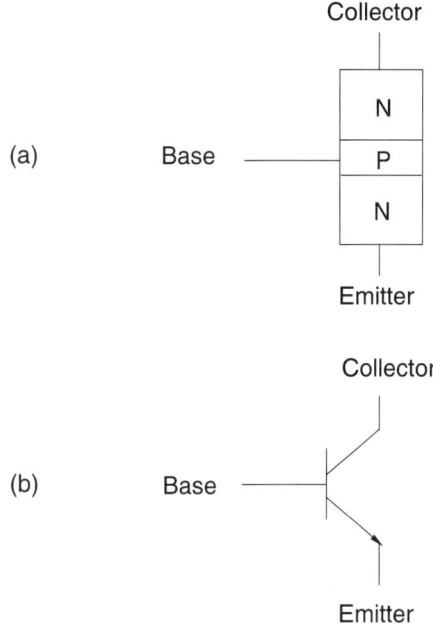

Figure 3.1. The NPN junction transistor: (a) physical layout and (b) circuit schematic.

current flow. The two ends are the two N-layers. The top is called the *collector*, and the bottom is the *emitter*. The collector is bigger than the emitter. This is also true for a PNP junction transistor, as introduced in the next section.

Each layer is connected to a conductor wire, so the transistor has three wires, or legs. The schematic of an NPN transistor is shown in Figure 3.1(b), where the arrow indicates the direction of the current flow. Because the P-N (base-emitter) junction acts like a diode, the base current flows on the conductor wire into the base and then to the emitter. Because electrons flow in the opposite direction, we say that the emitter emits electrons through the base to the collector. Remember that in an NPN transistor, a small current flows from the wire to the base and then to the emitter, with the understanding that electrons flow in the other direction.

To illustrate the concept, we apply a positive voltage, say 5 v., between the collector and the emitter. Then we apply a small positive voltage to the base with respect to the emitter. If this base voltage exceeds the threshold of the P-N junction, the base-emitter junction, or diode, becomes forward-biased. As a result, a small current flows into the base to the emitter, and we say that the NPN transistor is turned on. In fact, a small current into the base causes an amplified current to flow in the transistor from the collector to the emitter.

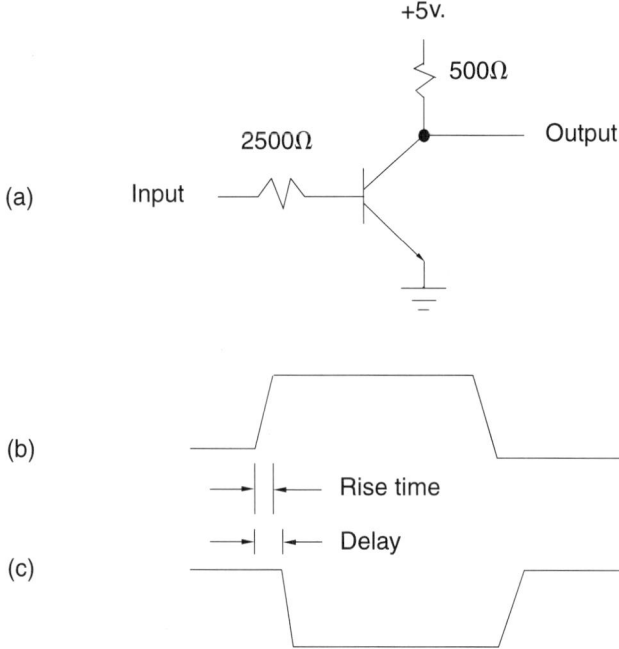

Figure 3.2. The RTL inverter: (a) circuit schematic, (b) the waveform of input, and (c) the waveform of output.

In a radio circuit, the NPN transistor works like a current amplifier. In logic design, it works like a switch. That is, if we either drive it very hard or do not drive it at all, the state of the switch can be closed or open depending on the input signal. The circuit schematic of an inverter in the RTL family is shown in Figure 3.2(a).

An inverter has one input and one output. The logic function produces an output as the complement of its input. Therefore, any change applied to its input will reflect on its output after a short timing delay. In logic design, an inverter is the nickname for a NOT gate. As depicted in Figure 3.2(b), the waveform of an input pulse rises from 0 v. to 5 v., stays high for one clock period, and then falls back to 0 v. We further define the rise time to be the time required for an input voltage to switch from low to high. This timing delay is due to the capacitance of the input circuit. With a single input, we have two possible cases to consider:

1. Input is high, say 5 v: The transistor is turned on. In the circuit, a base resistor of 2,500 ohms is needed to limit the base current. If we neglect the 0.3-v. drop across the junction, the base current Ib is:

$$Ib = 5/2500$$
$$= 2 \text{ ma (milliampere)}$$

The current amplification factor of the transistor, called β (beta), is defined as the ratio of the collector current over the base current. The current amplification β varies from transistor to transistor. If β is 50, a collector current Ic as large as 100 ma (2 * 50) can be induced. However, there is a resistor of 500 ohms between the collector and the power supply. This is the so-called *pull-up resistor*, which limits the collector current. When the collector current is less than its amplified amount, the voltage drop between the collector and the emitter is close to 0.1 v. Under such a condition, the transistor is saturated, or bottomed, and its collector voltage is close to ground. The waveform of the output voltage is plotted in Figure 3.2(c).

2. Input is low, say 0.1 v: There is no current flowing into the base, so the transistor is off. This is because the input is below the threshold required to turn on the transistor. As a result, the output is high because it is connected to the power supply. The rectangular waveforms of input and output are not in perfect shape because it takes time to charge the junction from cutoff state to saturated state and to discharge from saturated state to cutoff state. The input signal is A, and the output function f is \A (NOT A).

Recall that the collector area in a bipolar transistor is bigger than its emitter counterpart, even though both are negatively doped. In practice, we can swap the roles of collector and emitter in a circuit. That is, physically we tie the emitter to a high voltage and the collector to ground, and then the emitter becomes a collector. Note that the transistor can also operate in the reverse direction with a current amplification factor known as reversed β. Because of the size difference of its collector, the reverse β is much smaller than its regular β. In other words, the NPN transistor can work like a switch in either direction. In normal mode, the current flows from the collector to the emitter. In reverse mode, the current flows from the emitter to the collector.

3.3.2 PNP Transistor

We need to discuss PNP transistors because a logic circuit can have many NPN transistors and a few PNP transistors. A PNP junction transistor also has three layers: one thin N-layer and two P-layers. The physical layout of a PNP transistor is depicted in Figure 3.3(a). The top is the emitter, the middle is the base, and the bottom is the collector. Even though both the collector and the emitter are positively doped, the collector area is still bigger than its emitter, as in the NPN type. A PNP transistor can also act like a switch. Similarly, its base voltage controls the base current flow, but there are some design differences. First, the control current flows from the emitter to the base. As the base current flows outward on the wire, an amplified current flows from the emitter

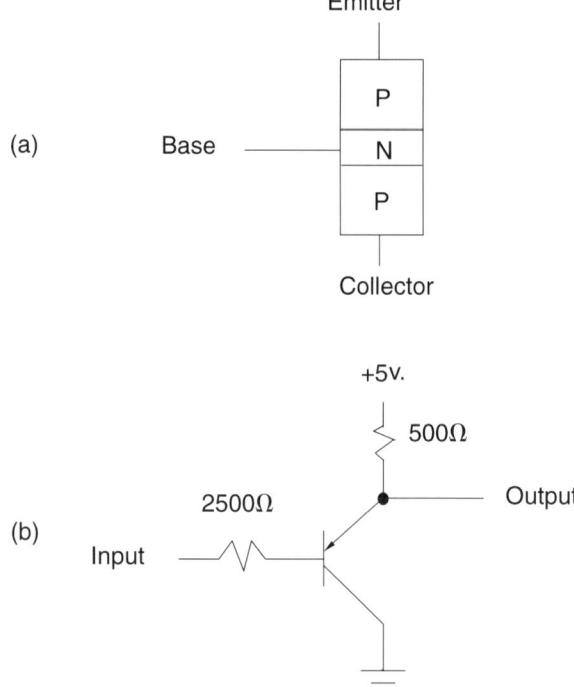

Figure 3.3. The PNP junction transistor: (a) physical layout and (b) circuit schematic.

through the base to the collector. That is, the emitter emits a current through the base to the collector in a PNP transistor.

The circuit schematic of a PNP transistor with two resistors is shown in Figure 3.3(b). The arrow indicates the direction of the base current. Recall that the collector of an NPN transistor receives electronics. In contrast, the collector of a PNP transistor receives current, or holes in semiconductor jargon. The PNP transistor is also a current amplifier. However, its emitter serves as the reference point when a base voltage is applied. The theory remains in that the P-N (emitter-base) junction acts like a diode. For example, a high voltage (5 v.) is applied to the emitter and the collector is connected to ground. The input signal can have one of two voltage levels, as discussed in the following:

1. A low voltage (0.1 v.) is applied to the base. Because this voltage exceeds the threshold, the P-N (emitter-base) junction becomes forward-biased. As a result, two things happen. First, a base current flows from the emitter to the base and outward on the wire. Second, an amplified current flows from the emitter through the base to the collector. A resistor is placed between the emitter and the power supply to limit the emitter current. When the voltage across the emitter

resistor is about 5 v., the transistor is saturated, or bottomed. As a result, the output voltage of its collector is 0.1 v., near ground level.

2. A high voltage (5 v.) is applied to the base. As the voltage between the emitter and the base does not exceed the threshold, no base current flows. This is because when the P-N junction is not forward-biased, the transistor is off and the collector output voltage is 5 v.

In conclusion, either an NPN or PNP transistor can operate like a switch with the understanding that the current flows in two different directions as stated here:

1. In an NPN transistor, if a high voltage with respect to the emitter is applied to the base, a current flows from the collector to the emitter, so the switch is on.
2. In a PNP transistor, if a low voltage with respect to the emitter is applied to the base, a current flows from the emitter to the collector, so the switch is on.

3.3.3   BIPOLAR TRANSISTOR LOGIC CIRCUITS

Many logic circuits are designed with bipolar junction transistors, so we will use TTL as an example to discuss logic design. Each logic gate in the family uses an input transistor whose emitter is connected to one or more input wires. The voltage applied to an input wire can be high (5 v.) or low (0 v.). To be precise, the low voltage is 0.1 v., near ground voltage. The state of the input transistor affects the other transistors in a circuit. The design of a NOT gate is not very different from a two-input NAND gate. A NOT gate has an input transistor with one input wire so the logic device is an inverter. A two-input NAND gate has an input transistor with two input wires, so the logic device is a two-input NAND gate. The schematic of a TTL inverter is shown in Figure 3.4. There are two NPN transistors, two resistors, and one power supply of 5 v. The input transistor Q1 has one input wire, and the collector of the output transistor Q2 is the output wire. Note that the collector output is deliberately tied to a light bulb, then to 5 v. The input can be one of two voltage levels, as follows:

1. Input is low: The Q1 transistor is on, so its collector current is pulled off the base of the Q2 transistor. As a result, the switch is cut off, so its output is high.
2. Input is high: The Q1 transistor is off, so the base-collector junction of Q1 becomes forward-biased. Then a base current flows into Q2 and its collector is bottomed. That is, the Q2 switch is on to pull its collector output voltage to low. Because the Q2 transistor can sink current into its collector, the light bulb is on.

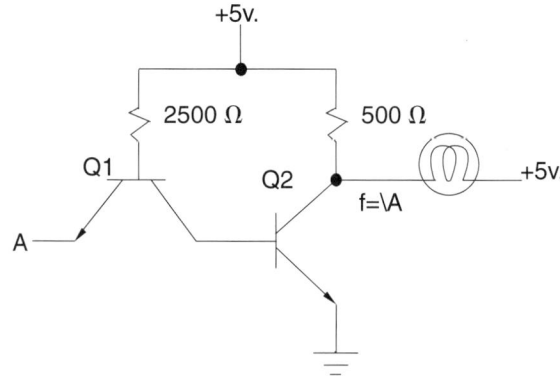

Figure 3.4. The circuit schematic of a TTL inverter.

It is interesting that the input transistor Q1 may have two input wires. If it does, the logic device is a two-input NAND gate whose circuit schematic is shown in Figure 3.5. The output of such a gate is low only when both inputs are high. Because the two input wires are separately connected to the emitter of the input transistor Q1 as *A* AND *B*, we have four input combinations, as described here:

1. *A* is high, *B* is low: The Q1 transistor is on. As a result, a collector current is pulled off the base of Q2. The transistor Q2 is off, so its output is high.
2. *A* is low, *B* is high: This is similar to Case 1; the Q1 transistor is on, and Q2 is off. Thus, the collector output of Q2 is high.
3. *A* is low, *B* is low: The Q1 transistor is on, and Q2 is off. Therefore, the collector output of Q2 is high.

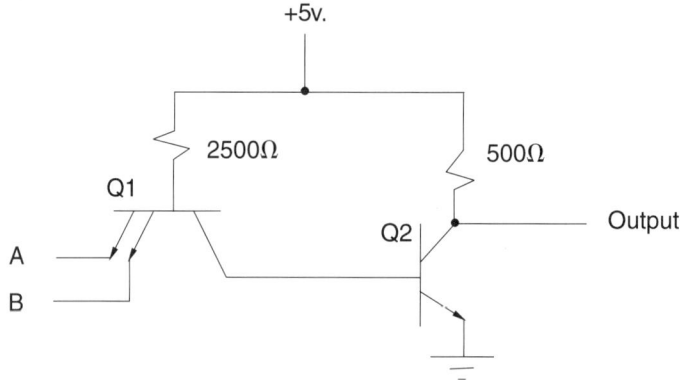

Figure 3.5. The circuit schematic of a two-input TTL NAND gate.

4. *A* is high, *B* is high: The Q1 transistor is off. As the base-collector junction of Q1 becomes forward-biased, a current flows into the base of Q2. Thus, the Q2 transistor is driven to saturated state so that its output is near ground.

Obviously, for the first three conditions (i.e., any low input), Q1 is on and Q2 is off so the output is high. The only condition necessary to obtain a low output is when both inputs *A* and *B* are high. As a result, Q1 is cut off, and Q2 is bottomed because its collector is pulled down to 0.1 v.

We should bear two things in mind. First, the TTL NAND gate is simple and intuitive. To make an AND gate out of it, we need to place an inverter after the output. Second, the emitter of the input transistor may have more than two wires. Therefore, there are a three-input NAND gate, a four-input NAND gate, and an eight-input NAND gate in TTL. For all the NAND gates, the output is low only when all inputs are high.

In addition to TTL, the ECL circuits were noted for their ultrahigh speed and high price. In such a circuit, each transistor is not driven hard enough, so it is not saturated. In other words, the transistor operates in the active region, so there is always a voltage drop between the collector and its emitter. If a transistor is not saturated, the switching time is reduced. Although TTL circuits are popular in many computers, unipolar ICs started making their way into the mainstream. In 1971, the early large-scale integration circuits were built with PMOS (P-channel metal oxide semiconductor) transistors [Pawl84]; unfortunately, such circuits are not compatible with TTL. In 1974, the NMOS (N-channel MOS) circuits were developed to provide not only faster speed but also compatibility with TTL. In 1984, when VLSI began to emerge, the power dissipation problem of NMOS became serious; it is a limiting factor to the continued increase of packing densities on the chip. As an alternative, many manufacturers turned to CMOS (complementary MOS), which is a combination of PMOS and NMOS and is compatible with TTL. The basic theories behind all the unipolar transistor circuits are described in the following.

3.4   *Unipolar Transistors*

A unipolar transistor is also known as a metal oxide semiconductor transistor. The full name should be MOSFET (metal oxide semiconductor field effect transistor), but in this book, we limit our discussions to silicon-based MOS. The *field effect* concept is different from that of the bipolar transistors. As a matter of fact, the unipolar transistor idea was conceived before the bipolar transistor [Dace55]. After many decades of effort, the idea was modified almost to perfection. That is, each MOSFET operates like a switch, and many such switches can be placed on one silicon wafer.

One distinctive feature of a MOS transistor is its small size, which means that the transistor consumes less power and generates less heat than a bipolar transistor. Consequently, the MOS circuits were widely used in CPUs, memory modules, and I/O controllers. As with the bipolar transistors, many different processes were developed to manufacture the MOS circuits. Let us explore the original unipolar idea, which was to use one piece of negatively doped semiconductor. The semiconductor was clamped by two metal parts at the two ends, known as the *drain* and the *source*, respectively. The middle section is attached to a gate made of metal. If we apply a positive voltage to the middle gate, then negative charges (i.e., electrons) would flow from the source to the drain. Because the channel is made of one piece of semiconductor, the device is called a *unipolar transistor*.

Some modifications have been made in modern MOS transistors. There are two types of MOS transistors, and both were derived from the original idea. Each MOS type uses a doped channel controlled by a voltage applied at the metal gate. The doped channel may be positively or negatively charged. Two questions remain to be answered. First, what does a doped area mean? Second, what does the term *field effect* mean? The answers are described in the next section.

3.4.1   NMOS

We discuss NMOS first, then PMOS. The physical layout of an NMOS transistor is shown in Figure 3.6(a). The channel is one piece of silicon substrate positively doped (P-Si). The S (source) region is at one end, and the D (drain) region is at the other end. The two regions are negatively doped and have equal physical sizes, so the transistor has a symmetrical shape. Above the regions and the channel, there is a silicon oxide layer designed as a dielectric, like a capacitor. Above the oxide, there is an aluminum-based metal for gate voltage control. A unipolar transistor is a switch, known as a basic gate. Several such basic gates can be interconnected to make a logic gate.

The circuit symbol of an NMOS transistor is shown in Figure 3.6(b). The NMOS transistor acts like a switch with or without a current flow. If a current flows in it, the switch is on, or closed. If no current flows in it, the switch is off, or open. At the gate input, note that the absence of a circle indicates that switch is positively activated. In other words, if an input voltage higher than the source by the threshold margin applied at the gate, the switch is turned on. There are several key ideas:

1. The two sides of the oxide act like a capacitor, and a metal wire to it is used for gate voltage control.

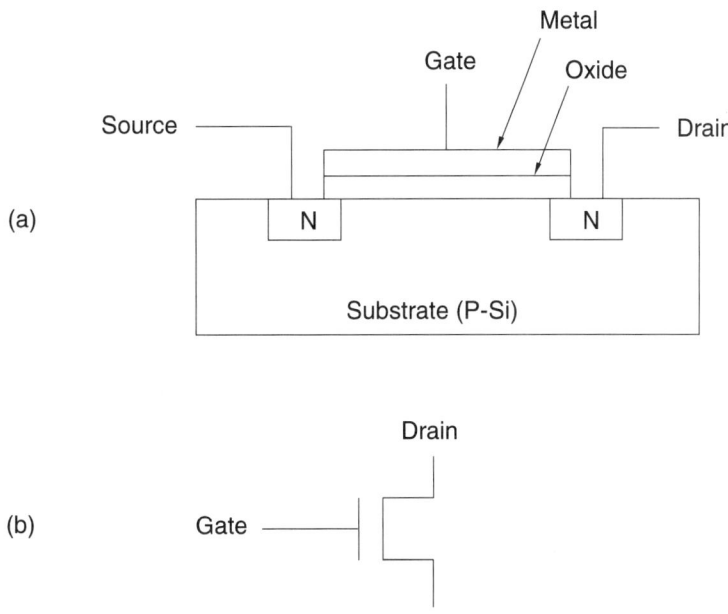

Figure 3.6. The N-channel MOS transistor: (a) physical layout and (b) circuit schematic.

2. When a relative negative input voltage is applied to the gate input, positively charged holes are induced in the channel right below the oxide layer to block any current from flowing in the channel. As a result, the switch is in cutoff state with no current flow.
3. When a positive input voltage above the threshold with respect to the source is applied to the gate, negative charges are induced in the channel. As a result, a current flows from the drain to the source, so the switch is on.

The drain voltage (Vdd) can be 3.3 v. or lower, and the source voltage (Vss) is near to 0 v., the ground voltage. When the input is switched from 0 to 3.3 v., the NMOS transistor is turned on. As a result, current flows from the power supply through the channel to the ground. An early four-bit microprocessor chip was an NMOS.

3.4.2   PMOS

The physical layout of a PMOS transistor is shown in Figure 3.7(a). The silicon substrate is negatively doped (N-Si), and the two regions are positively doped. If a gate input voltage is lower than the drain voltage by a threshold margin, positively charged holes are induced in the channel right below the oxide layer. Consequently, a current flows from the drain to the source, so the switch is closed.

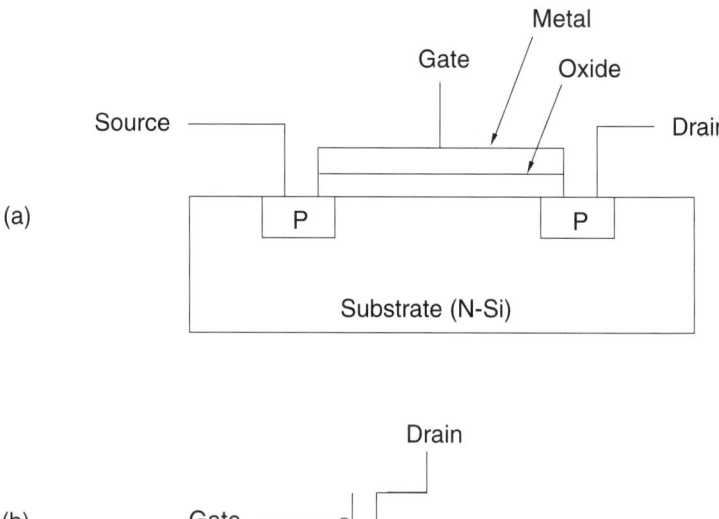

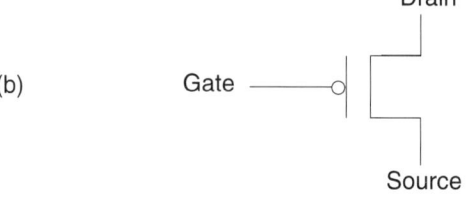

(a)

(b)

Figure 3.7. The P-channel MOS transistor: (a) physical layout and (b) circuit schematic.

The circuit symbol of a PMOS switch is shown in Figure 3.7(b). Note that the presence of a circle at the gate input indicates that the switch is negatively activated. We elaborate the concept as follows. If we use the same power supply, the drain voltage is 3.3 v., and the source voltage is 0 v. If a gate voltage is near Vdd, say, 3.3 v., no current can flow in the channel, so the switch is cut off, or open. On the other hand, if the gate input voltage is lower than Vdd but higher than Vss, the current flows from Vdd to Vss, so the switch is on, or closed. We stress the following three points:

1. The MOS technology is great for designing electronic switches.
2. A high input voltage turns on an NMOS switch, and a low input voltage turns on a PMOS switch.
3. When a switch is turned on, a current always flows from a high voltage, the drain, to a low voltage, the source.

3.4.3   CMOS

One silicon substrate may have many areas doped with either positive or negative charges. Such a large doped area on a silicon substrate is called a *well*. Interestingly, many areas on a well can be doped with a different type of material. Thus, it is possible to place PMOS transistors and NMOS transistors on the same silicon substrate. We can connect a PMOS transistor and an NMOS transistor in series and tie the two inputs together, as shown in Figure 3.8. Thus, we obtain a special CMOS logic circuit, also known as the inverter or the NOT gate. In Figure 3.8, we see two MOS transistors complementing each other in series. Between the two MOS transistors, only one can be on at a time regardless of the input conditions. Between the transistors, we provide the NOT function as output. Note that the lower output transistor is an NMOS, and we place a light bulb between the output and the drain voltage. If the input voltage is high, the NMOS switch is on, so its drain output is pulled down, near ground level with sinking current capability. In other words, the NMOS can sink current, so the light bulb is on. Recall that a TTL inverter has a similar property so that the two logic families are compatible. Where the switching concept is concerned, the NMOS output transistor in CMOS is not different from an NPN output transistor in TTL. Note that the resistance of the bulb limits the amount of current, so the NMOS transistor will not be burnt out. We discuss the two input conditions as follows:

1. Input is high: The upper **PMOS** switch is off, but the lower NMOS switch is on. Therefore, the output voltage is near 0 v., as it is effectively connected to ground.
2. Input is low: The upper **PMOS** switch is on, but the lower NMOS switch is off. Therefore, its output voltage is high because the output is effectively connected to the drain voltage.

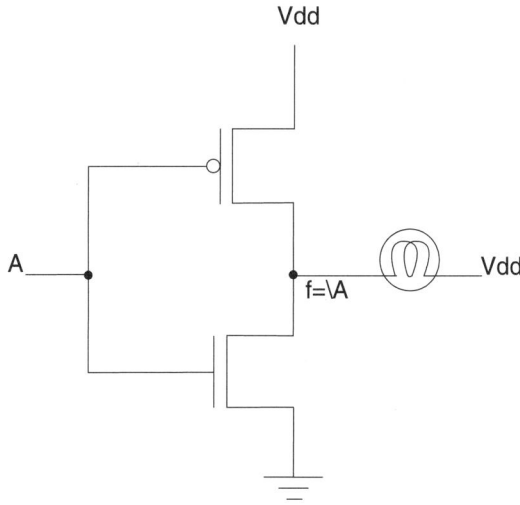

Figure 3.8. The circuit schematic of a CMOS inverter.

In a CMOS inverter circuit, the upper PMOS transistor represents the NOT function of input A ($\backslash A$), and the lower transistor represents its complement (A). The input variable A can be true or false. However, when one switch is on, the other switch is off. As a result, a current can never flow through the two transistors in series, so no energy is consumed except the charging and discharging of the metal gates. The design principles of CMOS circuits can be generalized as in the following:

1. A CMOS circuit can be divided into two halves. The upper half is made of PMOS transistors, and the lower half is made of NMOS transistors.
2. The upper half is the realized function (f), and the lower half is the complement of the realized function ($\backslash f$).
3. The two halves are connected in series, and the middle junction point provides the output.

We elaborate this concept with two more examples: a NAND circuit and a NOR circuit. As shown in Figure 3.9, we design a two-input CMOS NAND gate that uses four unipolar transistors. In the upper half, the

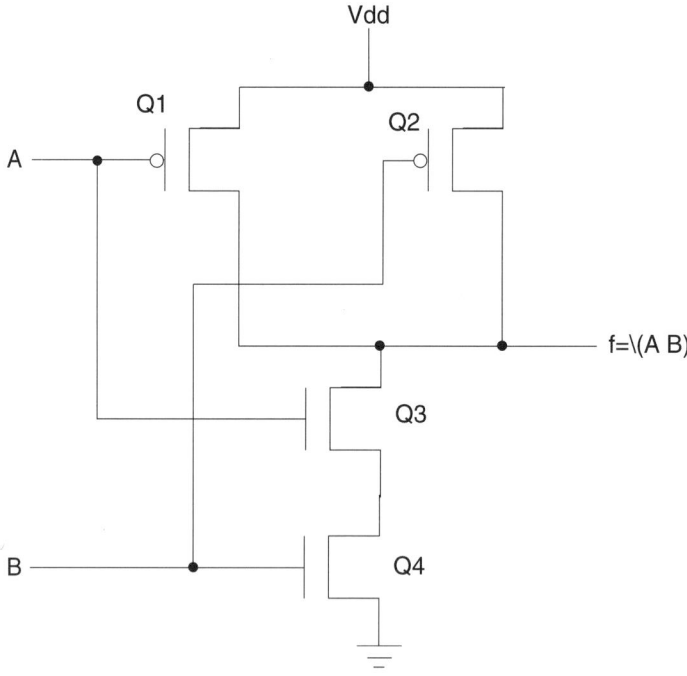

Figure 3.9. The circuit schematic of a CMOS two-input NAND gate.

top two **PMOS** transistors, named Q1 and Q2, are connected in parallel to realize the NAND function:

$$f = (\backslash A + \backslash B)$$

In the lower half, the two **NMOS** transistors, named Q3 and Q4, are connected in series to realize the complement of the NAND function:

$$\backslash f = (A \cdot B)$$

Given two inputs A and B, we have four combinations, and the only condition to generate a low output is when both inputs are high. Using positive logic—a high voltage is defined as 1 and a low voltage is defined as 0—we explain the NAND logic as follows:

1. A is high, B is high: The top Q1 and Q2 are cut off, but the bottom Q3 and Q4 are on. Therefore, the output f is effectively connected to ground.
2. A is high, B is low: One of the two gates on top is off, and one of the two gates on the bottom is off. Precisely, Q1 is on, Q2 is off, Q3 is on, and Q4 is off. As a result, the output f is connected to a high-voltage Vdd.
3. A is low, B is high: This case is similar to Case 2. That is, Q1 is off, Q2 is on, Q3 is off, and Q4 is on. As a result, the output f is connected to Vdd.
4. A is low, B is low: The top two switches are on but the bottom two are off. As a result, the output f is high.

We can rearrange the four transistors to make a two-input NOR gate, as shown in Figure 3.10.

In the upper half, the two **PMOS** transistors, Q1 and Q2, are connected in series to realize the true function:

$$f = (\backslash A \cdot \backslash B)$$

In the lower half, the two **NMOS** transistors, Q3 and Q4, are connected in parallel to realize the complement function:

$$\backslash f = (A + B)$$

The NOR circuit shows that the output f is low if one of its two inputs is high. Based on the high-low voltage relationship, we plot Table 3.1 as follows.

From Table 3.1, the letter L indicates a low voltage, and the letter H indicates a high voltage. As far as logic is concerned, we have two op-

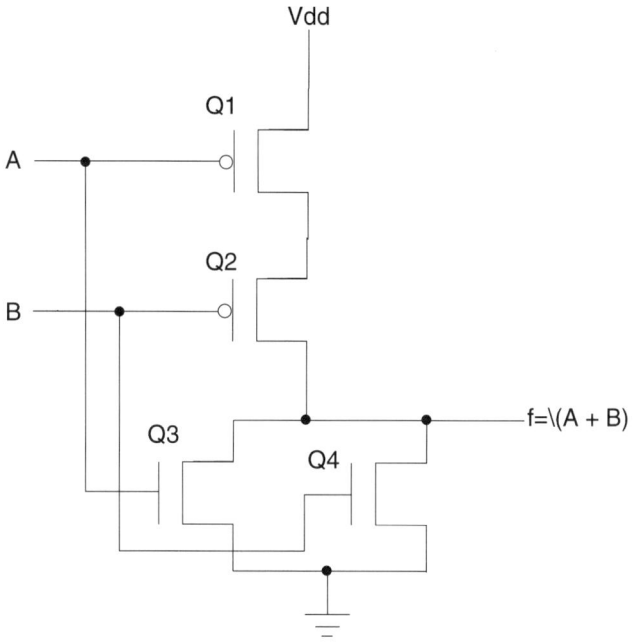

Figure 3.10. The circuit schematic of a CMOS two-input NOR gate.

tions. Using positive logic convention, we define a high voltage as True (i.e., 1) and a low voltage as False (i.e., 0). As a result, the logic circuit is a two-input NOR gate. However, we can use negative logic convention to define a low voltage as True (i.e., 1) and a high voltage as False (i.e., 0). Because of this change of definition, the same logic circuit becomes a two-input NAND gate in that the output f is False (i.e., high) if both of its inputs are True (i.e., low). When that happens, both Q1 and Q2 are on and Q3 and Q4 are off, so the output f is Vdd. Note that the high-low voltage relationship in Table 3.1 does not change. Therefore, we often use such a table to specify the physical properties of an electronic logic circuit.

Table 3.1. Two-input NOR function using positive logic.

Input		Output
A	B	f
L	L	H
L	H	L
H	L	L
H	H	L

In CMOS, a NAND gate is simpler than an AND gate. By placing an inverter after a NAND gate, we obtain an AND gate. Because an AND gate tends to use more switches, it has a longer circuit delay than a NAND. In Boolean algebra, an AND function is simpler than a NAND, but in practice, the realization of a NAND is simpler than an AND. Similarly, a NOR gate is simpler than an OR gate. By placing an inverter after a NOR gate, we obtain an OR gate. We conclude the following two points:

1. From a mathematical viewpoint, the two-input AND and the two-input OR operators are considered the basic logic functions.
2. From an electronic viewpoint, the two-input NAND gate is simpler than the two-input AND gate; the 2-NOR gate is simpler than the two-input OR gate.

Usually, a CMOS circuit is divided into two halves that are connected in series. Because one function is the complement of the other, the circuit cannot have a current flow, so it consumes less power. In VLSI or ULSI design, where many logic gates are cascaded together, we can cut corners to make a circuit simpler. Let us design an EOR (Exclusive OR) circuit, as proposed in Figure 3.11. The circuit uses four transistors arranged in two branches, which are symmetrical, Each branch has a PMOS transistor and an NMOS transistor in series. The two inputs A and B are fed to the bases, so the left branch represents ($\backslash A$ B) and the right branch represents (A $\backslash B$). The left branch is closed if A is low and B is high, but the right branch is closed if A is high and B is low. Hence-

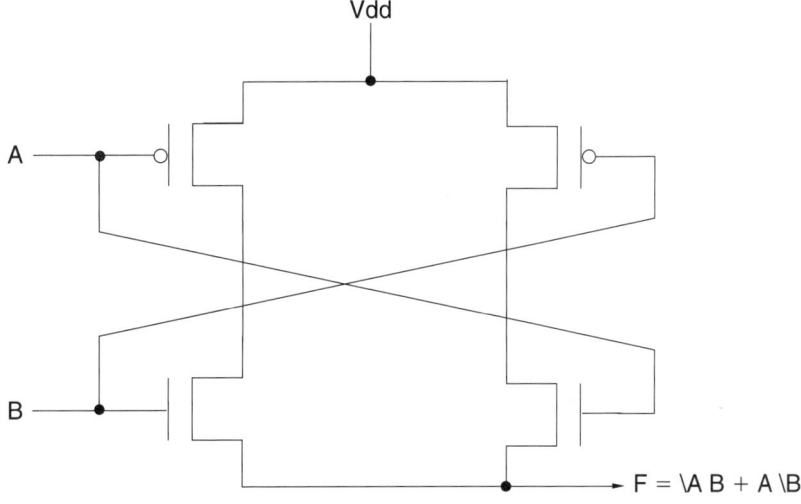

Figure 3.11. The circuit schematic of a CMOS two-input EOR gate.

forth, the output of the EOR circuit is Vdd, a high voltage, if the two inputs differ. In the case where the two inputs A and B are the same, both branches are open, so the output is open. One option is to place a resistor between the output and the ground. We discuss two design issues in the following:

1. The EOR output without a resistor may serve as input to a logic gate in the next stage.
2. The two sources of the PMOS transistors (i.e., the two drains of the NMOS transistors) can be tied together. As the current in the upper PMOS cannot cross the branches because one switch is the complement of the other, the output remains the same. With such a connection, we can apply the distributive law to derive the same EOR function as follows:

$$f = (\backslash A + \backslash B)\,(A + B)$$
$$= \backslash A\,A + A\,\backslash B + \backslash A\,B + \backslash B\,B$$
$$= \backslash A\,B + A\,\backslash B$$

EOR circuits are popular in logic design. Some applications include parity bit generation and detection, adders, checksum as error detection code, and comparators. The design details of logic circuits are discussed in the next chapter. In IC development, it is common to find TTL circuits in an SSI or MSI chip and CMOS circuits in a VLSI or ULSI chip. Due to a breakthrough, the CMOS process has established itself as the paramount leader in designing battery-operated devices, including laptops, personal digital assistants, digital cameras, and wireless phones.

3.4.4   COPPER TECHNOLOGY

The CMOS process has already achieved high speed, high density, and low power, but can we make progress to further reduce the power? The answer is yes. Power is defined as the product of voltage and current, so we have two approaches to make improvements. The first approach is to reduce the drain voltage, and the second approach is to use Cu (Copper) for interconnects. It is natural to decrease the drain voltage if the transistor size on a chip is getting smaller and the current through the transistor is kept constant. A smaller transistor means that it takes less energy to switch the transistor. Based on the 0.13-micron technology, we can decrease the drain voltage from 3.3 v. to 2.9 v., or even to 2.0 v.

Using copper for interconnections is intuitive because the power dissipated on a wire generates heat. The amount of heat power is proportional to the resistance of the wire if the current is constant. Each

MOSFET has metal parts: the front gate and the interconnect wires. The gate controls the current flow in the channel, and the wires are used to interconnect transistors on the chip. The CMOS processes using traditional aluminum-based wires have been perfected through more than three decades of experience. However, in the past decade, copper metallization technology for IC interconnects has been studied and tried. This new technology uses copper-based materials to interconnect transistors on the chip [Brau99]. A VLSI or ULSI chip has many layers. The bottom layer is the silicon substrate, and the top layers are for interconnect lines (i.e., wires). Each layer above the silicon has many interconnect lines deposited with copper-based material. Even though the design goal is simple, there are still many technical difficulties to be overcome. Credit is due to IBM for initiating this immense research effort.

3.5   Electronic Design Issues

There are many electronic issues in designing a logic circuit. Logic circuits are the basic design elements in a processing unit, memory module, I/O controller, and even power supply. Fortunately, all the circuits can be placed on a single chip. It is often necessary to interconnect design elements or logic circuits to make a more complex circuit. Where circuits are concerned, we should understand some basic design issues, including timing delays, input/output voltages, input/output currents, noise, and power consumption. The manufacturer of each IC provides a reference sheet to specify timing delay, input/output voltages, input/output currents, temperatures, powers, and so on. The ICs—bipolar or unipolar—from different families are compatible so long as they share the same electronic specifications.

Let us introduce the key difference between a combinational circuit and a sequential circuit. A combinational logic circuit is designed to realize a Boolean function. To put many logic gates together, we must consider the timing delays through the gates. A sequential circuit uses storage elements known as flip-flops in addition to logic gates. A flip-flop often uses a clock signal to control the timing of its output voltage changes. That is, the leading edge or the trailing edge of a clock signal triggers the internal circuitry of an ff (flip-flop). In other words, the output voltage of a flip-flop changes synchronously with the clock. We say that the sequential circuits are in sync with the clock. Many design issues include circuit delays, fan-out capability, input/output voltage levels, input/output current levels, and operating environment, including noise, temperature, and vibration.

3.5.1   CIRCUIT DELAYS

The input signal to a logic gate is an almost perfectly shaped rectangular pulse. The rising edge of such a pulse is slightly slanted due to input capacitance because it takes time to charge the transistor from cutoff state to saturated state. Similarly, the falling edge is also slanted because it takes time to discharge a transistor to turn it off. Comparing the output waveform with its input, we notice a short timing delay, which is considered the number one design parameter. In general, the MSI circuits have a delay of one nanosecond (ns or 10^{-9} s) per gate. In the ECL family, we can reduce the timing delay by feeding a very small current into the base. After amplification, if the collector current is not big enough to saturate the transistor, a voltage drop exists between the collector and its emitter. We say that the transistor operates in the active region, so both its input and its output signals look like sinusoidal waves. As a consequence, the timing delay of such a transistor may be reduced to 100 ps or less.

    As the transistors on a chip become smaller and smaller, switching times become shorter and shorter. As the length of the wire connection between two transistors becomes shorter, the time for the signal to propagate on the line is shorter. Because the sum of switching time and propagation time determines the basic clock rate, a CPU can operate at 1.5 GHz (gigaHertz) or faster.

3.5.2   COMPATIBILITY

If logic circuits from different families are used to design a digital system, we must be sure that all the circuits share the same specifications, such as voltage levels, current levels, and the direction of current flow. In the case where all the circuits are compatible, they can be interchanged. As an example, the CMOS and TTL circuits are compatible and can be interchanged.

Fan-Out Capability

Each logic device specifies its voltages and currents for input and output. In TTL, a current is drawn from the emitter of its input transistor when the voltage is low. The input transistor then activates the next transistor in the circuit. That means that the output transistor has the capability to sink a current into its collector. If the input current is one-tenth of the output current, the logic gate has a fan-out capability of 10. That is, the output of this TTL gate can drive ten inputs. What if there are more than ten places in the circuit that require the same signal? We can make one of two choices. First, we can duplicate the signal using extra gates. Second, we can replace the TTL gate with a powerful driver that serves as a buffer that outputs the same signal with more power. If the driver has a fan-out ratio of twenty, its output can drive 20 inputs. In fact, the CPU needs to duplicate the clock signal so that all the circuits can receive the clock at the same time. Remember that the TTL gate has a sinking current capability but not a driving current capability.

Operating Environment

Typical operating environment problems include temperature, noise, and vibration. The amplification factor of a transistor changes if the surrounding temperature changes. Therefore, a logic device should work correctly within a wide range of temperature. In commercial applications, the chip should sustain between 0° and 70° Centigrade. In military applications, the temperature range is even wider. In the following, we discuss noise-related issues.

Definition 3.2. A *noise* is a spurious voltage signal that is generated internally or externally in the circuit.

An external noise is due to electromagnetic radiation. An internal noise is present in the circuit when the operating temperature is above absolute zero. It is caused by the thermal agitation of electrons associated with each atom in the device. This is so-called *thermal noise*, or *white noise*. Logic circuits should be immune to noise to a certain degree.

Definition 3.3. *Noise immunity* is the amount of noise that can be applied to the input signal of a gate that will not change the logic state of its output.

Typically, valid input signals should cover a range for both high and low voltages. For example, if 3.3 v. from the power supply is the nominal high voltage and 0 v. is the nominal low voltage, a high input signal may be between 2.5 and 4.1 v., and a low input signal may be between −0.5 and 0.8 v. If the logic device is not susceptible to noise, then it has better noise immunity. A CMOS circuit has a high input impedance, so a voltage with little current (nanoamperes) can switch its state. A TTL circuit needs a voltage with some current (microamperes) to switch its state. It is much more difficult to induce noise in the form of current than in the form of voltage. Therefore, a TTL circuit has better noise immunity than CMOS. In other words, a TTL chip is less likely to be triggered by a noise.

If a device needs to operate in a vibrating environment, such as a car or rocket, all the signal pins may become loose after a period of time. One common solution is to place the digital system in an epoxy package that can sustain heavy shaking. In the next section, we will study the voltage waveform of a digital signal and different ways to encode a bit in the form of high-low voltage combinations.

3.6   *Digital Waveforms*

A CPU consists of combinational logic circuits and sequential logic circuits. In simple terms, a combinational circuit comprises logic gates only, and a sequential circuit comprises logic gates and flip-flops. A flip-flop is a logic device used to store one bit, as explained in the next chapter. Both logic gates and flip-flops are used to perform control in a CPU; they are referred to as hardwired logic. Before we discuss the design of flip-flops, let us study the voltage waveform of a digital signal. A waveform has two voltage levels, high and low. The combination of such high-low voltages can represent a digital signal. In other words, we use high-low voltage combinations to encode a bit (binary digit) as 1 or 0. The output voltage of a ff may change with time, as controlled by the clock signal. Using positive logic, a high voltage is defined as 1 and a low voltage is defined as 0. We study the clock signal, the digital signal, and the MC (Manchester code) in the following sections.

3.6.1   *CLOCKS*

The waveform of a single clock signal is shown in Figure 3.12.

The clock signal stays at 0 v., a low voltage, goes up to 3.3 v., a high voltage, and then goes back to low. The front edge of the high pulse is called the *leading edge* or *positive edge*. The rear edge of the high pulse is called the *trailing edge* or *negative edge*. The time duration of the high-

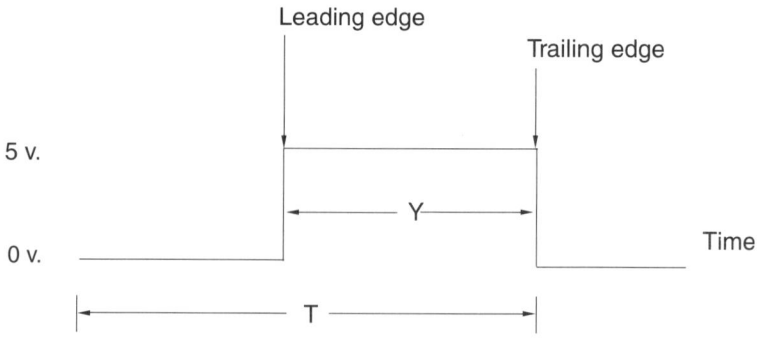

Figure 3.12. A single clock signal.

voltage pulse is designated as Y. The period T is defined to be the total time duration of the low voltage and the high voltage in a single clock. In a computer, the clock has a frequency F. However, the period T, computed as the inverse of F, is more visible on an oscilloscope.

Duty Cycle

The ratio of the time of high-voltage Y over the clock period T is defined to be the duty cycle of the clock:

$$duty\ cycle = time\ of\ high\ voltage\ /\ period\ of\ clock$$
$$= Y\ /\ T$$

Usually, the clock signal has a 50 percent duty cycle, which means that the clock stays low for a half period and switches to high voltage for a half period. As the clock rate goes higher, if a clock provides drive current to a very high-speed gate or flip-flop, its duty cycle may go up to 66 percent so to provide more energy, as required to switch the device.

Leading Edge Vs. Trailing Edge

When the clock signal goes from low voltage to high voltage, it is said to be the leading edge of the positive pulse. Thus, leading edge also means positive edge. When the clock signal goes down at the end of the clock cycle, it is the trailing edge. Thus, trailing edge also means negative edge. Depending on the design, some sequential logic devices use the leading edge to control the timing, while others use the trailing edge.

Because a clock signal is used to control the timing of sequential circuits, a CPU, memory, or I/O controller each has its own internal clock. The internal clock provides the basic timing reference for its control functions. A clock generator is a crystal-based oscillator that generates sinusoidal voltage waveforms at a fixed frequency. Through the reshaping circuit, its output is a continuous rectangular pulse train. In other words, each single clock signal has a low voltage followed by a high voltage.

Clock Frequency Vs. Clock Period

The speed of a clock can be measured by its frequency, or period. Given two CPUs with the same architecture, the clock rate usually indicates the raw speed of the CPU. Hence, the 1000-MHz CPU is about twice as fast as the 500-MHz CPU. Using frequency to measure the speed is common, but engineers like to measure the clock speed in term of its period, that is, the inverse of the frequency. Thus, the 1-GHz (1000-MHz) clock has a period of 1 nanosecond, and the 500-MHz clock has a period of 2 nanoseconds. The 1-ns clock is faster than a 2-ns clock by a factor of 2. More importantly, the difference in speed can be displayed on an oscilloscope.

3.6.2   DIGITAL SIGNAL

The digital signal is used in the CPU, memory, and I/O controllers. For short distance transmission, the digital signal is ideal because of its simplicity and intuitiveness. As shown in Figure 3.13(a), the clock is a continuous pulse train of high-low rectangular voltages. The digital signal waveform looks like a clock train except that its frequency is halved. As shown in Figure 3.13(b), the particular digital signal has alternate 0 and 1 combinations. Precisely, each digital signal is a rectangular waveform of two voltage levels. For positive logic, a high voltage represents one full-bit of time, that is, one clock period of time. In contrast a 0, has low voltage for one clock period. In other words, its period is doubled. A typical logic circuit uses a high voltage of 3.3 v. As the chip density increases, the high voltage supplied to the chip can be dropped from 3.3 to 2.9 v., or even lower. The digital signal used to drive those devices off the chip needs power, so its voltage is still 5 v.

The bit string of an ASCII b is displayed in Figure 3.13(c), provided that the b0 (bit 0) is transmitted first. If we store an ASCII character in an eight-bit byte, the msb or b7 (bit 7) is padded with a 0. On the line, the bit 0 is a 0 followed by a 1, 3 0s, 2 1s, and another 0. The last data bit (b7) transmitted on the line is the padded 0. Due to its simplicity, the digital signal is commonly used in CPU, memory, and I/O controllers. In addition, it is used for short distance transmission between two hardware components in one computer or between two computers. If we compare the digital signal for alternate 0 and 1 combinations with the clock train, the digital signal switches its voltage level at the trailing edge of the clock so that its frequency is halved.

If a bit string is transmitted serially from one device to another, the

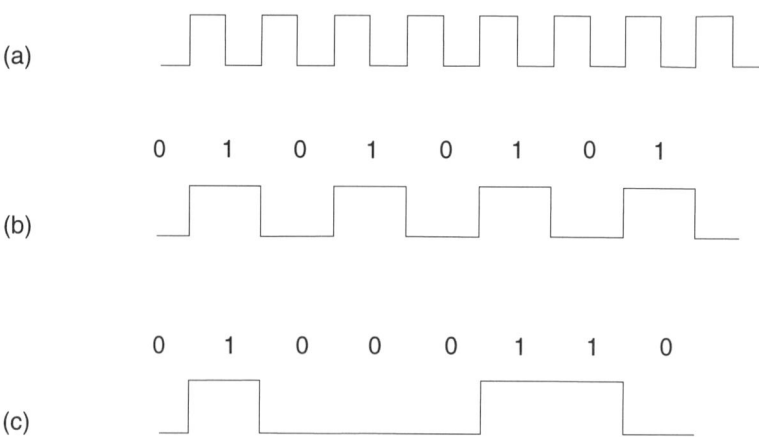

Figure 3.13. Digital signals: (a) clock, (b) alternate 0 and 1 combinations, and (c) ASCII b.

time interval per bit is equal to the clock period. A problem arises when a digital circuit uses inductive coupling, (i.e., transformer coupling). For example, the circuit cannot record the digital signal on disk or tape because when the digital signal contains a long string of consecutive 1s or 0s, it acts like a direct current and it cannot change the magnetic flux in the primary coil. As a result, no signal can be induced in the secondary. Bluntly put, the digital signal cannot be recorded. The Manchester code was developed in England as a first solution to this problem. That is, we oscillate the voltage levels per bit, from high to low, and vice versa. Note that an I/O controller uses the digital signal in its logic circuit, but during a read/write operation on the magnetic surface, it uses MC (Manchester code) instead.

3.6.3 MANCHESTER CODE

The Manchester code has a transition in the middle of a bit. If the transition goes up, that is, if a half-bit low voltage is followed by a half-bit high voltage, the bit is a 0. If the transition goes down, it is a 1. The EOR gate takes two inputs with such a property that its output is high when its two inputs differ. If one input is high, the other input must be low to generate a high output. In the case when both of its inputs are the same, its output is low. As depicted in Figure 3.14(a), an EOR

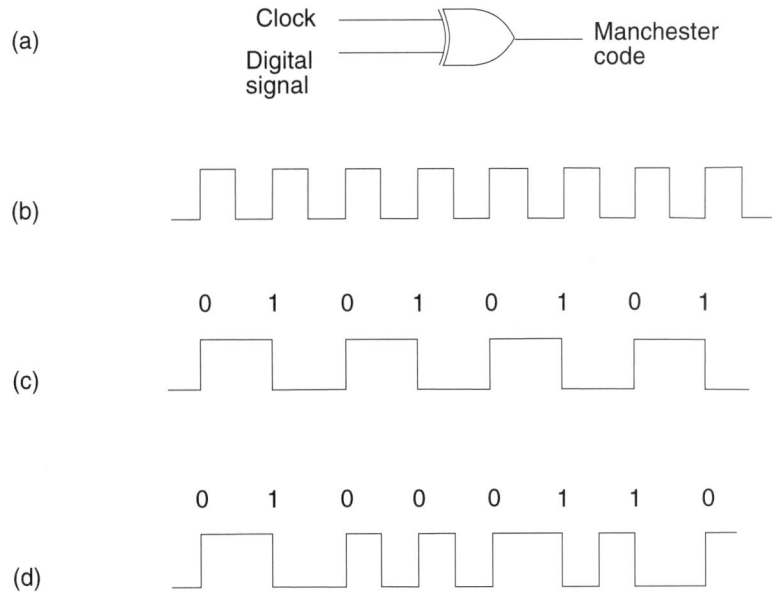

Figure 3.14. Manchester code: (a) generation circuit, (b) clock, (c) alternate 0 and 1 combinations, and (d) ASCII b.

gate symbol has an arc in front of a two-input OR gate. One input is the digital signal, the other is the clock signal, and the output is the MC for the digital signal.

One input to the EOR gate is the digital signal, and the other is the clock. The digital signal is not plotted, but the waveform of the clock is plotted in Figure 3.14(b). The clock pulse serves as the timing reference. The logic symbol for an EOR gate has an extra arc positioned before the two-input OR gate. To make an ENOR gate symbol, we append a circle at the output of an EOR gate to denote the NOT function. The form of a bit string of alternate 0 and 1 combinations is shown in Figure 3.14(c). If the b0 (bit 0) is transmitted first on the line, the MC waveform for an ASCII b is plotted in (d).

In fact, the Manchester code is known as a phase-modulated code whose frequency is in sync with the clock. Looking at a single clock signal, the true form is a 0, and the complement or inverse of a clock signal is a 1. Therefore, the clock train itself is a string of 0s in MC. Notice that MC is polarity-dependent, so by flipping the two wires, we obtain the inverse or complement of the signal. In other words, the inverse of the clock train represents a string of 1s. In Manchester encoding, we double the frequency or bandwidth of the signal to enforce a voltage change in the middle of a bit. The MC is widely used in magnetic recording, Ethernet, and other communication lines. It is interesting to know that in a token-ring LAN (local area network), the DMC (differential Manchester code) is used instead. Such an encoding is a derivative of MC, but it is polarity-independent. Henceforth, it makes no difference to a logic circuit if the two input signal wires are swapped [Hsu96].

3.7 Summary Points

1. The transistor in a logic circuit is made of semiconductor materials: silicon, germanium, or gallium arsenide.
2. A bipolar junction transistor consists of three layers designed as a current amplifier.
3. A MOS (metal oxide semiconductor) is a unipolar transistor using the field effect concept in physics.
4. The CMOS logic family has established itself as the leader in VLSI or ULSI design because of its low power consumption.
5. The copper interconnect technology provides faster circuits on an IC than its aluminum interconnect counterpart.
6. The logic circuits in a computer are usually synchronized in that a clock signal is used to determine the timing.

7. Noise immunity is defined as the maximum amount of noise that can be applied to the input signal of a gate such that the logic state of its output will not change.
8. A clock signal is a continuous pulse train of high-low rectangular voltage waveforms.
9. A rectangular waveform of two voltage levels is often used to represent 1s and 0s in a digital circuit.
10. The Manchester code is used for magnetic recording and for Ethernet transmissions.
11. The switching time is determined by the transistor size and the interconnect wire between two transistors.

Problems

3.1 What is a logic device or circuit?

3.2 What is a semiconductor process?

3.3 How many transistors are placed in a VLSI (very large-scale integration) chip and a ULSI (ultralarge-scale integration) chip?

3.4 What is a bipolar junction transistor, and what is the difference between an NPN transistor and a PNP transistor?

3.5 What is the reversed β of a bipolar junction transistor?

3.6 Explain how a bipolar junction can operate in cutoff, active, and saturated regions.

3.7 Draw the circuit schematic of a two-input TTL NAND gate.

3.8 What is a unipolar transistor, and what is the difference between a PMOS and an NMOS?

3.9 Why does a CMOS circuit save power?

3.10 Draw the circuit schematic of a two-input CMOS NAND gate.

3.11 Draw the circuit schematic of a two-input CMOS NOR gate.

3.12 What is a circuit delay in a transistor?

3.13 Define the propagation line delay time between two transistors.

3.14 Given a logic circuit with gates and flip-flops, explain the difference between the driving current and sinking current capabilities of its output power.

3.15 Why is copper interconnect technology superior in VLSI design?

3.16 In VLSI design, is it correct to say that the bottom layer is silicon substrate and the top layers are interconnect wires?

3.17 Define the noise immunity of a logic circuit.

3.18 Describe the frequency, period, leading edge, and trailing edge of a clock.

3.19 Define the duty cycle of a clock. Is it possible for the time duration of the high voltage to be shorter than the time duration of the low voltage?

3.20 Why does the clock period determine the raw speed of a circuit?

3.21 In regard to recent IC development, people are talking about nanotechnology. If 1 nanometer (nm) is equal to one-billionth of a meter (10^{-9} m), how many nanometers are in 0.03 micron?

3.22 Why is a straight digital signal not suitable for magnetic recording?

3.23 What is the digital signal waveform of an ASCII b displayed on an oscilloscope if b0 (bit 0) is transmitted first?

3.24 The five eight-bit strings are given in the following. First, plot the waveform of a positive clock train as a reference for timing. Then, for each bit string, plot its waveform in digital signal form and its Manchester code form:

1. 00000000   2. 11111111   3. 01010101
4. 10101010   5. 01000110

Combinational Logic Circuits

In a digital system, the logic circuits can be divided into two classes: combinational and sequential. A *combinational circuit* uses logic gates only; a *sequential circuit* uses flip-flops (ffs) and logic gates. The discussion of ffs is left to the next chapter. Most of the flip-flops are synchronous. Such a flip-flop has two sets of input—the clock and the data—and its output state changes in synchronization with the clock.

Even though a sequential circuit uses synchronous flip-flops to store bits of information, each ff needs combinational logic circuits to generate its excitation inputs. Henceforth, in logic design, the control part of a sequential circuit uses logic gates as the basic building blocks. Because the logic gates are connected in a series, the timing delay per gate is critical. The timing delay of the longest path in a sequential circuit determines the raw speed. Generally speaking, the total circuit delay should not exceed one clock period. Note that either a combinational or sequential circuit accepts many signals as input and generates many signals as output in the form of high-low voltage combinations.

4.1 Basic Logic Gates

The circuit schematic of a logic gate may be different, but its logic function gate is the same. Therefore, it is necessary to establish an industrial standard, so a set of standard graphic symbols is used to represent different logic gates [IEEE91]. Basically, the shape of a gate defines the logic function regardless of the transistor circuits used in the design. Algebraically, the NOT gate, two-input AND gate, and two-input

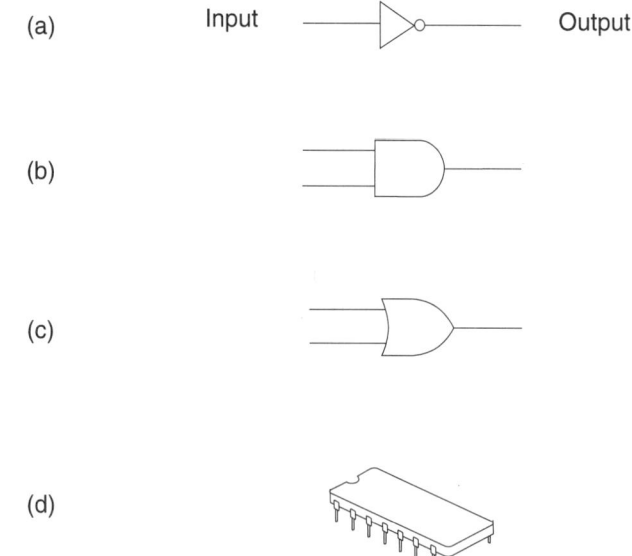

(a)   Input ———————▷o——————— Output

(b)

(c)

(d)

Figure 4.1. Basic logic gates: (a) NOT, (b) two-input AND, (c) two-input OR, and (d) dual inline package.

OR gate belong to the basic types, as shown in Figure 4.1. However, other types of logic gates have circuits that are simpler. Some logic gates can support three or more inputs; others have logic functions implemented for design convenience.

The graphic symbol of an inverter is shown in Figure 4.1(a). The logic gate has a triangular shape with a circle at the end. As a general rule, a circle at the output means to take the NOT (i.e., complement) function.

The logic symbol of a two-input AND gate is shown in Figure 4.1(b). Intuitively, the gate has high output when its two inputs are high. The logic symbol of a two-input OR gate is shown in Figure 4.1(c). Intuitively, the two-input OR gate has high output if either of its inputs is high or if both inputs are high.

The basic logic gates are the inverter, the two-input AND gate, and the two-input OR gate, but NAND gates and NOR gates are commonly used in design. In addition, any type of logic gate may support three inputs, four inputs, or eight inputs. If an extender is used to provide eight additional inputs, an eight-input gate with an extender can have a total of sixteen inputs. This includes all the gates: AND, OR, NAND, and NOR.

In SSI design, a DIP (dual inline package) is a chip that has 14 pins on two sides, as shown in Figure 4.1(d). The physical length is 0.75 in., the width is 0.25 in., and the depth is 0.25 in. The number of logic circuits on the chip is determined by the number of input and output pins. In addition to a voltage pin and a ground pin, the remaining twelve pins are used for input and output signals. Each chip can pack six inverters. Because a hexagon has six triangles, we chose it as the shape. Thus, some people call the gate a *hex inverter*.

4.2　Other Types of Logic Gates

Many other types of logic gates are available in an SSI chip. For example, we have buf (buffer), NAND, NOR, EOR (Exclusive OR), and ENOR (Exclusive NOR). Generally speaking, an SSI chip may contain six buffer gates, four two-input gates, three three-input gates, two four-input gates, or one eight-input gate. We introduce their logic functions in the following sections.

4.2.1　Buffer Gate

A *buffer* has an output that obeys its input after a timing delay, as shown in Figure 4.2(a). The buf gate also has a triangular shape but no circle at the end. The purpose of using such a gate is to reshape the input signal. Therefore, it is a buffer gate, nicknamed *buf*. Note that by using such a gate, we can either strengthen its output power or raise its voltage level. This feature is particularly desirable when the output signal is used to drive circuits off the chip.

A tristate buf has an enable signal added as the second input. It is similar to a two-input AND gate in that the enable signal serves as a second input. We have two types of tristate bufs: positively enabled and negatively enabled. The logic symbol of a positively enabled tristate buf is shown in Figure 4.2(b).

Note that there is no circle at the enable input of a positively enabled tristate buf. The gate provides two possible output states:

1. If the enable signal is high, the input signal of the buffer gate is passed to its output.
2. If the enable signal is low, the output of the gate acts like an open circuit, that is, high impedance.

The logic symbol of a negatively enabled tristate buf is shown in Figure 4.2(c). There is a circle placed at the enable input of such a buf. The circle at the input generally means to take the NOT function first. That is, if the enable input is low, its complement is high to open the

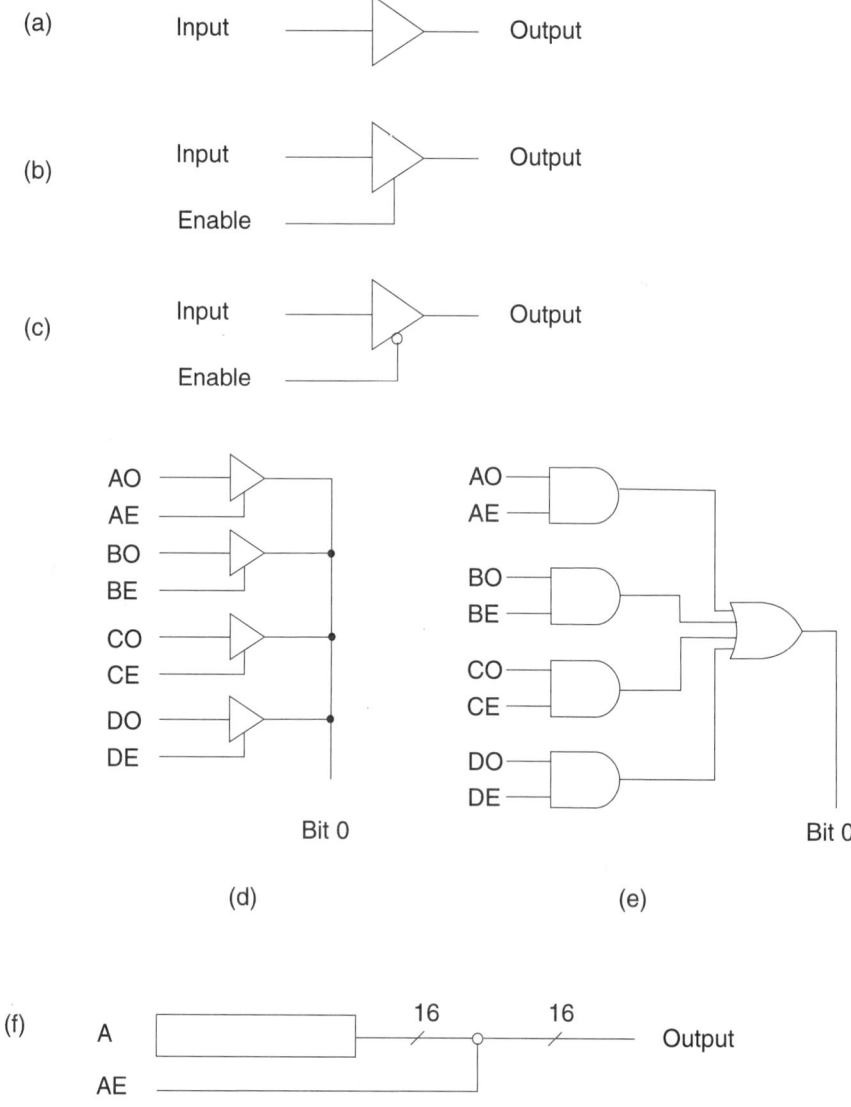

Figure 4.2. Bus signals: (a) a buffer gate, (b) tristate buf positively enabled, (c) tristate buf negatively enabled, (d) four bits are OR-tied, (e) using AND-OR gates, and (f) control gate structure.

gate. The two possible output states of a negatively enabled tristate buf are described here:

1. If the enable signal is low, the input signal of the buffer gate is passed to its output.
2. If the enable signal is high, the output of the gate acts like an open circuit, that is, high impedance.

4.2.2   OR-TIED FUNCTION

By tying the two outputs of tristate bufs together, we obtain an OR function of the two outputs. If any output of the two bufs is high, the tied OR function is high. As a rule of design, only one enable bit can be high at a time, so its input data signal is passed to the output. This feature is attractive in bus driver design because the digital signals are transmitted from one hardware component to another.

Let us use an example to describe the concept. A *register* is defined as an ordered set of flip-flops. The bits of information stored in a register can be placed on the bus via tristate bufs. Given four registers named A, B, C, and D, each bit in the register has a name followed by a digit indicating its bit position in the register. Thus, bit 0 of a register is denoted as A0, B0, C0, or D0. As shown in Figure 4.2(d), bit 0 of each register is fed to a tristate buf whose output is OR-tied to one bus wire. Each register uses one enable signal, and the four enable signals are named AE (A register enable), BE (B register enable), CE (C register enable), and DE (D register enable). If the enable signal for a particular register is on, all the bits in the register are enabled on the bus. We write down the logic equation for b0 (bit 0) as follows:

$$b0 = A0\ AE + B0\ BE + C0\ CE + D0\ DE$$

As an example, bit 0 in one register is placed on the bus if its enable signal is on. That is, the register is enabled, or selected. Without the tristate bufs, we need an AND-OR gate implementation, as shown in Figure 4.2(e). This bit slice is replicated for all the bits in a register. The size of a register is determined by the total number of bits in it. For a 16-bit register, the data bus needs 16 wires. As shown in Figure 4.2(f), register A has a sixteen-bit output that can be enabled on the bus. Symbolically, a slash is written on the line to represent a bus and the number 16 is the total number of wires on the bus. The circle on the line is a symbol for a gate control structure. This circle means a multiplexer (mul), which takes many sets of data inputs and enable inputs. Each enable input is asserted high to enable or select a set of data inputs. For example, if the enable signal AE is high, all the bits in register A are placed on the bus.

4.2.3   NAND GATES

The logic symbol of a two-input NAND gate is shown in Figure 4.3(a). A circle placed at its output indicates that the NOT function is performed after the AND function. Thus, the NAND gate is logically equivalent to an AND gate and an inverter in series, as shown in Figure 4.3(b). Using positive logic, a high voltage means true and a low voltage means false.

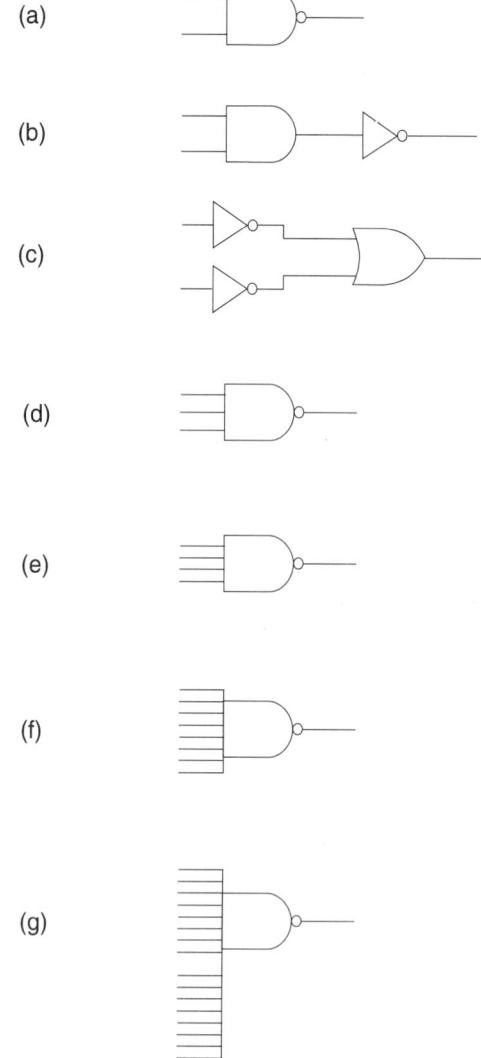

Figure 4.3. NAND gates: (a) two-input NAND, (b) two-input AND followed by an inverter, (c) two inverters followed by an OR, (d) three-input NAND, (e) four-input NAND, (f) eight-input NAND, and (g) sixteen-input NAND.

Thus, the NAND gate output is false if both of its inputs are true. Where voltage is concerned, the NAND gate output is low when both its inputs are high. The logic equation of a two-input NAND function is:

$$f = \backslash(A.B)$$
$$= \backslash A + \backslash B$$

The first line represents an AND function followed by a NOT function. The second line represents an OR function preceded by two inverters. That is, each input is fed to the inverter and then to the OR gate. Where low voltage is concerned, the NAND gate provides the OR function. Henceforth, a two-input NAND gate can be replaced by two inverters and a two-input OR gate, as shown in Figure 4.3(c).

An IC chip may contain four two-input NAND gates, three three-input NAND gates, two four-input NAND gates, or one eight-input NAND gate. The logic symbol of a three-input NAND gate is shown in Figure 4.3(d). The four-input NAND gate is shown in Figure 4.3(e), and an eight-input NAND gate is shown in Figure 4.3(f). By adding an eight-input extender, we can expand an eight-input NAND gate to support 16 inputs, as shown in Figure 4.3(g). Regardless of the number of inputs, the output of a NAND gate is low when all of its inputs are high.

The DeMorgan theorem allows us to convert two levels of NAND functions cascaded together into an AND-OR logic function. Thus, we can use NAND gates to derive the basic logic functions. Given four variables, A, B, C and D, we can use two levels of NAND gates cascaded together to obtain an AND-OR function. As shown in Figure 4.4, the logic schematic uses three two-input NAND gates for implementing the logic equation:

$$f = \backslash (\backslash (A \cdot B) \backslash (C \cdot D))$$
$$= (A \cdot B) + (C \cdot D)$$

On the first level, one gate takes inputs A and B and the other takes inputs C and D. The second-level NAND gate uses the output of the first-level NAND gate as input. The output function (f) of the second-level NAND gate represents the given function. Because NAND gates are simpler than AND gates, many digital systems use NAND gates exclusively. Can we turn a two-input NAND gate in TTL to an inverter? The answer is yes; we have three different approaches:

1. We can leave one input pin open. This approach works because an open input draws no current and is like a high-voltage input. However, the dangling metal pin is like an antenna because it is susceptible to noise.

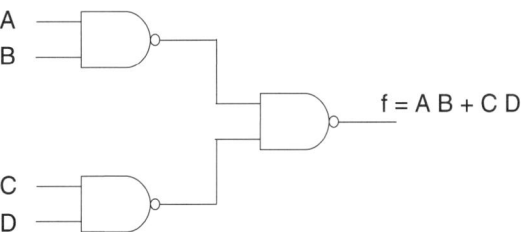

Figure 4.4. AND-OR function using cascaded NAND gates.

2. We can tie the two inputs together into one input:

$$f = \backslash(A.A) = \backslash A$$

This approach merely illustrates a concept of the basic theorem if signal A has enough power to drive the extra input. In other words, the signal A needs power to sink more current.

3. The best approach is to tie one input of a NAND gate to a high voltage, say 5 v. The logical equation is proven here:

$$f = \backslash(1.A) = \backslash A$$

Commonly, one input pin is tied to the power supply to draw no current, and it has better noise immunity.

Can we interchange the two input wires of a two-input NAND gate? Of course, the logic function remains the same as long as input signal A is fed to one wire and input signal B is fed to the other wire. This intuitive concept coincides with the basic Boolean theorem:

$$f = \backslash(A \cdot B)$$
$$= \backslash(B \cdot A)$$

4.2.4   NOR GATES

The NOR gates are low-power logic circuits that were widely used in the 1960s. The logic symbol of a two-input NOR gate is shown in Figure 4.5(a). A circle at the output of an OR gate indicates that a NOT function is performed after an OR function. Thus, the two-input NOR gate can be replaced by a two-input OR gate followed by an inverter, as shown in Figure 4.5(b). Where voltage is concerned, the output of the two-input NOR gate is low if either of its inputs is high. The De-Morgan theorem allows us to construct the NOR function differently:

$$f = \backslash(A + B)$$
$$= \backslash A \cdot \backslash B$$

As shown by the second line, the two-input NOR gate can be replaced by a two-input AND gate preceded by two inverters. The schematic is shown in Figure 4.5(c). Each variable is fed to an inverter whose output is fed to a two-input AND gate. Therefore, the output of a two-input NOR gate is high when both of its inputs are low. In negative logic, we define a low voltage as true and a high voltage as false. Using negative logic, a NOR gate works like a NAND gate. That is, the two-input NOR gate output is false if both of its inputs are true. A NOR gate may have many in-

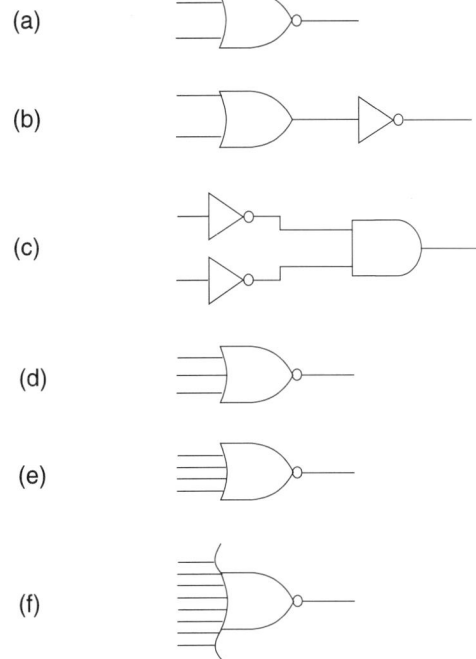

Figure 4.5. NOR gates: (a) two-input NOR, (b) two-input OR gate, one inverter, (c) two inverters, one two-input AND, (d) three-input NOR, (e) four-input NOR, and (f) eight-input NOR.

puts. For academic interest, a three-input NOR gate is shown in Figure 4.5(d), a four-input NOR gate is shown in Figure 4.5(e), and an eight-input NOR gate is shown in Figure 4.5(f). Regardless of the number of inputs, the NOR gate output is low if any of its input is high. To say it another way, the NOR gate output is high if all of its inputs are low.

4.2.5   EOR GATE VS. ENOR GATE

The logic symbol of an EOR gate is shown in Figure 4.6(a), and the logic symbol of an ENOR gate is shown in Figure 4.6(b). By connect-

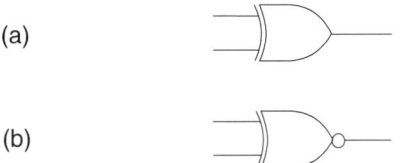

Figure 4.6. Logic symbols of: (a) EOR gate and (b) ENOR gate.

(a)
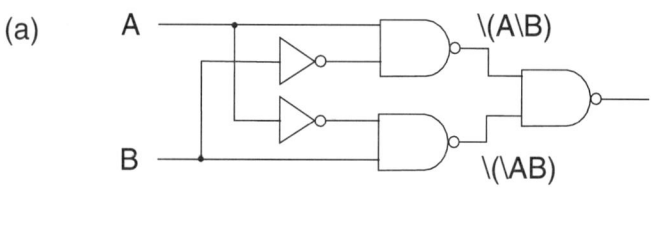

(b)
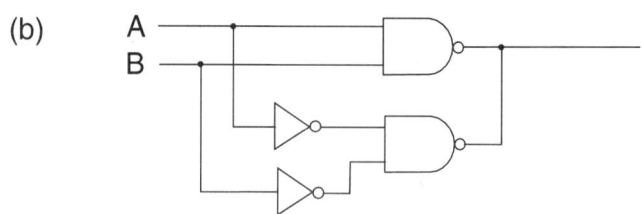

(c)
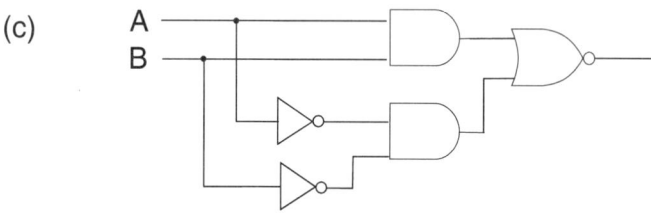

(d)
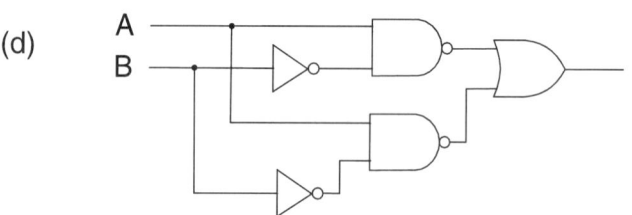

(e)
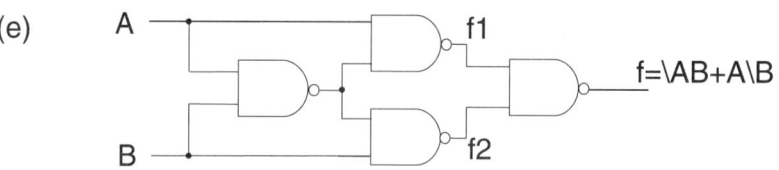

Figure 4.7. EOR circuits: (a) two inverters, three NAND gates, (b) two inverters, two NAND gates, (c) two inverters, two AND gates, one NOR gate, (d) NAO gates, and (e) four NAND gates.

ing an EOR gate and an inverter in series, we obtain an ENOR gate. Either type of gate takes two inputs and generates one output. The EOR gate output is high if its two inputs differ, while the ENOR gate output is high if its two inputs are alike.

There are many ways to implement an EOR gate with TTL NAND gates. Some are intuitive, and others are more difficult to understand. The first approach uses three two-input NAND gates and two inverters, as shown in Figure 4.7(a). The two-input NAND gates in the front provide the AND function followed by a NOT function, that is, $\backslash(A\ \backslash B)$ and $\backslash(\backslash A\ B)$, respectively. The NAND gate in the second stage provides the OR function:

$$f = \backslash(\backslash(A\ \backslash B)\ \backslash(\backslash A\ B))$$
$$= (A\ \backslash B) + (\backslash A\ B)$$
$$= A\ \backslash B + \backslash A\ B$$

The second approach uses two two-input NAND gates and two inverters, as shown in Figure 4.7(b). The two outputs of the NAND gates are negative OR-tied because the output of a NAND gate in TTL is the collector of an NPN transistor. The voltage of the joint wire is low if either output of the NAND gates is low. By treating the two inputs to the NAND gate as one set, we obtain the negative OR-tied function, which is low if any set of its inputs is high. That means that negative OR-tied means NOR-tied; the equivalent circuit using a NOR gate is shown in Figure 4.7(c). This logic schematic shows two two-input AND gates, two inverters, and one two-input NOR gate. The output of the NOR gate is low if the two inputs to either AND gate are high. Thus, in Figure 4.7(b) or (c), the two inverters are positioned to generate the two product terms, $\backslash(A\ B)$ and $\backslash(\backslash A\ \backslash B)$. That is, the NOR gate output is high if the two inputs A and B differ:

$$f = \backslash(A\ B + \backslash A\ \backslash B)$$
$$= (\backslash A + \backslash B)\ .\ (A + B)$$
$$= \backslash A\ B + A\ \backslash B$$

If the two outputs of the NAND gates are negative OR-tied, two pulled-up resistors are connected in parallel, so the overall resistance is halved. Consequently, more current tends to flow through the resistors, and the sinking current capability of the output is reduced. To remedy this problem, some NAND gates provide open collectors as output with no pull-up resistor. As a result, one external pull-up resistor is added in the circuit, and it is shared by all the output transistors in the NAND gates.

The third approach is to use NAO (NOT-AND-OR) gates, as shown in Figure 4.7(d). The top AND gate generates $(A\ \backslash B)$, the lower AND gate generates $(\backslash A\ B)$, and the OR gate generates the final function.

The last approach is shown in Figure 4.7(e). The logic schematic uses four two-input NAND gates. By applying the DeMorgan theorem, we write f1, f2, and the output function f as follows:

$$f1 = \backslash(A \ \backslash(A \ B))$$
$$f2 = \backslash(B \ \backslash(A \ B))$$
$$f = \backslash(f1 \ . \ f2)$$
$$= \backslash f1 + \backslash f2$$
$$= (A \ \backslash(A \ B)) + (B \ \backslash(A \ B))$$
$$= A \ (\backslash A + \backslash B) + B \ (\backslash A + \backslash B)$$
$$= A \ \backslash B + \backslash A \ B$$

4.3   Combinational Circuit Design Cases

A combinational circuit uses logic gates only, and each circuit performs a logic function. Design examples include parity bit generation and detection, decoders, encoders, adders, and comparators. Those circuits are considered basic components in a digital system.

4.3.1   Parity Circuit

A *parity circuit* takes a group of bits as inputs and generates an output, called the *parity bit*. Often, we use EOR gates to generate the even parity. By using an inverter to complement an even parity bit, we obtain the odd parity. In fact, we generate an even parity bit or an odd parity bit in applications. There are many ways to generate an even parity bit. One option is to perform a series of EOR operations on all the input bits. Assume that we have four input bits denoted as b0 (bit 0), b1 (bit 1), b2 (bit 2), and b3 (bit 3); they are input data bits to the parity circuit. What is the logical function to generate the even parity bit? Intuitively, we can plot the truth table in Table 4.1.

The four-bit input pattern is shown on the left-hand side, and its corresponding output is shown on the right-hand side. There are 16 rows; each row is for one input combination. If the input bit pattern contains an odd number of 1s, its output is 1. A number enclosed in braces denotes the decimal value of the input bit string. The logic equation for an even parity circuit is the sum of eight complete products:

$$p = \{1, 2, 4, 7, 8, 11, 13, 14\}$$
$$= (\backslash b3 \ \backslash b2 \ \backslash b1 \ b0) + (\backslash b3 \ \backslash b2 \ b1 \ \backslash b0) + (\backslash b3 \ \backslash b2 \ \backslash b1 \ b0)$$
$$+ (\backslash b3 \ b2 \ b1 \ b0) + (b3 \ \backslash b2 \ \backslash b1 \ \backslash b0) + (b3 \ \backslash b2 \ b1 \ b0)$$
$$+ (b3 \ b2 \ \backslash b1 \ b0) + (b3 \ b2 \ b1 \ \backslash b0)$$

Table 4.1. Truth table for generating an even parity bit for four input bits.

Input				Output
b3	b2	b1	b0	p
0	0	0	0	0
0	0	0	1	1 {1}
0	0	1	0	1 {2}
0	0	1	1	0
0	1	0	0	1 {4}
0	1	0	1	0
0	1	1	0	0
0	1	1	1	1 {7}
1	0	0	0	1 {8}
1	0	0	1	0
1	0	1	0	0
1	0	1	1	1 {11}
1	1	0	0	0
1	1	0	1	1 {13}
1	1	1	0	1 {14}
1	1	1	1	0

The first line shows the set notation for the sum of eight complete products. The second line shows each individual complete product enclosed in parentheses for easy inspection. We can plot a four-bit K-map to show that the equation cannot be simplified. With EOR operations, we can use one of two approaches as follows:

1. Serial approach: This approach performs three EOR operations from the rightmost bit to the leftmost bit in series. We do this in three steps. First, we perform an EOR operation on b0 and b1 to generate an output. Second, we perform an EOR operation on the output of the first gate and b2 to generate a second output. Finally, we perform an EOR operation on the output of the second gate and b3 to generate the even parity. The logical equation is rewritten as follows:

$$f = (((b0 \oplus b1) \oplus b2) \oplus b3)$$

The schematic is shown in Figure 4.8(a). The output of the first gate is fed to the second gate as input. The output of the second gate

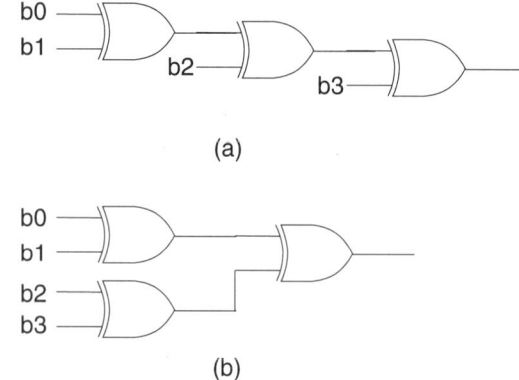

(a)

(b)

Figure 4.8. Parity circuits: (a) serial operations and (b) parallel operations.

is fed to the third gate as input. The output of the third gate is the even parity bit. Hence, the circuit uses three EOR gates in series, so the total number of circuit delays is three.

This approach is used in software simulations for two reasons. First, the CPU executes instructions one by one in sequence, so a computer program or routine will not suffer a speed disadvantage. A computer program or routine means a collection of instructions and data. The CPU fetches instructions from memory, interprets them, and then executes. Second, we can easily write a loop to perform the operations. In software design, a loop means many instructions grouped together that can be executed repeatedly by the CPU. In practice, we often write such a loop to generate the even parity bit for eight input data bits.

2. Parallel approach: Because the communicative law holds for EOR operations, the second approach performs two EOR operations in parallel followed by the third EOR operation. The logic equation is written as follows:

$$f = (b0 \oplus b1) \oplus (b2 \oplus b3)$$

The logic schematic is shown in Figure 4.8(b). This approach also uses three EOR gates divided into two levels. The first level uses two EOR gates, and each takes two data bits as inputs. The outputs from the first level gates are fed to the second-level gate as inputs. For this particular case, only one second-level EOR gate is needed. This approach is used in hardware design because the number of circuit delays is reduced.

A parity bit serves as an error detection code for data transmission between two hardware components. The hardware component may be the central processor, controller, or memory. Usually, the sending side generates an even parity bit for the eight-bit data. The eight data bits and the parity bit are transmitted on the line as a group. For the eight input bits, the parity circuit requires seven EOR gates divided into three levels. The first level has four EOR gates, the second level has two EOR gates, and the third level has one EOR gate. As a result, the circuit has only three EOR gate delays; its design is left as an exercise.

The receiving side feeds the received eight data bits to the same parity circuit to generate a parity bit. If the parity bit generated from the circuit is different from the parity bit received on the line, it means that an error has occurred during data transmission. That means that a bit has flipped on the line for whatever reason. The parity bit scheme is commonly used for error detection in computer communications.

4.3.2 DECODERS

An N-bit decoder takes N inputs and generates 2^N outputs. If N is two, the number of outputs is four. A decoder is a logic circuit that can detect a particular bit pattern as input. That is, a decoder takes a bit pattern as input and generates multiple outputs. Among all the outputs, one signal is decoded high and the rest are low. Therefore, because the decoded output represents a particular input pattern, an AND function can detect a given input. An instruction in a computer is an ordered set of bits that contains an opcode (operation code). The opcode tells the CPU what to do. The CPU fetches an instruction from memory into a register named IR (instruction register). Then the CPU uses a decoder to translate the opcode into one enable signal. This enable line represents the opcode in decoded form. Subsequently, the CPU uses the enable line to activate the operations that follow.

Let us design a two-bit decoder. The two inputs are I1 (input 1) and I0 (input 0). The outputs are D0 (decode 0), D1 (decode 1), D2 (decode 2), and D3 (decode 3). The two input signals, I1 and I0, constitute a two-bit count. The count value is the digit as coded in the output name. For example, D0 means a 00 input pattern, and D3 means a 11 input pattern. The truth table for a two-bit decoder is shown in Table 4.2.

Table 4.2. Two-bit decoder.

Input		Output			
I1	I0	D3	D2	D1	D0
0	0	0	0	0	1
0	1	0	0	1	0
1	0	0	1	0	0
1	1	1	0	0	0

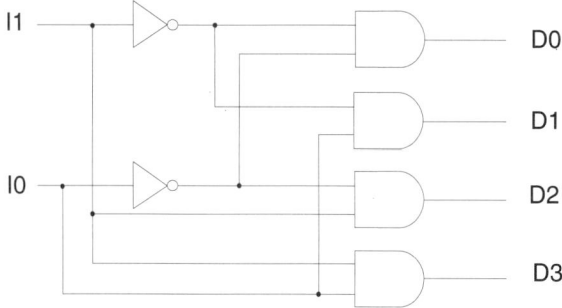

Figure 4.9. Two-bit decoder.

From the truth table, we can write the logical equations as follows:

$$D0 = \backslash I1\ \backslash I0$$
$$D1 = \backslash I1\ I0$$
$$D2 = I1\ \backslash I0$$
$$D3 = I1\ I0$$

As shown in Figure 4.9, the logic schematic uses four two-input AND gates and two inverters. In decoder design, each input signal requires an inverter to generate its complement. Each AND gate takes a two-bit pattern and generates an output. This decoded output serves as an enable signal that represents the input bit pattern whose value ranges from 0 to 3.

A four-bit decoder takes four inputs and generates 16 outputs. Such a circuit requires sixteen four-input AND gates plus four inverters. There are many approaches to design an eight-bit decoder. For fast speed, an eight-input AND gate can decode one output directly with one gate delay. To cover all the input combinations, we need a total of 256 eight-input gates and eight inverters. As an example, let us decode the specific eight-bit input pattern (I7 I6 I5 I4 I3 I2 I1 I0) that has a decimal value of 255. Its logic equation is:

$$D255 = (I7\ I6\ I5\ I4\ I3\ I2\ I1\ I0)$$
$$= (I7\ I6\ I5\ I4)\ .\ (I3\ I2\ I1\ I0)$$

To implement the first equation, we use an eight-input AND gate whose logic schematic is shown in Figure 4.10(a). To implement the second equation, we can use two four-input AND gates and one two-input AND gate. The output of the four-input AND gate is fed to the two-input AND gate as input. The schematic for such a circuit is shown in Figure 4.10(b). As we can see, the same function is achieved with two gate delays. Ei-

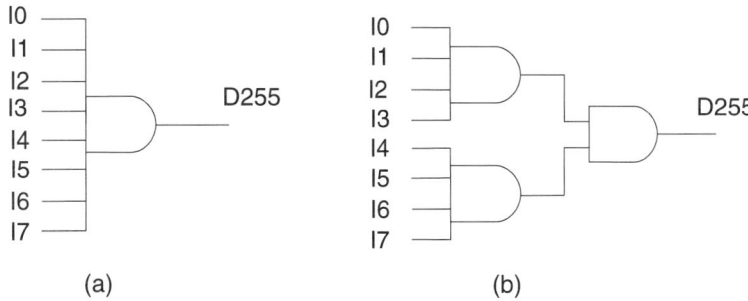

Figure 4.10. Eight-bit decoding: (a) one eight-input AND gate and (b) two four-input AND one two-input AND gates.

ther circuit is acceptable in logic design, as determined by parameters such as the availability of gates, fan-out capability, and timing delays.

4.3.3 ENCODERS

An encoder does the reverse function of a decoder. That is, an *encoder* is a logic device that receives many input signal lines and generates several outputs. Among the inputs, one line is high and the rest are low. The output signal lines or bits constitute a binary number, representing the bit position of the input signal that is high. In practice, the encoding concept is used to design an opcode in an instruction or in a message transmitted between two computers.

For example, a two-bit encoder takes four input lines and generates two output bits, representing the bit position of the input signal line that is high. Assuming the four inputs are I3 (input 3), I2 (input 2), I1 (input 1), and I0 (input 0), we obtain the two outputs as E1 (encoded output 1) and E0 (encoded output 0). In Table 4.3, the reduced truth table shows only four rows because the remaining twelve rows are don't cares.

Given four input bits, we should have a total of 16 entries in the reduced truth table. Because only four input conditions are allowed, the

Table 4.3. Two-bit encoder.

Input				Output	
I3	I2	I1	I0	E1	E0
0	0	0	1	0	0
0	0	1	0	0	1
0	1	0	0	1	0
1	0	0	0	1	1

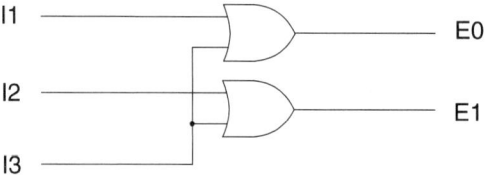

Figure 4.11. Two-bit encoder.

remaining 12 entries are don't cares. Nevertheless, we can use the don't cares to simplify the equations:

$$
\begin{aligned}
E0 &= \backslash I3 \ \backslash I2 \ I1 \ \backslash I0 + I3 \ \backslash I2 \ \backslash I1 \ \backslash I0 \\
&= I1 \ (\backslash I3 \ \backslash I2 \ \backslash I0 + \backslash I3 \ \backslash I2 \ I0 + \backslash I3 \ I2 \ \backslash I0 + \backslash I3 \ I2 \ I1 \\
&\quad + I3 \ \backslash I2 \ \backslash I0 + I3 \ \backslash I2 \ I0 + I3 \ I2 \ \backslash I0 + I3 \ I2 \ I1) \\
&\quad + I3 \ (\backslash I2 \ \backslash I1 \ \backslash I0 + \backslash I2 \ \backslash I1 \ I0 + \backslash I2 \ I1 \ \backslash I0 + \backslash I2 \ I1 \ I0 \\
&\quad + I2 \ \backslash I1 \ \backslash I0 + I2 \ \backslash I1 \ I0 + I2 \ I1 \ \backslash I0 + I2 \ I1 \ I0) \\
&= I1 + I3 \\
E1 &= \backslash I3 \ I2 \ \backslash I1 \ \backslash I0 + I3 \ \backslash I2 \ \backslash I1 \ \backslash I0 \\
&= I2 + I3
\end{aligned}
$$

The don't cares are chosen so that in the parentheses we obtain a sum of all complete products that is 1. Looking at the truth table, we can obtain the two reduced equations by inspection. The logic schematic of a four-input encoder is shown in Figure 4.11.

We can also plot a four-bit K-map to verify the equations. Note that the I0 input is not shown in the equations for E0 and E1, because when the input signal I0 is on, the output bit pattern is 00.

We can extend the concept to design a four-bit encoder. Such a circuit takes sixteen input signal lines, and each line is translated into a four-bit output. The four-bit output pattern has a value that represents the bit position of the input signal that is high. The encoding concept itself is important because it is applied to opcode design. An opcode between two bits and eight bits is often used in an instruction or message that is transmitted from one computer to another.

4.3.4 SEVEN-SEGMENT DISPLAY

The block diagram of a seven-segment display logic is shown in Figure 4.12(a). This circuit takes four input variables and produces seven output variables. The inputs are named X3, X2, X1, and X0. The outputs are named A, B, C, D, E, F, and G. The four-bit input pattern represents a decimal digit between 0 and 9. That is, each digit is encoded as a four-bit binary coded decimal that has a value ranging from 0 to 9.

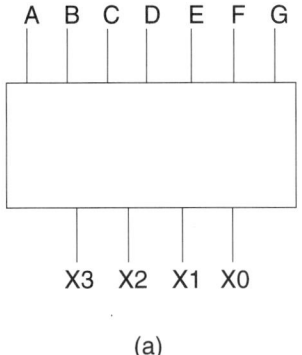

(a)

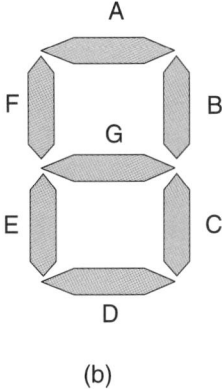

(b)

Figure 4.12. Seven-segment display: (a) block diagram and (b) graphical display pattern.

Each bit in the output represents a segment in the graphic display pattern, as shown in Figure 4.12(b).

If the output bit is 1, it turns on a graphical segment or light in the display. Because some segments are on while others are off, the graphical shape of a decimal digit can be displayed. To start, we plot a reduced truth table, as shown in Table 4.4.

Table 4.4 does not show the six don't cares. In the table, the digit 0 has six segments on, and the middle segment G is off. The digit 8 has all seven segments on. Next, we plot a total of seven K-maps, as shown in Figure 4.13. The equation for segment A is shown in Figure 4.13(a), and the equation for segment G is shown in Figure 4.13(g).

In each map, an empty box represents a 0, so only 1s and don't cares are marked in the map. After inspection, we select the don't cares so

Table 4.4. Truth table for the seven-segment display

Input				Output						
X3	X2	X1	X0	A	B	C	D	E	F	G
0	0	0	0	1	1	1	1	1	1	0
0	0	0	1	0	1	1	0	0	0	0
0	0	1	0	1	1	0	1	1	0	1
0	0	1	1	1	1	1	1	0	0	1
0	1	0	0	0	1	1	0	0	1	1
0	1	0	1	1	0	1	1	0	1	1
0	1	1	0	0	0	1	1	1	1	1
0	1	1	1	1	1	1	0	0	0	0
1	0	0	0	1	1	1	1	1	1	1
1	0	0	1	1	1	1	0	0	1	1

that the equation can be simplified. If there are several ways to group an entry, we pick one of them. The seven simplified equations are:

$$A = X3 + X2\ X0 + \backslash X2\ \backslash X0 + X1\ X0$$
$$B = \backslash X2 + \backslash X1\ \backslash X0 + X1\ X0$$
$$C = X2 + \backslash X1 + X0$$
$$D = X2\ \backslash X1\ X0 + \backslash X2\ X1 + \backslash X2\ \backslash X0 + X1\ \backslash X0$$
$$E = \backslash X2\ \backslash X0 + X1\ \backslash X0$$
$$F = X3 + X2\ \backslash X1 + X2\ \backslash X0 + \backslash X1\ \backslash X0$$
$$G = X3 + X2\ \backslash X1 + \backslash X2\ X1 + X1\ \backslash X0$$

This circuit does code conversion by merging the decoding and encoding circuits into one. In other words, the four-bit input pattern is translated into a seven-bit output pattern for graphical display. The same code translation logic function can be performed by a read only memory (ROM), as described later.

4.4 Binary Adders

In functions, there are two types of adders: the CPA (carry propagated adder) and the CSA (carry save adder). In general, a binary adder is a CPA that can add two numbers in binary. The CSA or CPA is composed of many one-bit adders as defined here:

1. A one-bit full adder can add three input bits and generate a sum bit and a carry bit as output.

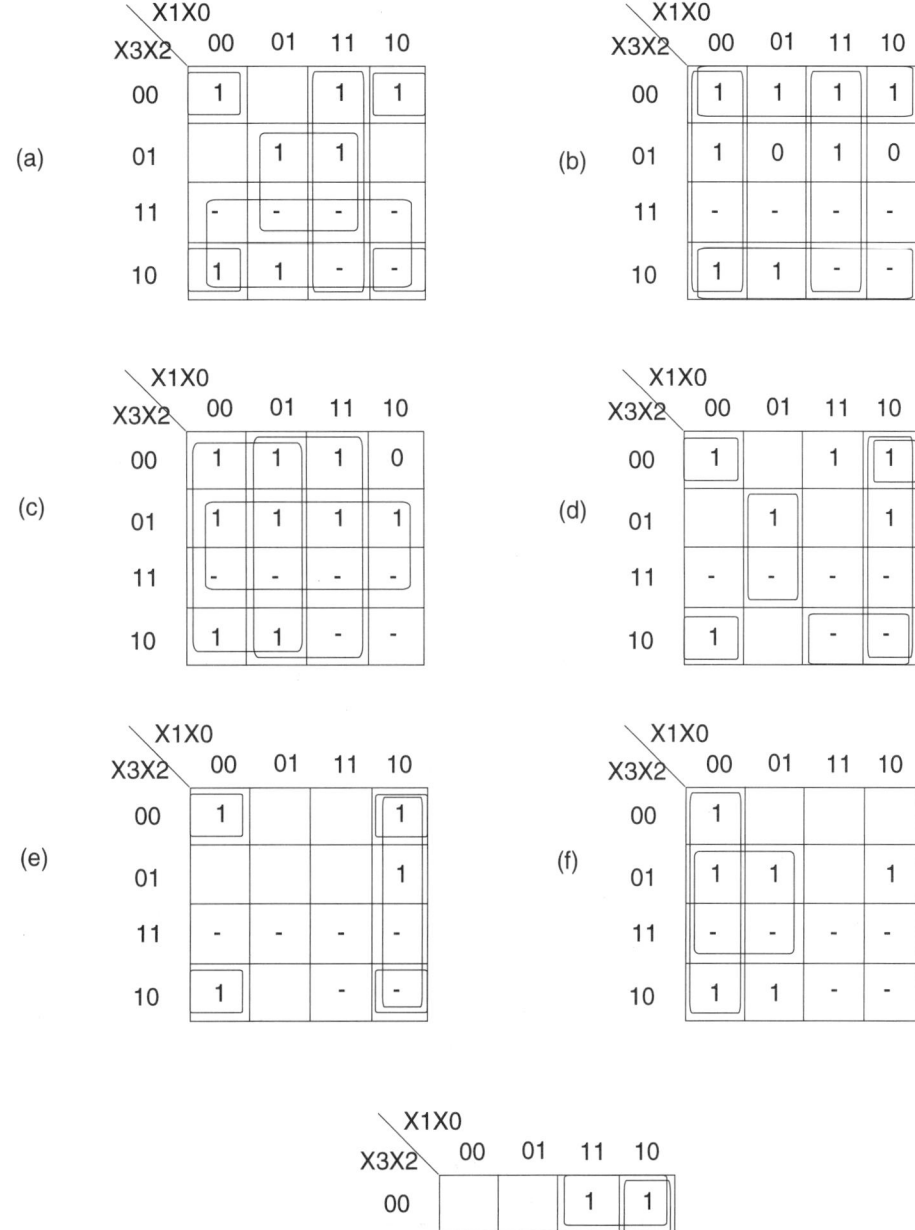

Figure 4.13. K-maps for seven segments: (a) A, (b) B, (c) C, (d) D, (e) E, (f) F, and (g) G.

2. A one-bit half adder can add two input bits and generate a sum bit and a carry bit as output.

A CPA has many one-bit full adders interconnected to compute the arithmetic sum of two numbers. A CSA also has many one-bit full adders, but each adder is independent and there are no interconnections. Each one-bit full adder in a CSA produces one sum bit and one carry bit. In other words, a CSA performs bitwise logical operations on three input bit strings. As a result, a CSA cannot compute the arithmetic sum of two numbers. In the following sections, we will discuss the one-bit half adder, the one-bit full adder, the CSA, and the CPA.

4.4.1 ONE-BIT HALF ADDER

The one-bit half adder adds two input bits and generates two output bits. Assume that the two inputs are named A0 and B0, and the two outputs are named C1 (carry 1) and S0 (sum 0). The symbol A0 means bit position 0 to adder input A and the symbol B0 means bit position 0 to adder input B. The two-bit output (C1 S0) denotes a number. The S0 carries a weight of 1 (2^0) and C1 carries a weight of 2 (2^1). This number counts the number of 1s in the two input bits, so its value ranges from 0 to 2, as shown in the truth table in Table 4.5.

By looking at the entries in Table 4.5, the two logic equations for a half-adder are stated as follows:

$$S0 = \backslash A0\ B0 + A0\ \backslash B0$$
$$= A0 \oplus B0$$
$$C1 = A0\ B0$$

From the equations, if A0 is 1 and B0 is 1, the two-bit output count shows 2, or 11 in binary. The S0 (sum 0) function can be implemented by NAO (NOT-AND-OR) gates or by one EOR gate. That is, if both input bits differ, then the sum bit is 1; otherwise the sum bit is 0. The C1 (carry 1) function can be implemented by a two-input AND gate. That means that if the two inputs are 1s, the carry bit is 1. Figure 4.14 depicts the logic schematic of a one-bit half adder for bit 0 by using four

Table 4.5. Truth table for a one-bit half adder

Input		Output	
A0	B0	C1	S0
0	0	0	0
0	1	0	1
1	0	0	1
1	1	1	0

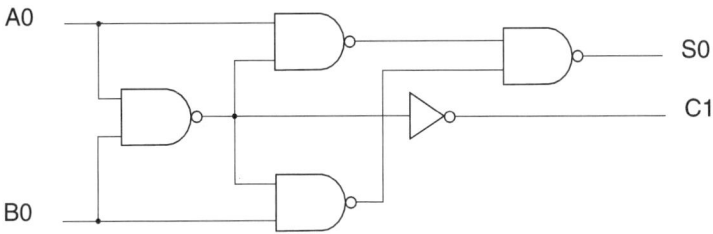

Figure 4.14. One-bit half adder.

two-input NAND gates and one inverter. The four NAND gates provide the EOR function. By placing an inverter after a NAND gate, we obtain the AND function. A one-bit half adder may be used in a CSA, but in a CPA the least significant bit is a one-bit full adder.

4.4.2 ONE-BIT FULL ADDER

Assume the input bits are A0, B0, and C0 (carry 0) and the two output bits are C1 (carry 1) and S0 (sum 0). We plot the truth table for a one-bit full adder as shown in Table 4.6.

Each row on the left-hand side shows the three-bit input combination, and the right-hand side shows the two-bit output as the count. In Table 4.6, there are four 1 entries in the output for S0. There are also four 1 entries in the output for C1. The two logic equations are written as follows:

$$S0 = \backslash A0 \ \backslash B0 \ C0 + \backslash A0 \ B0 \ \backslash C0 + A0 \ \backslash B0 \ \backslash C0 + A0 \ B0 \ C0$$
$$= A \oplus B \oplus C$$
$$C1 = \backslash A0 \ B0 \ C0 + A0 \ \backslash B0 \ C0 + A0 \ B0 \ \backslash C0 + A0 \ B0 \ C0$$
$$= A0 \ B0 + A0 \ C0 + B0 \ C0$$

Table 4.6. Truth table for a one-bit full adder

Input			Output	
A0	B0	C0	C1	S0
0	0	0	0	0
0	0	1	0	1
0	1	0	0	1
0	1	1	1	0
1	0	0	0	1
1	0	1	1	0
1	1	0 .	1	0
1	1	1	1	1

From the equations, a one-bit full adder generates a two-bit output. The S0 function is a sum of four complete products, and each product contains an odd number of 1s. The sum function is equivalent to the even parity function for three input bits. We can realize this function with NAO (NOT-AND-OR) gates or two EOR gates. The C1 function is a sum of four complete products, but it can be reduced. Intuitively, a carry is generated if a complete product contains at least two 1s. Thus, this function can be a sum of three products, and each product has two true variables. The two-bit output (C1 S0) counts the number of 1s in the input, so its value ranges from 0 to 3.

A CPA has many one-bit full adders. To generalize the adder equations for bit i, we denote the three inputs as Ai, Bi, and Ci and the two outputs as Si and $Ci+1$. The Ci bit can be obtained as the carry output from the previous stage whose bit position is $(i-1)$. The logic equations for the ith sum bit and the ith carry bit are shown here:

$$Si = \backslash Ai\ \backslash Bi\ Ci + \backslash Ai\ Bi\ \backslash Ci + Ai\ \backslash Bi\ \backslash Ci + Ai\ Bi\ Ci$$
$$= Ai \oplus Bi \oplus Ci$$
$$Ci+1 = \backslash Ai\ Bi\ Ci + Ai\ \backslash Bi\ Ci + Ai\ Bi\ \backslash Ci + Ai\ Bi\ Ci$$
$$= Ai\ Bi + Ai\ Ci + Bi\ Ci$$

The sum function in the form of SOP can be implemented by NAO (NOT-AND-OR) gates. The sum function can also be implemented by two EOR gates in series. The carry function can be implemented by three two-input AND gates and one three-input OR gate. The block diagram of a one-bit full adder for bit i is shown in Figure 4.15(a), and its logic schematic using NAND gates is shown in Figure 4.15(b).

4.4.3 CARRY SAVE ADDER

A CSA (carry save adder) is a collection of many independent one-bit full adders; an example is shown in Figure 4.16.

The adder has six one-bit full adders, and each one-bit full adder takes three input bits and generates a sum bit and a carry bit. The three inputs are denoted as X, Y, and Z. Each one-bit full adder performs a bitwise logical operation. At the rightmost bit position, the two output bits are S0 (sum 0) and C1 (carry 1). Therefore, the six-bit CSA produces a six-bit sum vector and a six-bit carry vector. A *vector* means a set of bits. Because the carry vector is saved for a subsequent operation, the adder is thusly named. A group of CSAs and one CPA (carry propagated adder) are used to add many binary numbers at the same time, as explained later.

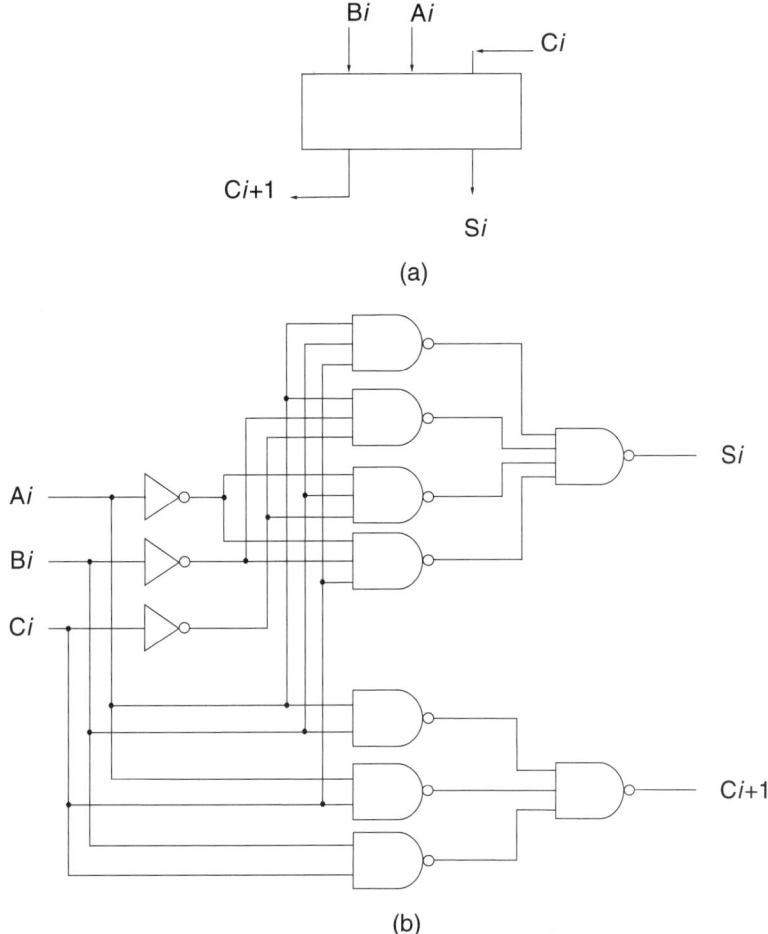

(a)

(b)

Figure 4.15. One-bit full adder: (a) block diagram and (b) logic schematic.

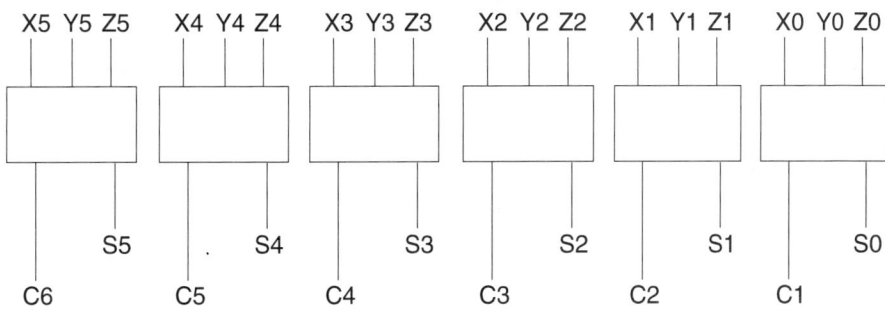

Figure 4.16. Six-bit carry save adder.

4.5 Carry Propagated Adder

A CPA has many one-bit full adders that are interconnected. For example, the logic symbol of a four-bit CPA is shown in Figure 4.17(a). The adder consists of four one-bit full adders. The adder has two sets of inputs, and each set of input has four bits. The adder symbol shows input A on the left and input B on the right. In addition, the Cin (carry in) bit is an input to the least significant bit. The Cin or C0 (carry 0) bit plays an important role in binary arithmetic. The four bits of input A are A3, A2, A1, and A0; the four bits of input B are B3, B2, B1, and B0. Inside the adder, the two sets of input bits are interleaved. That is, a bit in A and a bit in B are fed to each one-bit full adder as two input bits and the carry is its third input. By looking at the way carry output is generated, we have the carry rippled adder and the carry look-ahead adder, as discussed in the following sections.

4.5.1 CARRY RIPPLED ADDER

The design of a four-bit carry rippled adder is shown in Figure 4.17(b). The carry output of each one-bit full adder is fed to the next one-bit full adder as its carry input. The four sum equations are listed here:

$$S0 = A0 \oplus B0 \oplus C0$$
$$S1 = A1 \oplus B1 \oplus C1$$
$$S2 = A2 \oplus B2 \oplus C2$$
$$S3 = A3 \oplus B3 \oplus C3$$

The sum equations are generalized as follows:

$$Si = Ai \oplus Bi \oplus Ci \text{ for } i = 0, 1, 2, 3$$

The four carry equations are:

$$C1 = A0 \ B0 + A0 \ C0 + B0 \ C0$$
$$C2 = A1 \ B1 + A1 \ C1 + B1 \ C1$$
$$C3 = A2 \ B2 + A2 \ C2 + B2 \ C2$$
$$C4 = A3 \ B3 + A3 \ C3 + B3 \ C3$$

The carry equation is generalized as follows:

$$Ci+1 = Ai \ Bi + Ai \ Ci + Bi \ Ci \text{ for } i = 0, 1, 2, 3$$

If we allow the carry to ripple from the lsb to the msb, the C1 equation uses three two-input AND gates and one three-input OR gate, so there are two delays. The C2 equation has four (2 * 2) delays. The C3 equa-

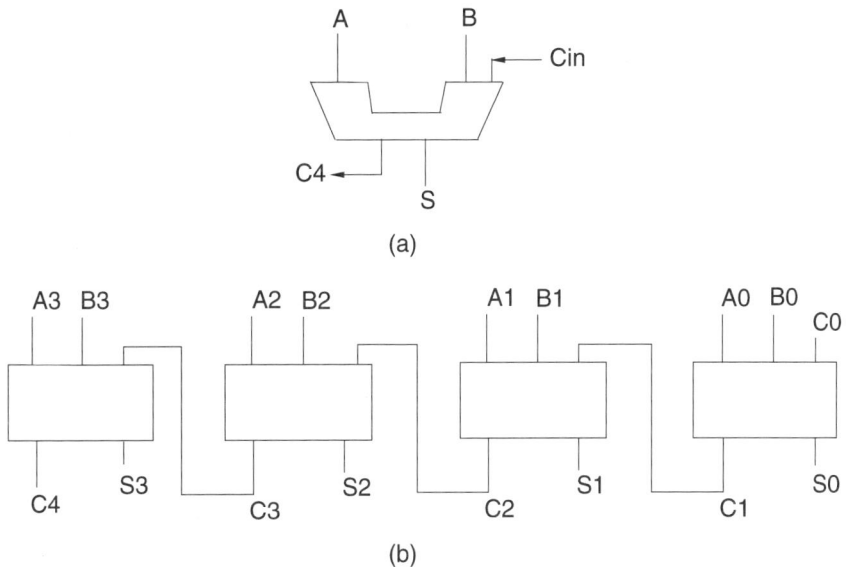

Figure 4.17. Carry propagated adder: (a) logic symbol of a four-bit adder and (b) design of a four-bit carry rippled adder.

tion has six delays, and the C4 equation has eight delays. For a 32-bit CPA, there are sixty-four delays to generate the last carry output C33.

4.5.2 CARRY LOOK-AHEAD ADDER

Because the adder is a crucial component in a CPU, we would like to design a carry look-ahead adder that can perform an add operation in one clock cycle. Let us study the carry equations first and then figure out a way to reduce the number of circuit delays. In concept, the carry output at any bit position is a function of all the input data bits at the previous stages plus the Cin bit. After this expansion, the number of gate levels is reduced and so is the number of circuit delays.

To get an idea, we start with a four-bit carry look-ahead adder design. First, we introduce two functions whose logic schematic is shown in Figure 4.18(a):

$$G0 = (A0\ B0) \qquad \text{\{generate function 0\}}$$
$$P0 = (A0 + B0) \qquad \text{\{propagate function 0\}}$$

The output of the two-input AND gate is G0, the generate function at bit 0. That is, a carry output is true if A0 is true and B0 is true regardless of its carry input. The output of the two-input OR gate is P0, the propagate function at bit 0. That is, a carry output is true if

(a)

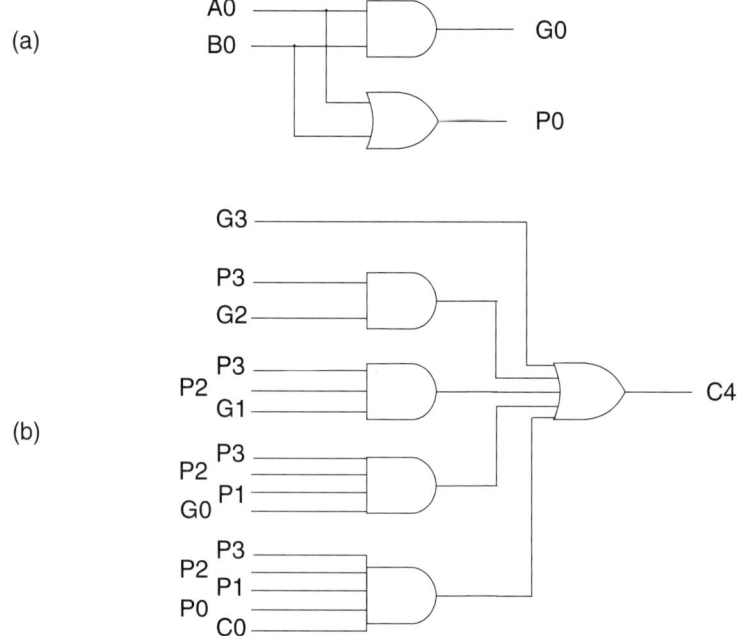

(b)

Figure 4.18. Carry look-ahead adder: (a) generate and propagate functions at bit 0 and (b) logic schematic of C4.

A0 or B0 is true and its carry input (C0) is true. The carry input serves as an assist from the right-hand side. In other words, a generate function does not need an assist from its right-hand side, but a propagate function does. The carry output at bit 0 is C1; the logical equation is:

$$C1 = A0 \; B0 + B0 \; C0 + A0 \; C0$$
$$= A0 \; B0 + (A0 + B0) \; C0$$
$$= G0 + (P0 \; C0)$$

In the third line, the C1 function is true if G0 is true or if both P0 and C0 are true. To generalize, we define the following equations:

$$Pi = Ai + Bi \qquad \{\text{propagate function } i \text{ for } i = 0, 1, 2, 3\}$$
$$Gi = Ai \; Bi \qquad \{\text{generate function } i\}$$

1. The Pi function propagates a carry from input to output, if there exits a carry input at bit i.
2. The Gi function, if true, generates a carry output 1 regardless of its carry input at bit i.

We can use AND-OR logic to represent the carry outputs C2, C3, and C4:

C2 = A1 B1 + A1 C1 + B1 C1
   = A1 B1 + (A1 + B1) C1
   = A1 B1 + (A1 + B1) (A0 B0 + A0 C0 + B0 C0)
   = A1 B1 + (A1 + B1) A0 B0 + (A1 + B1) (A0 + B0) C0
   = G1 + P1 G0 + P1 P0 C0
C3 = A2 B2 + A2 C2 + B2 C2
   = A2 B2 + A2 (G1 + P1 G0 + P1 P0 C0)
           + B2 (G1 + P1 G0 + P1 P0 C0)
   = G2 + (A2 + B2) G1 + (A2 + B2) P1 G0 + (A2 + B2) P1 P0 C0
   = G2 + P2 G1 + P2 P1 G0 + P2 P1 P0 C0
C4 = A3 B3 + A3 C3 + B3 C3
   = G3 + A3 (G2 + P2 G1 + P2 P1 G0) + B3 (G2 + P2 G1 + P2 P1 G0)
   = G3 + (A3 + B3) G2 + (A3 + B3) P2 G1 + (A3 + B3) P2 P1 G0
   = G3 + P3 G2 + P3 P2 G1 + P3 P2 P1 G0 + P3 P2 P1 P0 C0

The C4 function is the sum of five products; therefore it is true if any of the following five conditions is true:

1. The generate function at bit 3 is true.
2. The generate function at bit 2 is true and the propagate assist at bit 3 is also true.
3. The generate function at bit 1 is true and the propagate assists from bit 3 and bit 2 are true.
4. The generate function at bit 0 is true and the propagate assists from bits 3, 2, and 1 are true.
5. The C0 or Cin bit is true, with the propagate assists from all four bits.

The logic schematic of C4 is shown in Figure 4.18(b), which has three circuit delays. By expanding the look-ahead carry concept to level 2, we obtain a 16-bit adder. By expanding to level 3, we obtain a 64-bit adder [Hsu01]. In VLSI design, the OR operator in the propagate function can be replaced by an EOR operator if its circuit is simpler. The adder *width* is the number of one-bit full adders in it. Thus, a 16-bit adder can add two 16-bit integers in one add cycle. If a 16-bit adder is used to add two 32-bit integers, a sequential logic circuit may be designed to control two add operations in sequence. In other words, add the lower 16-bit part, remember the carry, and then add the upper 16-bit part with the carry.

4.5.3 SUBTRACTION VIA AN ADDER

Given A and B as two four-bit signed integers, by subtracting B from A, we obtain the difference $(A-B)$. The difference is also a four-bit signed number. We can use a four-bit adder to perform the subtraction in one clock cycle. We feed *A* to one adder input, feed the ones complement of *B* to the other adder input, and turn on the Cin bit. That is, by adding the twos complement of *B* to *A*, we obtain the difference. If a carry output is generated from the leftmost bit position, it is discarded by the hardware. Let us try to subtract 1 from 7 to obtain 6 as follows:

```
                    1     {Cin}
          0  1  1  1     {7}
    +)    1  1  1  0     {ones complement of 1}
        ─────────────
        1  0  1  1  0     {6}
```

In arithmetic, we have (7 − 1) = 6. The top row shows the Cin bit as 1. The second row shows the binary number on the left and its decimal value on the right. The third row shows the ones complement of 1 on the left followed by a comment. The carry output at its most significant bit is discarded, so the output is (0110) in binary, whose decimal value is 6, as enclosed in braces.

4.5.4 CARRY VS. OVERFLOW

An adder generates a carry output 1 at its most significant bit position. A carry output is different from an overflow. An adder can add or subtract two signed numbers. An overflow condition occurs if the result is out of range or invalid. The adder takes two inputs and generates one output. Using four-bit arithmetic, adding 1 to 7 is invalid because the sign changes as shown here:

```
        0  1  1  1     {7}
    +)  0  0  0  1     {1}
      ─────────────
        1  0  0  0     {overflow}
```

The two sign bits of the inputs are 0s. The sign bit of the output changes to 1. In twos complement notation, the number is negative, so it is an overflow. That means that the adder output is not what four bits can correctly represent as a valid result with a value ranging from −8 to +7. The result really represents −8, not +8, so it is defined as an overflow. Let us examine the sign bits of adder inputs and output. Both sign bits of inputs are 0s, but the sign bit of the output changes to 1. We bust the machine, so to speak. Let us try to add two negative numbers. By adding −1 to −8, it is an overflow, as shown here.

```
        1  0  0  0     {−8}
    +)  1  1  1  1     {−1}
      ─────────────
        0  1  1  1     {overflow}
```

The two sign bits of the inputs are 1s, but the sign bit of the output changes to 0. Therefore, an overflow occurs if the sign of the output changes after adding two positive or negative numbers. In the preceding example, the machine cannot use four bits to represent a valid −9.

During a subtract operation, integer A is fed to one adder input, the complement of integer B is fed to the other adder input, and the Cin bit is turned on. Thus, the subtract operation is implemented as follows:

$$(A - B) = A + (\text{ones complement of } B) + 1$$

Subtracting a negative number means adding a positive number. Subtracting a positive number means adding a negative number. When two input bit strings are added, an overflow occurs if the output bit string is invalid. The same set of rules is applied to detecting an overflow condition during a subtract operation. That is, if the two input signs are the same and the output sign changes, it is an overflow. Adding two numbers with different signs would never generate an overflow. Based on this notion, we plot a reduced truth table in Table 4.7.

The first three columns are adder inputs; the next two columns are adder outputs; and an entry 1, in the rightmost column, marks an overflow condition. Table 4.7 shows only eight meaningful entries; the remaining twenty-four entries are don't cares. In Table 4.7, the two product terms (\A3 \B3 S3) and (A3 B3 \S3) are unique, denoting an overflow. The same is true for (\C4 C3) and (C4 \C3). Therefore, we can write the logical equations for OA (overflow-arithmetic) as follows:

$$OA = \text{\textbackslash A3 \textbackslash B3 S3} + \text{A3 B3 \textbackslash S3}$$
$$= \text{\textbackslash C4 C3} + \text{C4 \textbackslash C3}$$
$$= \text{C3} \oplus \text{C4}$$

Table 4.7. Reduced truth table to detect an overflow condition.

Input					Output
A3	B3	C3	C4	S3	OA
0	0	0	0	0	0
0	0	1	0	1	1
0	1	0	0	1	0
0	1	1	1	0	0
1	0	0	0	1	0
1	0	1	1	0	0
1	1	0	1	0	1
1	1	1	1	1	0

The OA function is a sum of two product terms. First, the sign of adder input A is 0, the sign of adder input B is 0, and the sign of the sum output is 1. Second, the sign of adder input A is 1, the sign of adder input B is 1, and the sign of the sum output is 0. The third line shows the EOR operator between C3 and C4. Interestingly, the second line can be derived from the first line by logical deduction as follows:

1. If both input signs are 0s and the output sign is 1, then C4 must be 0 and C3 must be 1.
2. If both input signs are 1s and the output sign is 0, then C4 must be 1 and C3 must be 0.

Algebraically, we can derive the second line from the first line in three steps. First, expand each product into four complete products of five variables. Second, because the sum of four complete products of two variables is 1, we apply the distributive law to introduce the carry bits into the equation. Now, each product is expanded into four five-variable complete products. Third, for each product, we drop three don't cares and introduce seven new don't cares. As a result, we eliminate the two data bits, and the sum bit:

$$
\begin{aligned}
OA &= \backslash A3 \ \backslash B3 \ S3 \ (\backslash C4 \ \backslash C3 + \backslash C4 \ C3 + C4 \ \backslash C3 + C4 \ C3) \\
&\quad + A3 \ B3 \ \backslash S3 \ (\backslash C4 \ \backslash C3 + \backslash C4 \ C3 + C4 \ \backslash C3 + C4 \ C3) \\
&= \backslash A3 \ \backslash B3 \ S3 \ C4 \ \backslash C3 + A3 \ B3 \ \backslash S3 \ \backslash C4 \ C3 \\
&= C4 \ \backslash C3 \ (\backslash A3 \ \backslash B3 \ S3 + \backslash A3 \ \backslash B3 \ \backslash C3 + \backslash A3 \ B3 \ \backslash S3 + \backslash A3 \ B3 \ S3 \\
&\quad\quad + A3 \ \backslash B3 \ \backslash S3 + A3 \ \backslash B3 \ S3 + A3 \ B3 \ \backslash S3 + A3 \ B3 \ C3) \\
&\quad + \backslash C4 \ C3 \ (A3 \ B3 \ \backslash S3 + \backslash A3 \ \backslash B3 \ \backslash S3 + \backslash A3 \ \backslash B3 \ S3 + \backslash A3 \ B3 \ \backslash S3 \\
&\quad\quad + \backslash A3 \ B3 \ S3 + A3 \ \backslash B3 \ \backslash S3 + A3 \ B3 \ \backslash S3 + A3 \ B3 \ C3) \\
&= C4 \ \backslash C3 + \backslash C4 \ C3
\end{aligned}
$$

The plotting of a five-bit K-map to verify the two equations is left as an exercise. For academic interest, we discuss four key concepts in the following:

1. If the adder input B is 0, it is not possible to generate an overflow because the adder input A is the output.
2. If the adder output is 0, no overflow is generated except in one condition when we add the two most negative numbers. With four bits, adding (-8) and (-8) generates an overflow as shown here:

$$
\begin{array}{rcccccl}
 & 1 & 0 & 0 & 0 & & \{-8\} \\
+) & 1 & 0 & 0 & 0 & & \{-8\} \\
\hline
1 & 0 & 0 & 0 & 0 & & \{overflow\}
\end{array}
$$

3. If the adder input A is 0, any add operation will not trigger an overflow because the result is B.
4. If the adder input A is 0, a subtract operation will not trigger an overflow except in one condition. If the most negative number (-8) is subtracted from 0, the adder output is invalid, triggering an overflow as shown here:

$$
\begin{array}{rll}
& 1 & \{Cin\} \\
& 0\ \ 0\ \ 0\ \ 0 & \{0\} \\
+)\ & \underline{0\ \ 1\ \ 1\ \ 1} & \{ones\ complement\ of\ -8\} \\
& 1\ \ 0\ \ 0\ \ 0 & \{overflow\}
\end{array}
$$

4.5.5   COMPARATORS

A comparator takes two input bit strings and generates an output if the condition is true. We will discuss two comparators: the equal to compare and the greater than or equal to compare.

Equal To

Given A and B as two four-bit numbers, the comparator generates an output if A is equal to B. That is, the two input bit strings of A and B are identical, bit by bit. One design option is to use an adder. After performing a subtract operation, one decoder is used to detect the equal condition. If the adder output contains four 0s, the two inputs are equal. Where adder output is concerned, this is also known as the Z (zero) condition. This single decoder consists of one four-bit AND gate with four inverters. Each sum bit from the adder output is fed to an inverter. Then each inverter output serves as an input to the AND gate. The decoded function is shown here:

$$f = (\backslash S3\ \backslash S2\ \backslash S1\ \backslash S0)$$

If all four output bits are 0s, the decoded output is true. As an alternative, we can design an equal comparator whose logic schematic is shown in Figure 4.19(a). The logical equation is:

$$f = (A3 \odot B3)\ .\ (A2 \odot B2)\ .\ (A1 \odot B1)\ .\ (A0 \odot B0)$$

The four ENOR gate outputs are denoted E3, E2, E1, and E0. The outputs are fed to the four-input AND gate to generate f. Each ENOR gate takes two input bits; its output is high if the two input bits are alike. The output of the four-input AND gate is true when the two input numbers are equal.

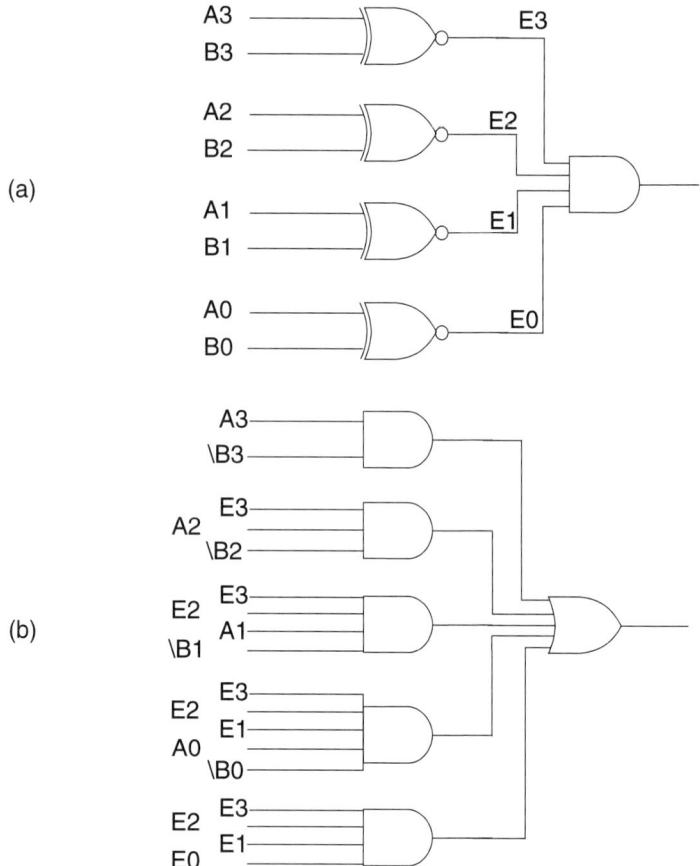

Figure 4.19. Comparators: (a) equal to and (b) greater than or equal to.

Greater Than or Equal To

If A is greater than or equal to B in unsigned compare, the comparator generates an output. One design option is to use an adder. After the subtract, if the carry output C4 is true, then A is greater than or equal to B. Recall that A is fed to one adder input, the ones complement of B is fed to the other adder input, and the Cin bit is turned on. The true carry output means there is no borrow; such a condition indicates that A is greater than or equal to B. As an alternative, we can compare A and B, bit by bit, from left to right. The logic circuit is based on the equation as follows:

$$
\begin{aligned}
f = \ & (A3 \ \backslash B3) + ((A3 \odot B3) . (A2 \ \backslash B2)) \\
& + ((A3 \odot B3) . (A2 \odot B2) . (A1 \ \backslash B1)) \\
& + ((A3 \odot B3) . (A2 \odot B2) . (A1 \odot B1) . (A0 \ \backslash B0)) \\
& + ((A3 \odot B3) . (A2 \odot B2) . (A1 \odot B1) . (A0 \odot B0))
\end{aligned}
$$

The schematic is shown in Figure 4.19(b); for simplicity, the ENOR circuits to generate E3, E2, E1, and E0 are not shown. Note that the output function of (A3 $\odot$ B3) is E3, and it serves as an input to four different AND gates. The logical function for greater than or equal to compare is a sum of five conditions:

1. The most significant bit in A (A3) is 1 and the msb in B (B3) is 0.
2. The msb in A and in B are equal, but A2 is 1 and B2 is 0.
3. The leading two bits in A and B are equal, but A1 is 1 and B1 is 0.
4. The leading three bits in A and B are equal, but A0 is 1 and B0 is 0.
5. All four bits in A and B are equal.

The first four conditions are for the greater than compare; the last condition is for the equal to compare.

4.6   Multiplication Tree

A CPU can perform two types of multiply (mul) operations: unsigned and signed. The opcode for unsigned mul is different from the one for signed mul. Thus, after decoding the opcode, the CPU generates two signal lines for mul, one for unsigned multiply and one for signed multiply. Note that an unsigned mul operates on two unsigned numbers to produce an unsigned product. In contrast, a signed mul operates on two signed numbers to produce a signed product. In design, the multiplication tree can handle either unsigned mul or signed mul in one clock cycle.

4.6.1   Unsigned Multiply

Using four-bit arithmetic as an example, the tree takes two four-bit numbers as inputs and produces an eight-bit product as output. For unsigned mul, the two inputs are positive and the output is positive. Let us try to multiply the unsigned 3 by the unsigned 15. The product is an unsigned 45. During the operation, the number 3 is the multiplicand and the number 15 is the multiplier. In an unsigned number, each bit carries a positive weight including the sign. The unsigned multiply operations are described here:

					0	0	1	1	{3, multiplicand}
*)					1	1	1	1	{15, multiplier}
	0	0	0	0	0	0	1	1	{3, M0}
	0	0	0	0	0	1	1		{6, M1}
	0	0	0	0	1	1			{12, M2}
+)	0	0	0	1	1				{24, M3}
	0	0	1	0	1	1	0	1	{45, unsigned product}
	p7	p6	p5	p4	p3	p2	p1	p0	

The binary multiply operation is similar to a decimal multiply; the symbol * means multiply. The bits in the multiplier are examined from right to left. Each bit in the multiplier carries a weight of 2^N where N denotes its bit position in the multiplier. Thus, the least significant bit in the multiplier carries a weight of 1 (2^0) and the most significant bit carries a weight of 8 (2^3). If the bit in a multiplier is 1, the bit is used to enable and shift the multiplicand to the left by N bits. If the bit in a multiplier is 0, the multiplicand is not enabled, so it is 0.

The four multiplicands after being shifted are named M0 (multiplicand 0), M1 (multiplicand 1), M2 (multiplicand 2), and M3 (multiplicand 3). Note that only M0 is not shifted because its decimal value is 3 ($3 * 2^0$). M1 has a decimal value of 6 ($3 * 2^1$). M2 has a decimal value of 12 ($3 * 2^2$). M3 has a decimal value of 24 ($3 * 2^3$). In each shifted multiplicand, any implied trailing 0 is replaced by a space. The multiplication tree adds the four shifted multiplicands at the same time to generate a sum. This sum is the final product, denoted as (p7 p6 p5 p4 p3 p2 p1 p0), where p0 is the least significant bit.

The tree consists of a seven-bit CSA, a six-bit CSA, and a five-bit CPA, plus some logic. At the lsb, each CSA may use a one-bit half adder to do the job because there are only two input bits. Let us study the operations performed by the two carry save adders and the final CPA. The lsb in M0 is p0 in the final product, so the upper seven bits in M0 are fed to the seven-bit CSA as one input. The M1 has one trailing 0, so its upper seven bits are fed to the seven-bit CSA as the second input. M2 has two trailing 0s, so its upper six bits, after being left-justified, are fed to the seven-bit CSA as the third input. Each one-bit adder in the CSA generates one sum bit and one carry bit, so the seven-bit CSA as a whole generates a seven-bit SV1 (sum vector 1) and a 7-bit CV1 (carry vector 1). A *vector* is a group of bits, as shown in the following:

```
      0   0   0   0   0   0   1      {upper 7 bits of 3}
      0   0   0   0   0   1   1      {upper 7 bits of 6}
 +)   0   0   0   0   0   1   1      {upper 6 bits of 12}
      ─────────────────────────
      0   0   0   0   1   0   0      {SV1}
  0   0   0   0   0   1   1          {CV1}
```

The SV1 is written straight down, but the CV1 is skewed one bit to the left. It should be mentioned that the most significant bit of CV1 is discarded by the hardware. The purpose of having a CSA is to reduce one row of inputs. The lsb in SV1 is the same as p1 in the final product, so the upper six bits in SV1 are fed to the six-bit CSA as the first input. The lower six bits in CV1 are fed to the six-bit CSA as the second input. The upper five bits in M3, after being left-justified, are fed to the six-bit CSA as the third input. As a result, the six-bit CSA generates SV2 (sum vector 2) and CV2 (carry vector 2) as follows:

```
        0   0   0   0   1   0     {upper 6 bits in SV1}
        0   0   0   0   1   1     {upper 6 bits in CV1}
+)      0   0   0   1   1         {upper 5 bits of 24}
        ─────────────────────
        0   0   0   1   1   1     {SV2}
    0   0   0   1   0             {CV2}
```

A multiplication tree uses CSAs to reduce input rows, but the last stage must be a CPA to generate an arithmetic sum. Therefore, a five-bit CPA is used to add the last two vectors. As the least significant bit of SV2 is the same as p2 in the final product, the upper five bits in SV2 are fed to the CPA as one input. The most significant bit in CV2 is discarded, so its lower five bits, after being left-justified, are fed to the CPA as the other input. The CPA contains five one-bit full adders that are interconnected to generate the upper five bits in the final product:

```
        0   0   0   1   1   1     {SV2}
+)      0   0   0   1   0         {CV2}
        ─────────────────────
        0   0   1   0   1
        p7  p6  p5  p4  p2
```

We should understand two important notions, which will be discussed later. First, an unsigned mul treats each multiplicand as a positive number. The four-bit multiplicand, after being shifted to the left, cannot fully occupy eight bits. Therefore, its upper bits are padded with 0s. We say that the multiplicand is 0-extended in the tree. Second, the four-bit multiplier is a positive number even if its sign bit is on. Therefore, the last M4 is added to the other multiplicands as a positive number.

4.6.2   SIGNED MULTIPLY

Recall that the sign bit of a negative number in twos complement notation carries a weight of (-8) if four-bit arithmetic is used. Thus, we make two modifications so that the tree can also perform a signed mul. First, the multiplicand is sign-extended in the tree instead of 0-extended. If the sign bit of the multiplier is 0, the M4 entry is not enabled, so it is 0. However, if the sign bit of the multiplier is 1, the M4 addition is replaced by subtraction. This is the second key concept in design. The notion of subtract really means that the twos complement of M4 is placed in the last row. However, this is done in two steps:

1. Place the ones complement of M4 as the last row in the tree.
2. Turn on the Cin bit as input to the five-bit CPA. Thus, the twos complement of M4 is obtained by adding 1 to its ones complement.

By multiplying (-3) and (-1), we obtain a signed product of $+3$:

						1	1	0	1	$\{-3,$ multiplicand$\}$
*)						1	1	1	1	$\{-1,$ multiplicr$\}$
	1	1	1	1	1	1	0	1		$\{-3,$ M0$\}$
	1	1	1	1	1	0	1			$\{-6,$ M1$\}$
	1	1	1	1	0	1				$\{-12,$ M2$\}$
+)	0	0	0	1	1					$\{$twos complement of $-24,$ M3$\}$
	0	0	0	0	0	0	1	1		$\{3,$ signed product$\}$
	p7	p6	p5	p4	p3	p2	p1	p0		

The seven-bit CSA generates SV1 and CV1 as follows:

		1	1	1	1	1	1	0	$\{$upper 7 bits in $-3\}$
		1	1	1	1	1	0	1	$\{$upper 7 bits in $-6\}$
		1	1	1	1	0	1		$\{$upper 6 bits in $-12\}$
		1	1	1	1	0	0	1	$\{$SV1$\}$
	1	1	1	1	1	1	0		$\{$CV1$\}$

The six-bit CSA generates SV2 and CV2 as follows:

		1	1	1	1	0	0	$\{$upper 6 bits in SV1$\}$
		1	1	1	1	1	0	$\{$lower 6 bits in CV1$\}$
+)		0	0	0	1	0		$\{$ones complement of $-24,$ M3$\}$
		0	0	0	1	1	0	$\{$SV2$\}$
	1	1	1	1	0	0		$\{$CV2$\}$

The five-bit CPA adds SV2, CV2, and Cin to generate an arithmetic sum as follows:

	0	0	0	1	1	$\{$upper 5 bits in SV2$\}$
	1	1	1	0	0	$\{$lower 5 bits in CV2$\}$
+)					1	$\{$Cin bit$\}$
	0	0	0	0	0	$\{$upper 5 bits in product$\}$

4.7 Programmable Logic Arrays

The PLA (programmable logic array) is a VLSI device that can be programmed to realize any logic function in the form of sum of product (SOP). A PLA has an AND plane, an OR plane, and two sets of metal wires. Sometimes, a wire is called a *line*. The simplified diagram of a small PLA is shown in Figure 4.20(a).

The vertical wires run from bottom to top. The horizontal wires run from left to right. The intersection of the two wires is called a *cross point*. Each horizontal wire goes from the AND plane to the OR plane. On the left-hand side the AND plane supports a total of 16 input variables. The internal logic decodes each input variable into two vertical input lines: true and complement. The first input pair has I0 (input 0)

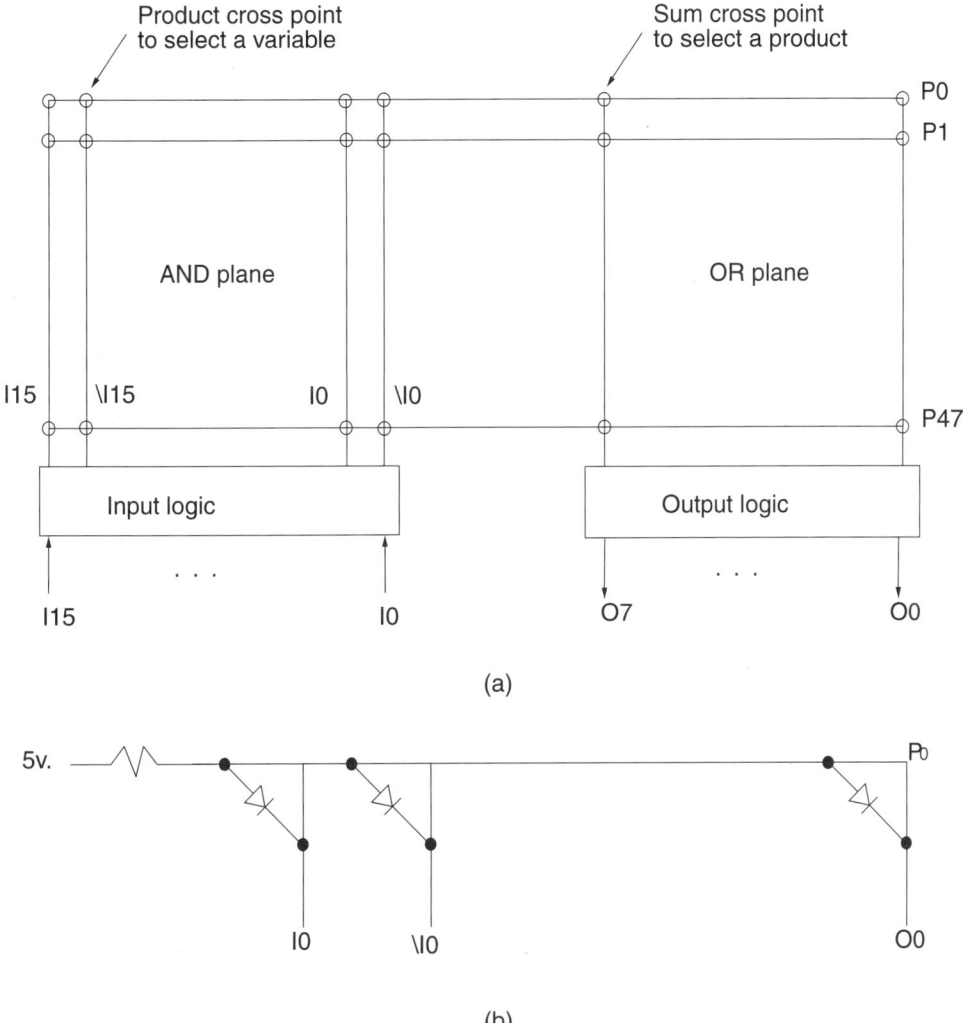

(a)

(b)

Figure 4.20. The simplified diagram of a sixteen-input, forty-eight-product PLA: (a) AND plane vs. OR plane and (b) one specific output.

and its complement \I0. The 16th input pair has I15 (input 15) and its complement \I15. The AND plane provides 48 product lines, denoted P0 to P47. The numbering of horizontal lines starts from the top. The number 48 is chosen as a design parameter. Omitted from Figure 4.20 is a high voltage followed by a resistor connected to each product line on the left. Because each input variable has true and false, the number of cross points in the AND plane is 1,536 (2 * 16 * 48), where the symbol * means multiply.

On the right-hand side an OR plane provides eight output lines, denoted O0 to O7. The number 8 is also chosen as a parameter in design. The number of cross points in the OR plane is 384 (8 * 48), so the total number of cross points on the chip is 1,920 (1,536 + 384). On the right-hand side each product line can be ORed into any of the eight output lines. Thus, the PLA chip can take eight input variables and generate eight output functions. Each function is a sum of forty-eight products, and each product can have up to eight variables. We can program a PLA by burning the selected cross points in both planes. In other words, coincident current can flow into the selected vertical and horizontal lines to burn the cross points at the intersections. The term *burn* really means to disconnect, or disable the joint. The original raw state of a cross point is 1; after burning it changes to 0.

To illustrate the logic concept, each cross point can be a diode link from a horizontal line to a vertical line. An example is shown in Figure 4.20(b) to produce the function (I1 \I0) on the P0 line. On the left-hand side the two diodes are used to select the AND function (I1 I0). On the right-hand side one diode links the P0 line to the O0 output. Each cross point or link is a PN junction between a horizontal line and a vertical line. Because each cross point can be disabled, or burnt, each horizontal line can be programmed to encode a product of up to eight input variables.

The diodes on the left-hand side perform an AND function for each row, and the diodes on the right-hand side perform an OR function for each column. If P0 is (I1 \I0), then the P0 line has two cross points, I1 and \I0, and all the rest are disconnected. That is, P0 is high if both I1 and \I0 are high. If any input is low, the P0 line is pulled low. On the left-hand side, the P0 line is ORed to the output line O0. Thus, if any product line is high, it will show up on the output line. On the other hand, if any product line is low, it is effectively disconnected from the output line, because the diode is backward-biased.

4.7.1   ERASABLE PROGRAMMABLE LOGIC ARRAY

An erasable PLA is a logic device in that the cross points can be burnt, erased, and burnt again. That is, after burning the cross points, if an ultraviolet ray is applied to the circuit, the electrons become mobile again. Thus, the cross points are restored to their raw state. The erasable programmable logic array is used in prototyping digital designs, so the device can be burnt and erased repeatedly until all the mistakes are corrected. One final question: Why use ultraviolet light? The answer: Because visible light has a longer wavelength, it is blocked on the silicon surface. On the other hand, an X-ray has a shorter wavelength, so it passes through the layer. The ultraviolet ray has a wavelength that is the correct size, so it stays in the layer to excite the electrons. As technology advances, the OR plane has the diodes replaced by NMOS transistors, and they can be electrically erased.

4.8 Memories

The fast growth of portable computers has placed a demand on all kinds of semiconductor memories [Sher01]. Because each CPU chip needs many memory chips to match, semiconductor memories have been the fastest growing segment in the market for size and cost. Generally, a memory is designed as a storage device. Where function is concerned, there are many types of memory, including read only, read and write, and write once read only. Where circuits are concerned, we have static memories and dynamic memories. Where process is concerned, we have TTL, ECL, NMOS, and CMOS.

The CPU also uses registers on a chip to store results. In fact, a *register* is a small memory with the fastest speed. What is an address? An *address* is a location number in the form of an unsigned bit string. A register has an address, and so does a memory cell. An address must be provided to access the storage cell in a pile.

A memory contains a lot of storage cells, or elements. Each cell is assigned an address; it is the basic addressable unit. In general, the basic unit is a byte that can store eight bits. In some read only memories, the basic unit is a word that can have any number of bits. In order to access one particular memory cell, the CPU transmits an address on the address bus. During a read operation, the memory decodes the address into an enable signal that is used to fetch the bits stored at this address. After the read cycle, the bits at this address remain intact. In other words, the bits are merely copied on the data bus to the CPU. This is called a *load operation*. During a write operation, the memory decodes the address into an enable signal that is used to write the data bits at this address. This is called a *store operation*. We summarize six key points as follows:

1. The memory always receives an address.
2. During a read operation, the memory places data bits on the data bus to the CPU.
3. During a write operation, the CPU places data bits on the data bus to the memory.

4. It takes time to decode the address, read the data bits, and write the data bits.
5. A memory address is fixed by hardware so it cannot change. However, the bits stored at the address can change in a write cycle.
6. A memory does not have processing capability.

4.8.1   READ ONLY MEMORY

A ROM (read only memory) has many words, and each word has many bits stored in it. The memory provides the read function, but not the write function. In each memory word, the bits stored are nonvolatile. That means that the bits are stored on a permanent basis, even when the power is turned off. A ROM receives many input bits as addresses and generates a group of data bits stored at this address as output. We can use a ROM to perform the code translation function. For example, the seven-segment display logic may use a ROM that receives four-bit addresses as input and generates seven data bits as output. A ROM has a left plane and a right plane. In this case, the left plane decodes the four address bits into 10 enable signals, but only one enable signal is high. The right plane is the storage plane that has ten words, and each word has seven data bits. The enable signal with a high voltage is used to select the seven data bits in the word as addressed.

We can program a PLA into a ROM. Assume that a PLA has eight address input lines and 16 data output lines. The ROM function is: Given an address, fetch the data bits at this address. Therefore, the AND plane provides the decode function, and the OR plane provides the storage function. The eight address input bits are named A0 (address bit 0) to A7 (address bit 7). A0 is the least significant bit and A7 is the most significant bit. Each of the eight inverters in the input logic generates the complement of each address bit. The purpose of the AND plane is to decode the input address into 256 enable lines. The address bits, in the form of true variable or complement, are negative OR-tied to the enable line. That means that any enable line with the wrong address will be pulled to low, so the only enable line that can be high is the one with the correct address after decoding. The enable line with a high voltage represents the given address in decoded form.

Each enable line goes from the AND plane to the OR plane. The purpose of the OR plane is two-fold. First, in the OR plane, each enable line encodes sixteen data bits on it, namely, D0 (data bit 0) to D15 (data bit 15). D0 is the least significant bit and D15 is the most significant bit. Second, the plane performs the OR-tied function on all two-hundred-fifty-six enable lines. As a result, one set of 16 data bits is generated as output. In the storage plane, each vertical line is called a *bit line*, and each horizontal or enable line is also called a *word line*. Each memory word has 16 bits that are addressable by a given address.

In sum, a ROM is used to store bits that do not change state, such as a program in a game cartridge, or data in a computer for computation. In general, a ROM has high speed, high density, and low cost. Usually, a ROM can take eight address bits and produce 16 data bits in one clock cycle. Note that there are some ROM devices that can be written to once. After that, it is read only. Such a device is called a write once read memory (WORM).

4.8.2 Erasable Programmable ROM

An EPROM (erasable programmable ROM) is a ROM that can be erased and programmed again. The memory is often used for prototyping because the data bits can be burnt and erased repeatedly. An EPROM can be used to store a computer program in the development phase. If an error is found in the program, the program can be erased, and the chip burned again. This cycle is repeated until all the errors are corrected. Because a ROM or EPROM uses circuits to store the bits, they are called *static memory*. They are classified as random access memories (RAMs) as elaborated in the following sections.

4.8.3 Random Access Memory

Since 1970, many types of RAM were developed separately. One attribute is that the device takes equal time to read a word, so they are all referred to as random access memory. Based on different technology, one RAM may allow a read function; others allow both read and write. Generally speaking, a bipolar RAM has high speed but low density. A CMOS RAM has high density, low power consumption, and low cost. A new technology emerged to combine bipolar circuits and CMOS circuits on one chip. One application is to use bipolar drivers in a CMOS memory to provide more drive current. The two types of RAM used in design are static and dynamic, as introduced next.

Static RAM

An SRAM (static RAM) uses four to six transistors to construct each bit cell. Because a flip-flop uses the latch concept to connect logic gates, its structure is considered static. A typical CMOS bit cell uses three PMOS transistors and three NMOS transistors, so the ratio of PMOS and NMOS transistors is 1:1. In a DRAM (dynamic RAM), each bit cell consists of one NMOS transistor and one capacitor, so there are more NMOS transistors than PMOS transistors. Because SRAM is about ten times faster than DRAM, it serves as on-chip storage. In an SRAM or DRAM, the bit cell is volatile. That means that when the power is turned off, all the bits in memory are lost.

Dynamic RAM

In a DRAM, each bit cell is composed of an NMOS transistor and a capacitor, as shown in Figure 4.21. If the capacitor carries a positive charge, it is a 1. If the capacitor carries no charge, it is a 0. Writing a bit cell is described next.

1. Connect the capacitor to ground to discharge.
2. Apply the data input bit to the gate of the NMOS transistor.

If the input bit is 1, the NMOS transistor is turned on to charge the capacitor. If the bit is 0, the NMOS transistor is off so the capacitor has no charge. This one transistor per bit concept results in higher density and low cost. However, a serious drawback is that the capacitor leaks as time passes. As a remedy, a special refresh circuit is designed to charge the capacitors every 40 ms (millisecond). Nevertheless, due to its high density, low power, and low cost, DRAM is used as the main memory in a computer.

4.8.4 FLASH MEMORY

Flash memory was developed in 1988; it is both programmable and nonvolatile. A flash memory is used in a digital camera, a personal digital assistant, an automobile, or in a wireless phone, etc. There are many flash memory types, but each type is a derivation of EEPROM (electrically erasable programmable ROM). An EEPROM bit cell is composed of many transistors; a flash memory bit cell is composed of one transistor. A flash memory has the following attributes:

1. Electrically, the semiconductor storage device can be read, erased, and programmed in the host system without being taken out.
2. The device has no moving parts.

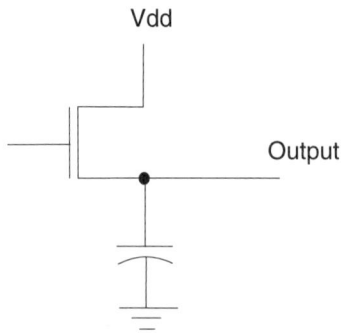

Figure 4.21. DRAM bit cell.

A flash memory has two planes: the left plane and the right plane. The left plane is the decoder that has logic circuits to decode an address into enable lines. Each enable line is also known as a word line that goes from the left plane to the right plane. The right plane is the storage plane, which is designed as a two-dimensional matrix of rows and columns. Each row is a word line to access the bit cells in a word. Each column is a bit line for input and output. The intersection of a word line and bit line is the bit cell for storage. A simplified block diagram of flash memory is shown in Figure 4.22(a).

On top, the single line represents a group of wires, so we have address lines, data lines, and control lines. The address lines are unidirectional to the memory as input. The data lines are bidirectional for input and output. The control lines are used to specify a command code for read, erase, or program. During a reading operation, a high voltage is applied to one enable or word line connected to the front gate of each bit cell in the word. Depending on the state of the bit cell, an output 1 or 0 is generated on the bit line. An erase operation sets the bit cell to 1; a program operation resets each bit cell to 0.

Floating Gate

Inside a flash memory, the circuits can be different, but the basic design principles of a bit cell are the same. The physical layout of a modified NMOS transistor is shown in Figure 4.22(b). The modified NMOS has such properties, as described here:

1. On top of the channel, a thin layer of oxide is deposited as the tunnel.
2. A layer of polysilicon is deposited on top of the oxide as the floating gate.
3. Another layer of oxide is deposited on the floating gate and finally on the front aluminum-based gate for voltage control.

The circuit schematic of such an NMOS transistor is shown in Figure 4.22(c), and the middle vertical line represents the floating gate. If the floating gate carries no negative charge, the bit stored is 1. If the floating gate has an excess negative charge over a threshold, the bit stored is 0. The floating gate is insulated on all sides by oxide. The thin oxide layer between the floating gate and the P-substrate channel serves as the tunnel. A bit cell changes state by a process known as *tunneling*, either adding or removing the negative charge from the floating gate. Because the floating gate is insulated by oxide, the negative charge on a floating gate does not leak, even when the power is turned off. In other words, the floating gate serves the nonvolatile storage function.

The circuit schematic of four bit cells in a partial matrix is shown in Figure 4.22(d). Word line (WL) is the horizontal line and bit line

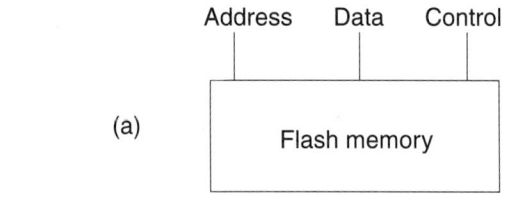

(a)

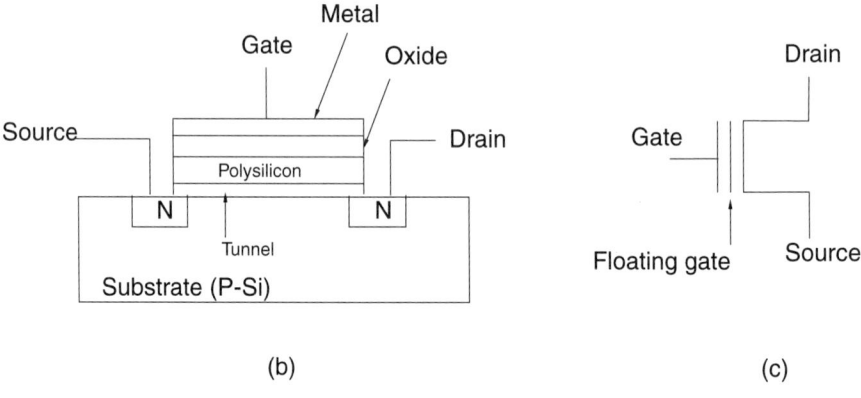

(b)   (c)

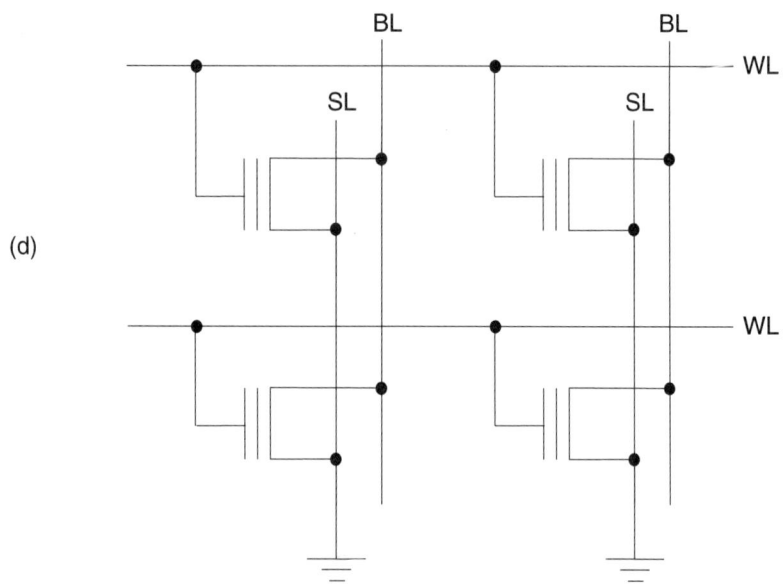

(d)

Figure 4.22. Flash memory: (a) simplified block diagram, (b) physical layout of the bit cell, (c) logic symbol of the bit cell, and (d) partial matrix.

(BL) is the vertical line. The modified NMOS at the intersection of the two lines has a front gate, a drain region, and a source region. The front gate is connected to WL, the drain is connected to BL, and the source is connected to source line (SL). All the SLs are connected to the common ground. The voltage combinations applied to WL and BL jointly define an operation: read, erase, or program.

Operation Modes

The negative charge on a floating gate is like a barrier, or a negative bias, to the input voltage at the front gate. The amount of negative charge by the excess of electrons on the floating gate defines the state of the bit cell. If we store one bit per cell, then a floating gate with no negative charge is defined as state 1 because a nominal high voltage applied to the front gate will turn on the transistor. A floating gate with negative charge is defined as state 0 because a nominal high voltage applied to the front gate will not turn on the transistor. The three operation modes are described in the following:

1. During a read operation, a nominal high voltage is applied to the WL, connected to the front gate. The BL is negative OR-tied, so if the selected transistor is turned on, its drain output is pulled down to low on the BL defined as 1 using negative logic. For this reason, this design is coined the NOR cell design in that if the selected transistor is on, the voltage on the drain is low.
2. During a program operation, a nominal high voltage is applied to the front gate via the word line. If a bit 0 is to be written, a high voltage is also applied to the drain via the BL. Through the tunneling effect, the excited electrons push through the thin oxide layer and are trapped on the floating gate, so the floating gate carries a negative charge. If the bit input is 1, the drain voltage is low, and consequently, the number of electrons on the floating gate does not change. In other words, a program operation can only change the bits in a word from 1s to 0s. A bit 0 cannot change back to 1 without an erase operation, as described next.
3. An erase operation means to change all the bits in a block of words to 1s. Note that the floating gates are neutral initially, so all the raw bits stored are 1s. During an erase operation, a negative voltage is applied to the front gate by the word line and the drain is left open. The excess electrons tend to flow from the floating gate to the SL and then to the ground of 0 v. As a result, the floating gate is restored to neutral with no negative charge.

In nearly all memory devices, each cell usually stores one bit of information. For example, a 16-Mb (megabit, i.e., 2^{20}-bit) flash supports a memory array composed of 16 Mega transistors. In such a device, a single threshold input voltage level separates the 0 state from the 1 state. Therefore, the storage is based on one bit per cell. Interestingly, advanced technology allows two bits of information to be stored in one modified NMOS transistor. This is known as the two-bit per cell design, as introduced in Intel StrataFlash. In such a design, the amount of negative charge on a floating gate has four levels. Each charge level represents an input voltage required to turn on the transistor. Henceforth, each input voltage level represents the encoding of two bits stored in one cell. The access time may be longer, but the storage capacity is doubled. If the amount of negative charge on a floating gate has eight distinguishable levels, then three bits of information can be stored in each cell.

Commercial flash memory is available in the form of a card or a stick. A flash memory card has a dimension of 45 by 37 by 0.76 mm (millimeter). Accordingly to lab tests, a flash memory can sustain heavy usage for a long period of time without data loss. Typically, a flash memory card can store 256 MB and can support dual voltages of 3.3 or 5 v.

4.9   Summary Points

1. In Boolean algebra, the three basic logical operators are NOT, AND, and OR.
2. There are other logical operators, such as NAND, NOR, EOR, ENOR.
3. A decoder is used to detect a particular bit pattern.
4. An encoder does the reverse of a decoder.
5. A register is an ordered set of flip-flops in a CPU or controller, and it has an address assigned to it.
6. A CSA performs add operations on a bitwise basis.
7. A CPA performs arithmetic add operations on two numbers.
8. In a carry look-ahead adder, the carry output is generated from the data inputs of the previous stages plus the carry in bit.
9. A multiplication tree can perform a multiply operation on two integers: unsigned or signed.
10. A PLA is a VLSI device for general-purpose applications.
11. Each cell or access unit in memory has an address.
12. A ROM is nonvolatile but supports read only operations.
13. An EEPROM can be electrically erased and programmed again repeatedly.
14. A RAM is volatile, but it can perform both read and write operations.
15. An SRAM has a lower density but is faster than a DRAM.

16. A flash memory is programmable and nonvolatile.
17. A flash memory cell has a floating gate to store negative charges.

Problems

4.1 Using positive logic, design a decoder circuit for the switching function:

$$f = A.B.C.D.E$$

1. Use one eight-input gate.
2. Use two three-input gates.
3. Use two three-input N gates and inverters.

4.2 Repeat 4.1 using one eight-input NOR gate and five inverters. *Hints:* The three unused inputs of the NOR gate should be tied to 0 v. and the function is:

$$f = \backslash(\backslash A + \backslash B + \backslash C + \backslash D + \backslash E + 0 + 0 + 0)$$

4.3 Repeat problem 4.1 by using one eight-input NOR gate and inverters. *Hints:* The three unused inputs of the NOR gate should be tied to 0 v. and the function is:

$$f = \backslash(\backslash A + \backslash B + \backslash C + \backslash D + \backslash E + 0 + 0 + 0)$$

4.4 When the power is turned on in a system, we often design a one-shot circuit to generate a single pulse for the purpose of initialization. As shown in Figure 4.23, the two-input NAND gate takes two inputs. One input is the power signal A, a step function, and the other is $\backslash A$, which is delayed.

In theory, the NAND gate output should be $\backslash(A.\backslash A)$, or high. However, if the circuit delay of each inverter is 4 ns, the sum of five delays is 20 ns. Thus, the leading edge of input A triggers the generation of a negative pulse of 20 ns as the NAND gate output. After inversion, we obtain a single positive pulse of 20 ns. Neglect-

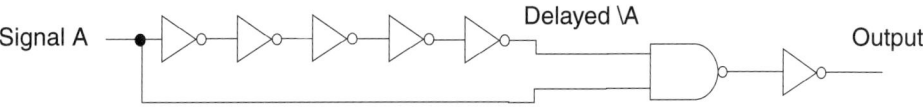

Figure 4.23. One-shot design using circuit delays.

ing the rise time, plot the waveforms for A, the delayed $\backslash A$, the NAND gate output, and the one-shot output.

4.5 Given eight input data bits denoted b0, b1, b2, b3, b4, b5, b6, and b7, use seven EOR gates to design an even parity generator for the eight input bits. Use the parallel approach to implement the equation:

$$f = ((b0 \oplus b1) \oplus (b2 \oplus b3)) \oplus ((b4 \oplus b5) \oplus (b6 \oplus b7))$$

4.6 Given four input bits denoted I3, I2, I1, and I0, what is the logic equation for decoding the four-bit number whose decimal value is 12?

4.7 Design a four-bit decoder that takes four inputs and generates sixteen outputs.

4.8 Design of a four-bit encoder that takes 16 inputs and generates four outputs.

4.9 Use NAO (NOT-AND-OR) gates to design a one-bit half adder.

4.10 Use NAO gates to design a one-bit full adder.

4.11 What is the difference between a CSA and a CPA?

4.12 Design a four-bit carry rippled adder.

4.13 When we design a carry propagated adder, we have the following functions at bit position 1:

$$P1 = A1 + B1 \ \{\text{can be replaced by } A1 \oplus B1\}$$
$$G1 = A1 \ B1$$
$$C2 = G1 + P1 \ C1$$

If we change the OR operator in the P1 function into an EOR operator, verify that C2 is logically the same.

4.14 In four-bit arithmetic, plot the five-bit truth table for the overflow condition after a four-bit adder operation.

1. Verify the following two equations:

$$OA = \backslash A3 \ \backslash B3 \ S3 + A3 \ B3 \ \backslash S3$$
$$= \backslash C4 \ C3 + C4 \ \backslash C3$$

2. Can you obtain another equation for the overflow condition?

4.15 Verify that if the output of an EOR gate is fed to the NOR gate as input, we can use four EOR gates and one four-input NOR gate to compare two four-bit numbers (A3 A2 A1 A0) and (B3 B2 B1 B0). Write down the logic equation for the four-bit equal to comparator.

4.16 What is the difference between a ROM and a WORM?

4.17 What is the difference between an SRAM and a DRAM?

4.18 Describe the floating gate in a flash memory cell.

4.19 Describe the three operation modes of a flash memory.

4.20 In flash memory design, if each modified NMOS is charged with four levels, different voltage levels are applied to the gate of an NMOS transistor to turn it on. How many bits are encoded for each NMOS transistor cell? If such a chip has 64 mega NMOS transistor cells, what is its total storage capacity in bits?

4.21 A logical shift means 0 flows at the end as determined by the direction, left or right. Assume that we have four input bits denoted S3, S2, S1, and S0. After a one-bit shift logical left, each bit is skewed to its left and a 0 flows into the least significant bit. After a one-bit shift logical right, each bit is skewed to its right and a 0 flows into the most significant bit.

4.22 Design a mul (multiplexer) circuit that can select one of three functions. There are four input data bits, three enable bits, and four output data bits. The four input bits are S3, S2, S1, and S0. The three enable signals are used for shift control, namely, NS (no shift), SHL (shift left), and SHR (shift right). The four output bits are Sh3, Sh2, Sh1, and Sh0. Only one enable signal can be on at a time so, it selects one of the inputs as output. The four logic equations are:

$$Sh0 = S0\ NS + S1\ SHR$$
$$Sh1 = S1\ NS + S0\ SHL + S2\ SHR$$
$$Sh2 = S2\ NS + S1\ SHL + S3\ SHR$$
$$Sh3 = S3\ NS + S2\ SHL$$

Form a project team of three students and select a leader.

1. Draw the logic schematic using AND-OR gates.
2. Draw the logic schematic using NAND gates only.
3. Using logic gates, lights, and switches, build this one-bit shifter and have fun.

4.23 A three-bit multiplication tree can multiply two three-bit unsigned numbers into a six-bit unsigned product. By multiplying 3 by 7, we obtain the product 21. The shifted multiplicands and the final product are listed in the following:

				0	1	1	{3, multiplicand}
*)				1	1	1	{7, multiplier}
	0	0	0	0	1	1	{3, M0}
	0	0	0	1	1		{6, M1}
+)	0	0	1	1			{12, M2}
	0	1	0	1	0	1	{21, unsigned product}
	p5	p4	p3	p2	p1	p0	

The six-bit product is denoted (p5 p4 p3 p2 p1 p0). Verify that the five-bit CSA generates two vectors:

	0	0	0	0	1	{3}
	0	0	0	1	1	{6}
+)	0	0	1	1		{12}
	0	0	1	0	0	{SV1}
	0	0	0	1	1	{CV1}

Verify that the four-bit CPA generates an arithmetic sum of the two last vectors, as shown here:

	0	0	1	1	{upper 4 bits in SV1}
+)	0	0	1	1	{lower 4 bits in CV1}
	0	0	0	1	{upper 4 bits in product}
	p5	p4	p3	p2	

Form a project team of three students and select a leader. Answer the following questions:

1. Why does the tree need one five-bit CSA and one four-bit CPA?
2. What are the ten logical equations for SV1 and CV1?
3. What are the four logical equations for (p5 p4 p3 p2) in terms of the bits in SV1 and CV1?
4. Use the logic gates, lights, and switches to build this tree for unsigned mul (multiply).

CHAPTER 5

Sequential Logic Circuits

5.1 Sequential Circuit Elements

A sequential circuit consists of logic gates and flip-flops. A *flip-flop* (ff) is a bistable device that has two outputs. One output indicates the true variable of the output, and the other indicates its complement. Such a device is used to store one bit of information. In concept, a sequential circuit uses logic gates to provide the control functions, and it uses flip-flops to store the digital signals. If the output of an ff changes as soon as its input changes, it is called an *asynchronous ff*. If the output of an ff changes as its input changes but is controlled by a clock, it is a *synchronous ff*. An asynchronous ff requires no clock, but a synchronous one does. A synchronous ff has a clock input in addition to its data inputs. Thus, the data inputs and clock input jointly control the timing of the change in its output voltage. By grouping an ordered set of flip-flops, we obtain a register. Thus, a register is used to store many bits where each ff is a one-bit storage cell in a register. The length of a register is the number of bits that can be stored. Precisely, an eight-bit register can store eight bits, a 16-bit register can store 16 bits, and a 32-bit register can store 32 bits. If the output of register A is connected to the input of register B, the presence of a clock at the input can transfer the bits from register A to register B. The bits in register A remain after the operation.

With timing, the output state of a synchronous ff changes at the leading edge or trailing edge of a clock. In either case, the output of such an ff obeys its data inputs with a one-bit delay. Synchronous ffs are commonly used in a sequential circuit. The design of such circuits is easy, but only after practice. The timing of a voltage change is abstract, but it can be displayed on an oscilloscope. The basic notion is that the next state of a sequential circuit is determined by its data inputs and clock. The data inputs may include external inputs and the current state of a register. Because an ff has a one-bit delay, the output of an ff can be written as a function of its input. Henceforth, we turn a sequential logic circuit design into a combinational logic circuit design. We say that a sequential logic circuit uses flip-flops to store bits and uses logic gates to control the inputs to the ffs. There are different types of ffs; each type operates under a set of rules, or characteristic equations. Because the ffs are the basic elements, we study the theory behind the design and its application in a synchronous circuit.

5.2 RS Flip-Flops

An RS flip-flop has two inputs and two outputs. The two inputs are S (set) and R (reset). The two outputs are Q and \Q. That means that one output is always the complement of the other. Using positive logic, we have four input conditions:

1. If S is high and R is low, then Q is high and \Q is low.
2. If S is low and R is high, then Q is low and \Q is high.
3. If both S and R are low, the output state of the ff remains unchanged.
4. If both S and R are high, the output state of the ff is undefined, and such a condition is considered as a design error.

5.2.1 ASYNCHRONOUS RS FLIP-FLOP

Since the first generation of computers in the late 1940s many different types of flip-flops have been developed. The asynchronous RS (reset-set) type was developed first, and many other types followed, including as D, JK, and T. Those flip-flops were derived from the design of an RS flip-flop. The name RS instead of SR is used because the letter *R* precedes *S* in the 26-letter alphabet sequence. The logic schematic of an asynchronous RS flip-flop using two OR gates and two inverters is shown in Figure 5.1(a).

Such an ff has no clock input, so its output changes as soon as the input signal arrives after a timing delay. The design is symmetrical and intuitive. The two two-input OR gates are latched to store one bit. That is, the output of each OR gate is the input to an inverter, and the inverter output is the input to the other OR gate. From its logic symbol, as shown in Figure 5.1(b), the two inputs are S (set) and R (reset) and the two outputs are Q and \Q. At the upper output, there is no circle to indicate the true variable of the output state Q. At the lower output, there is a circle to indicate the complement of Q (\Q). Inside the rectangular box, no mnemonic symbol is given before the circle with the following understanding:

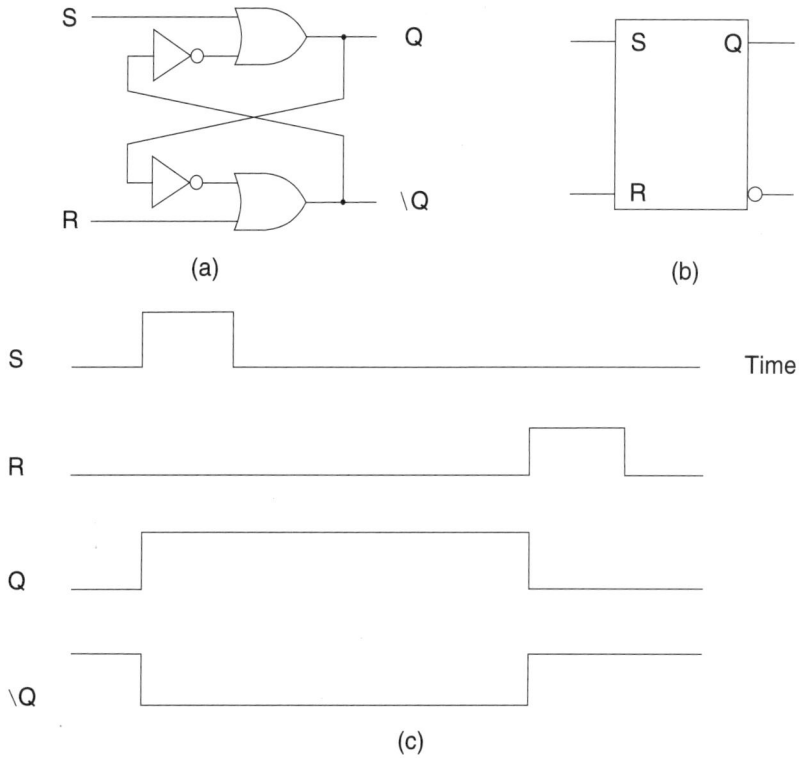

Figure 5.1. Asynchronous RS flip-flop: (a) using two OR gates, (b) logic symbol, and (c) the waveforms of S and R inputs and Q and \Q outputs.

1. Before the circle, the mnemonic symbol should be Q.
2. After the circle, the mnemonic symbol should be \Q.

Intuitively, let us figure out the operations of such an ff. Assuming that the output state Q of the ff is low, if S is high to the upper OR gate, its Q output becomes high. The complement of Q is fed to the lower OR gate as input, so \Q is low. Interestingly, the complement of \Q is latched to the first OR gate as one input. Thus, the output Q is latched high even if the S input is turned off from high to low. The simplified truth table of an RS flip-flop is shown in Table 5.1.

On the left-hand side, all the inputs for R and S are specified. On the right-hand side, the output $Qn+1$ is specified according to its input. Remember that S and R cannot be high at the same time, and such an input condition is a don't care; In practice, if both S and R really are high at the same time, it is a design error. The mnemonic symbol Qn represents the nth time output of the ff (the current output state). The mnemonic symbol $Qn+1$ represents the $(n+1)$th time

Table 5.1. Simplified truth table for an asyncronous RS flip-flop.

Input		Output
R	S	Qn+1
0	0	Qn
0	1	1
1	0	0
1	1	—

output of the ff (the next output state). The truth table is a simplified version because it only shows two inputs, S and R, and not Qn. In the truth table, if S is 0 and R is 0, the output $Qn+1$ is specified as Qn, which means the two outputs of the ff remain unchanged. We plot the four waveforms for S, R, Q, and \Q in Figure 5.1(c) in order to see the timing relationship. The vertical axis represents the voltage level of the input and output signals, and the horizontal axis represents the elapsed time. Assuming that the initial state of the RS flip-flop is 0 and the circuit delay is relatively small so that it is ignored in the plot, we have the following explanations:

1. If there is no S or R input, the output state of the ff remains. There-fore, the Q output stays low and the \Q output stays high.
2. An S input signal arrives, so Q switches from low to high and \Q switches from high to low. This \Q output is complemented by the up-per inverter, so a high voltage is latched back as input to the upper OR gate. As a result, even if the S signal is turned off to low, the Q output stays high and the \Q output stays low; the ff flips from 0 to 1.
3. An R input signal arrives, so Q switches from high to low and \Q switches from low to high. The Q output is complemented by the lower inverter, so a high voltage is latched back as input to the lower OR gate. As a result, even if the R signal is turned off to low, the \Q out-put stays high and the Q output stays low; the ff flips from 1 to 0.

When the RS ff is in the true state, an input S signal arrives. The two inputs of the upper OR gate are true, so the two output states of the ff remain. Similarly, if the ff is in the false state, an input R signal ar-rives. The two inputs of the lower OR gate are true, so the two output states of the ff remain.

5.2.2   CHARACTERISTIC EQUATION

What is the theory behind the design of an asynchronous RS flip-flop? First, let us plot the full truth table with three inputs and one output $Qn+1$. The three inputs are S, R, and the current output state of the ff, denoted as Qn. Therefore, the truth table has eight entries, as shown in Table 5.2.

Table 5.2. Truth table for an asynchronous RS flip-flop.

Input			Output
R	S	Qn	Qn+1
0	0	0	0
0	0	1	1
0	1	0	1
0	1	1	1
1	0	0	0
1	0	1	0
1	1	0	—
1	1	1	—

The last two entries are don't cares. From Table 5.2, we plot the three-bit Karnaugh map in Figure 5.2(a).

From the K-map, we write down the characteristic equation of an RS flip-flop as follows:

$$Qn+1 = S + \backslash R \; Qn$$

The characteristic equation represents the storage function or properties of an RS flip-flop in algebraic form. Thus, the output $Qn+1$ is 1 under

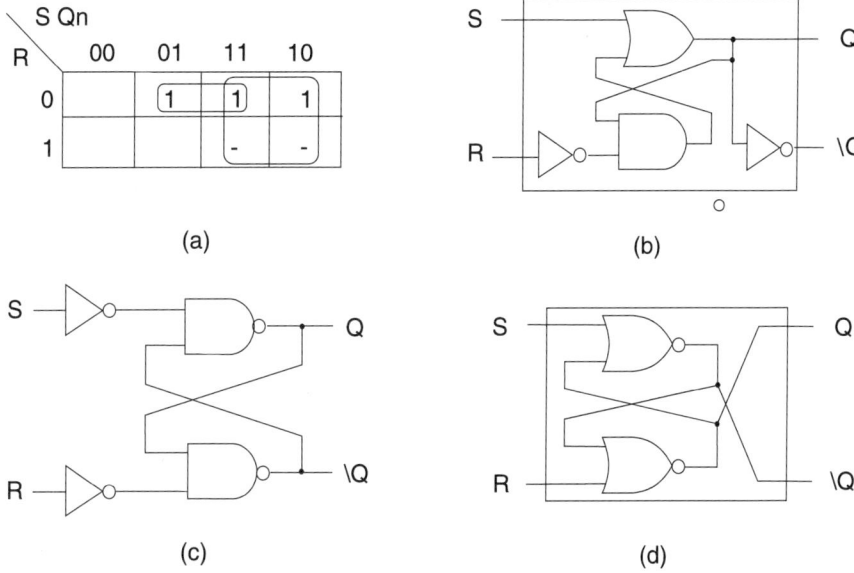

Figure 5.2. Other asynchronous RS flip-flops: (a) Karnaugh map, (b) using one AND gate and one OR gate, (c) using two NAND gates, and (d) using two NOR gates.

two conditions. The first condition is when S is 1. The second condition is when R is 0 and the current output Qn is 1. Intuitively, the RS ff produces a true output if S is 1 or the current state is 1 with no reset. The implementation of such a flip-flop using basic NAO gates is shown in Figure 5.2(b). Even though the circuit is not symmetrical, it works as well as other RS flip-flops. The algebraic derivation is explained as follows:

1. The AND gate has two inputs. The inverter produces \R as one input, and the other input is the current state Qn. Thus, the output of the AND gate is (\R . Qn).
2. The OR gate has two inputs. The AND gate output is latched back as one input, and the other input is S. As a result, the output $Qn+1$ is (S + \R Qn).

There are other design approaches, but each must obey the same characteristic equation. The third RS flip-flop design is shown in Figure 5.2(c). Such a design using two NAND gates and two inverters is symmetrical. The lower NAND gate takes two inputs and generates its output as \(\R . Qn). The upper NAND gate takes two inputs. One input is \S, and the other input is \(\R . Qn). Therefore, the output $Qn+1$ of the upper NAND gate is \(\S . \(\R . Qn)). After applying the DeMorgan theorem, we obtain the characteristic equation as follows:

$$Qn+1 = \backslash(\backslash S . \backslash(\backslash R . Qn))$$
$$= (S + \backslash R \ Qn)$$

The fourth example is shown in Figure 5.2(d). The circuit using two NOR gates only is also symmetrical. The characteristic equation can be derived in three steps. First, we find the output of the upper NOR gate, \(S + Qn). Second, we find the output of the lower NOR gate, $Qn+1$. Third, we simplify the characteristic equation as follows:

$$Qn+1 = \backslash(R + \backslash(S + Qn))$$
$$= \backslash R . (S + Qn)$$
$$= S \backslash R + \backslash R \ Qn + (S \ R) \qquad \{(S \ R) \text{ is a don't care}\}$$
$$= S (\backslash R + R) + \backslash R \ Qn$$
$$= S + \backslash R \ Qn$$

In the preceding, we apply the DeMorgan theorem to obtain the second line. After introducing the don't care (S R) in the third line and applying the distributive law in the fourth line, we obtain the final result.

5.2.3   SYNCHRONOUS RS FLIP-FLOP

A synchronous RS flip-flop is derived from the asynchronous RS ff; they share the same truth table and the same characteristic equation. However, a synchronous flip-flop needs a clock input in addition to its data input. Without a clock, the flip-flop will not flip, and sometimes this design feature allows us to simplify the input logic.

Leading Edge Trigger

Each clock signal is a low voltage followed by a high-voltage pulse in rectangular shape. The front edge of the positive pulse is called the *leading edge* or *positive edge*, which goes from low to high. The rear edge of the pulse is called the *trailing edge* or *negative edge*, which goes from high to low. Depending on the circuit, either edge of the clock may decide the exact time to change its output. For leading edge triggered flip-flops, if input data are present with the leading edge, the device can change its output in time. The logic symbol of a leading edge triggered synchronous RS flip-flop is shown in Figure 5.3(a).

The two inputs are S and R, and the two outputs are Q and \Q. We notice two things. First, the clock input has no circle on it. Second, there are two dc (direct current) inputs: the Pr (preset) signal and the Cl (clear) signal. The Pr input signal has no circle, which means that

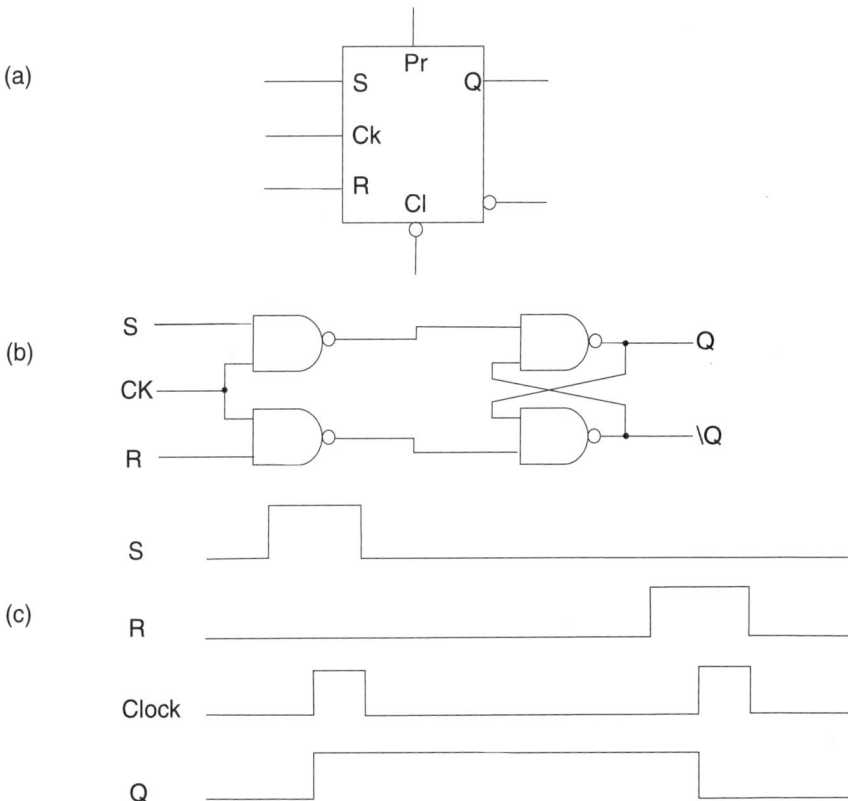

Figure 5.3. A leading edge triggered RS flip-flop: (a) logic symbol, (b) the waveforms of S, R, clock and Q output, and (c) a simplified logic schematic using NAND gates.

the output state is set to high, or 1, if the preset input is asserted high (positive edge). The Cl input signal has a circle, which means that the output state is reset to low, or 0, if the clear input is asserted low (negative edge). In other words, extra circuits are provided in the design to set or reset the device asynchronously.

Assume that the ff is initialized to the low state. The waveforms of R, S, clock input, and output Q are plotted in Figure 5.3(b). When the S input is high, the Q output changes state from low to high at the leading edge of the first clock pulse. Later, when a high R input arrives, the device flops to 0 at the leading edge of the second clock pulse.

A simplified logic schematic using NAND gates is shown in Figure 5.3(c). The dc set or reset circuits are omitted for the sake of simplicity. The clever design uses four NAND gates. The two NAND gates in the front are for gating control of the clock input. The two NAND gates in the back are latched for storing one bit of information. This design is derived from the asynchronous RS flip-flop using two NAND gates and two inverters, as shown in Figure 5.2(c). The inverter function is merged into the front NAND gate. When the S input signal is high, it cannot pass the front gate without the presence of a positive clock. Later, when the clock turns positive, the NAND gate opens to pass the S input to the flip-flop. As a consequence, the flip-flop changes its state at the leading edge of the clock.

Trailing Edge Trigger

The logic symbol of a trailing edge triggered RS ff is shown in Figure 5.4(a).

The logic symbol shows a circle at its clock input. That means that the flip-flop changes state at the trailing edge of the clock. For such a flip-flop, input data should arrive before the trailing edge so the device can change its output state in time. The initial output of the ff is assumed to be 0, or low. The waveforms of S, R, clock, and Q are plotted in Figure 5.4(b). As we can see, the flip-flop output Q changes state at the trailing edge of the clock. Regarding circuit delays, a circle at the clock input means alot to the logic designer.

5.3   Other Types of Flip-Flops

In addition to the RS flip-flop, popular flip-flops include the D flip-flop, the JK flip-flop, and the T flip-flop, as described in the following sections.

5.3.1   D FLIP-FLOP

The D type flip-flop is derived from the design of an RS flip-flop by adding one inverter in the front. The D flip-flop has only one input. Be-

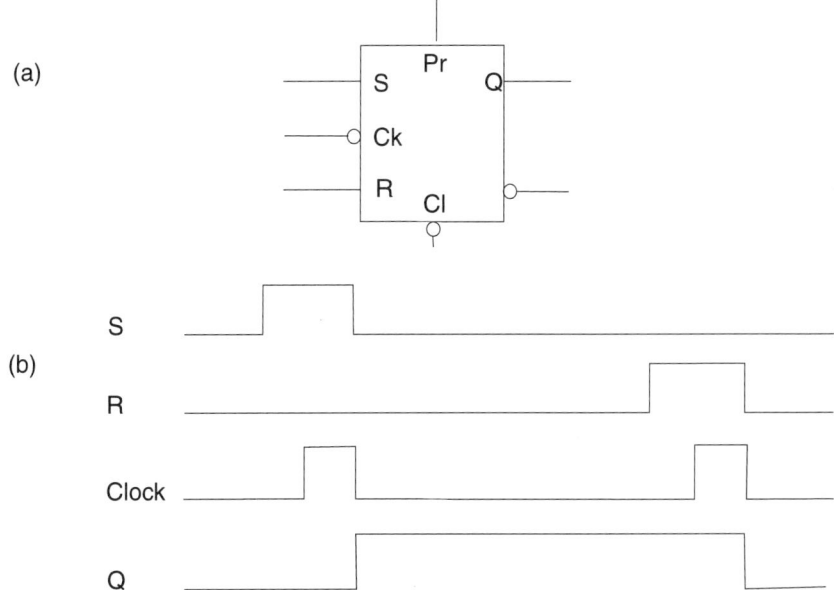

Figure 5.4. A trailing edge triggered RS flip-flop: (a) logic symbol and (b) the waveforms of S, R, clock, and the Q output.

cause it saves wiring, D ffs are used in buffer design. The letter *D* stands for data or delay because the output of this kind of ff always obeys the input after one bit delay. The logic symbol of a leading edge triggered D flip-flop is shown in Figure 5.5(a).

The absence of a circle at the clock input means that it is a positive edge trigger. The waveforms of D, clock, and Q are plotted in Figure 5.5(b). The initial state of the flip-flop is assumed to be low. When the D input arrives, the output Q does not go high until the leading edge of the first clock is present. When that happens, the output Q obeys the D input. The output Q stays high for a while, until the arrival of the second clock pulse. Because the D signal is low, the device flops to 0 at the leading edge of the second clock.

We can design a synchronous D flip-flop out of a synchronous RS flip-flop. Intuitively, we should tie the D input to the S input and tie the complement data (\D) to the R input. Thus, we need an inverter, as shown in Figure 5.5(c). The algebraic proof is left as an exercise. In practice, we pack eight such D flip-flops on one SSI chip for the following reasons:

1. Each D flip-flop requires only one input pin.
2. One output Q is adequate for buffer applications.
3. All the clock signals can be tied as one input.

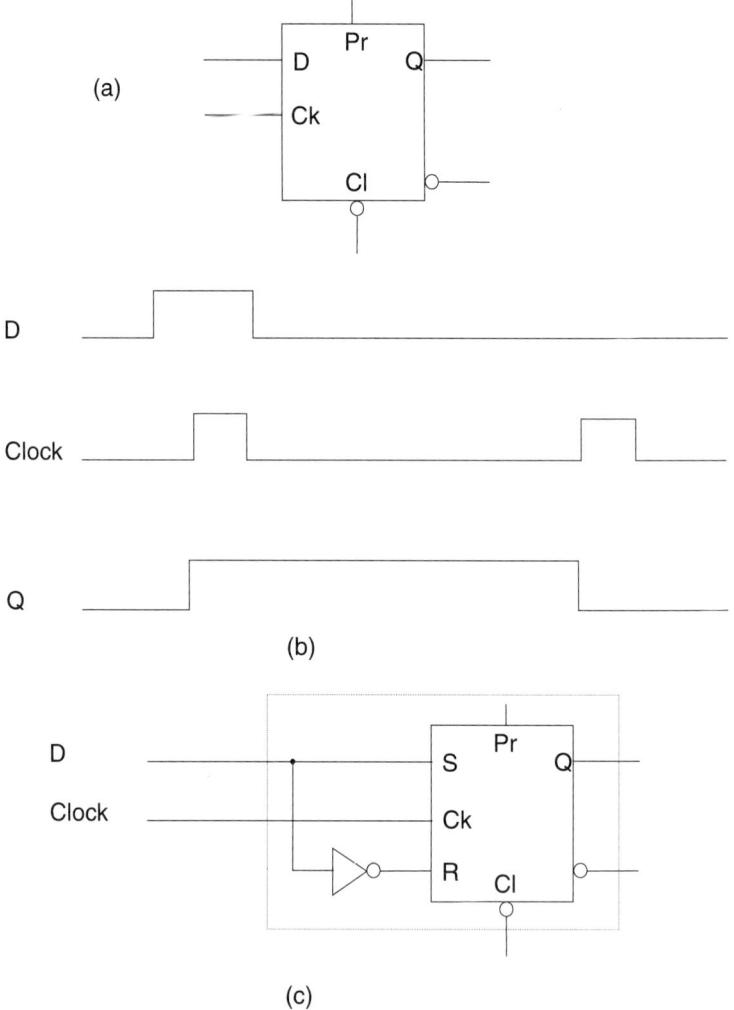

Figure 5.5. A leading edge triggered D flip-flop: (a) logic symbol, (b) the waveforms of D, clock, and the Q output, and (c) using an RS flip-flop.

4. All the dc clear signals can be tied, as one input and no preset input is provided.

5.3.2   JK FLIP-FLOP

A JK flip-flop is a superset of an RS flip-flop where both inputs can be activated high at the same time. When that happens, it switches or toggles the output state, regardless of the previous state. Most JK flip-flops are trailing edge triggered; they were popular in the 1960s. However,

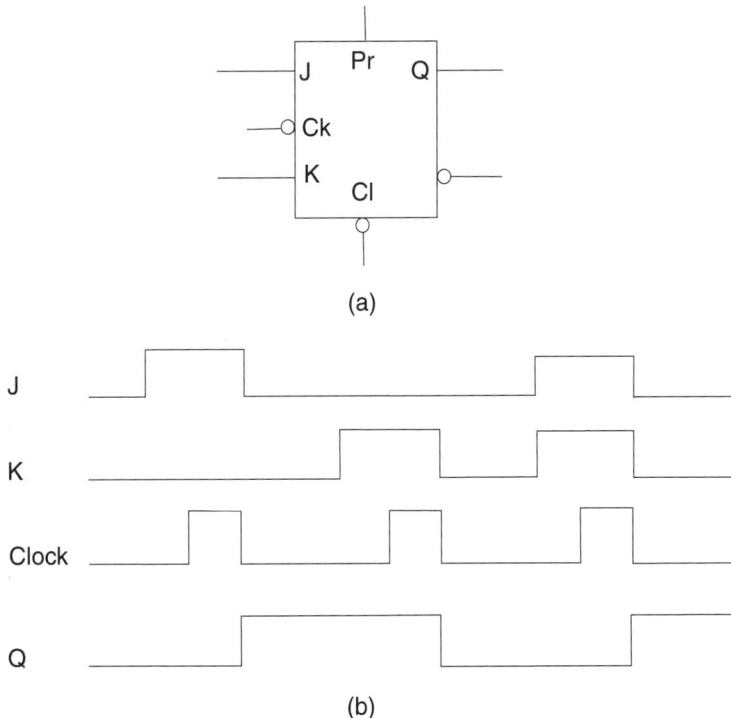

(a)

(b)

Figure 5.6. A trailing edge triggered JK flip-flop: (a) logic symbol and (b) the waveforms of J, K, clock, and the Q output.

no one seems to know why the flip-flop was called JK. Therefore, my colleague R. Sandige suggested that it is named for Jester and King. The logic symbol of a JK ff is shown in Figure 5.6(a).

The simplified truth table of a JK flip-flop is shown in Table 5.3. As shown in Table 5.3, the first three entries look like an RS flip-flop, but the fourth entry is an added capability. That is, when both J and K are high, the ff switches state at the trailing edge of the clock. If the initial state of the flip-flop is low, we can plot the waveforms of J, K, clock,

Table 5.3. The simplified truth table of a JK flip-flop.

Input		Output
J	K	$Qn+1$
0	0	Qn
0	1	0
1	0	1
1	1	$\backslash Qn$

and Q in Figure 5.6(b). When the J signal arrives, the ff switches its output state Q from low to high at the trailing edge of the first clock. When the K signal arrives, the Q output stays high and waits for the trailing edge of the second clock. When that happens, the Q output switches from high to low. Finally, when both inputs J and K are high, the out-put switches from low to high at the trailing edge of the third clock. The JK flip-flops are popular for two reasons. First, they can replace the RS flip-flops in design, but not vice versa. Second, because both inputs of a JK flip-flop can be high at the same time, its logic input equations can sometimes be simplified; this is not possible with an RS flip-flop.

We can make a JK flip-flop out of an RS flip-flop. Because the RS flip-flop has a one-bit delay, we are able to change a sequential design into a combinational design. First, we plot a truth table that specifies three columns. The first column specifies the input conditions of a JK flip-flop. The second column indicates the next state of output after a one-bit delay. The third column specifies the excitation equation for input R and S to generate the next state of output. Such a truth table is shown in Table 5.4.

The left-hand side shows the input conditions for J, K, and Qn. The right-hand side shows two columns: the output $Qn+1$ and the excitation for input R and S. After examining the input conditions on the left-hand side, we plot $Qn+1$ accordingly. The next step is crucial in that from the Qn and $Qn+1$ pair, we plot the excitation function for R and S. The full truth table has eight rows; the first six rows are identical to an RS flip-flop. In the last two rows, two input conditions are allowed, in that both J and K can be high at the same time. When that happens, the output of the ff switches state, so that $Qn+1$ becomes the complement of Qn. From the current state Qn to the next state $Qn+1$, we can

Table 5.4. The truth table for a JK flip-flop.

Input			Output	Excitation	
J	K	Qn	Qn+1	R	S
0	0	0	0	—	0
0	0	1	1	0	—
0	1	0	0	—	0
0	1	1	0	1	0
1	0	0	1	0	1
1	0	1	1	0	—
1	1	0	1	0	1
1	1	1	0	1	0

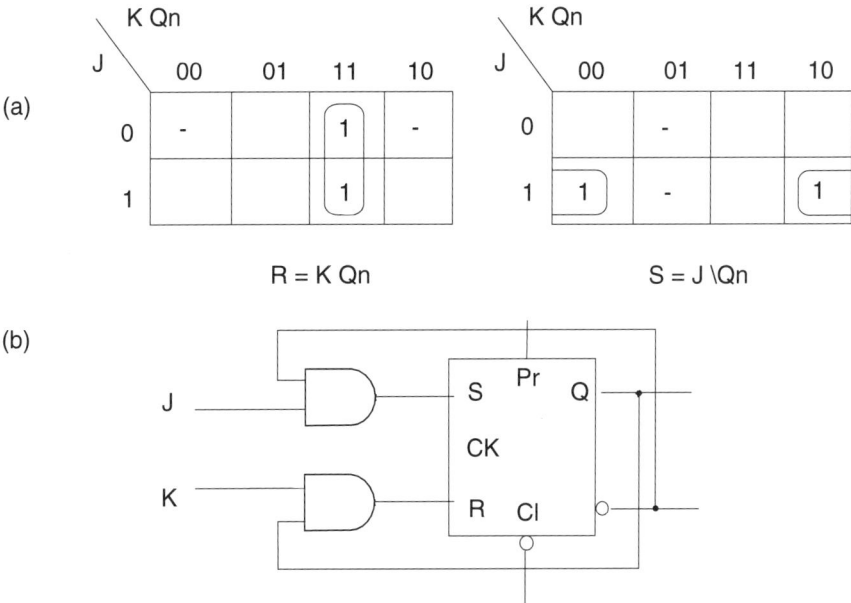

Figure 5.7. A JK flip-flop design: (a) Karnaugh maps for the R and S inputs and (b) a logic schematic using an RS flip-flop.

determine the input conditions for R and S. This notion is important because the excitation table is crucial in sequential circuit design. By inspecting the Qn and $Qn+1$ entries in the truth table, we can determine the excitation equation for R and S, as explained in the following:

1. In the first row, the J input is 0 and the K input is 0 (i.e., no input). The current output state Qn is 0, so the next output state $Qn+1$ is 0. In the excitation table, the S entry must be 0, but the R entry is a don't care. The don't care input condition really means that even if R is asserted true, it does not change the output of the flip-flop.
2. In the second row, because both J and K are 0s and Qn is 1, $Qn+1$ remains as 1. Thus, the R entry must be 0, but the S entry is a don't care.
3. In the third row, J is 0, K is 1, and the current output Qn is 0. Thus, the next output $Qn+1$ remains 0. Intuitively, the S input entry must 0, and the R entry is a don't care.
4. In the fourth row, J is 0, K is 1, and the current output Qn is 1. The next output $Qn+1$ changes to 0, the R input is 1, and the S input is 0.
5. In the fifth row, J is 1, K is 0, and the current output Qn is 0. The next output state $Qn+1$ changes to 1, so S must be 1, and R is 0.

6. In the sixth row, J is 1, K is 0, and the current output Qn is 1. The next output $Qn+1$ remains 1, the excitation input for R is 0, and the excitation input for S is a don't care.

7. In the seventh row, J is 1, K is 1, and the current output Qn is 0. Therefore, the flip-flop switches state, as $Qn+1$ becomes 0. Because the current output Qn changes from 0 to 1 after a one-bit delay, its S excitation input must be 1 and its R excitation input is 0.

8. In the eighth row, J is 1, K is 1, and the current output Qn is 1. As the flip-flop switches state, $Qn+1$ becomes 1. Therefore, the R input must be 1 with an S input of 0.

Note that both R and S cannot be high at the same time. By looking at the output states Qn and $Qn+1$, the first and third rows are the same. The second and sixth rows are the same; so are the fifth and seventh rows; the fourth and eighth rows. If two rows are the same in regard to output states, their excitation inputs should also be the same.

Our next step is to write down the logic functions for R and S in the form of SOP (sum of product) and to simplify. We plot two Karnaugh maps for R and S, as shown in Figure 5.7(a).

Each K-map has two don't cares, but none of them can be used to simplify the equation, as shown here:

$$S = J \setminus Qn$$
$$R = K \, Qn$$

The logic schematic is shown in Figure 5.7(b). Note that the J input is gated with $\setminus Qn$ and the K input is gated with Qn. This makes sense because when both J and K are 1s, only one input signal can go through the gate to toggle the flip-flop.

Edge Trigger Vs. Pulse Trigger

A positive clock is defined to be a half-bit low voltage followed by a half-bit high voltage. In order for the output of the flip-flop to change at the trailing edge of the clock, we have two different design approaches, pulse triggered and edge triggered. There is a subtle difference in circuit design between pulse triggered flip-flops and edge triggered flip-flops.

The pulse triggered flip-flops were once popular in TTL circuits. Such a flip-flop has the so-called master-slave design in that two flip-flops are cascaded in series. The flip-flop in the front is the *master* and the flip-flop in the back is the *slave*. The input data signal is clocked into the master flip-flop at the leading edge of the clock pulse. The same bit is transferred from the master to the slave at the trailing edge of the clock pulse. Such a design is termed *pulse triggered*, and the symbol of the flip-flop does not have a triangle shape at the clock input.

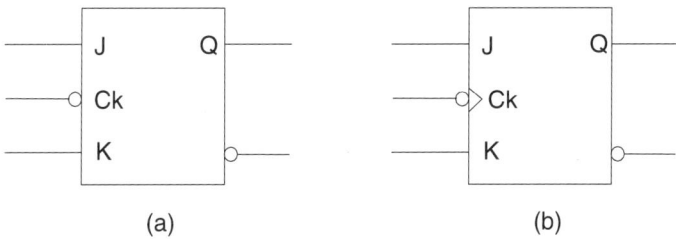

Figure 5.8. Logic symbols: (a) a pulse triggered JK ff at the trailing edge and (b) an edge triggered JK ff at the trailing edge.

An edge triggered flip-flop locks the data before the edge and changes its output state when the clock pulse falls from high to low. The logic symbol of a pulse triggered JK ff is shown in Figure 5.8(a), and an edge triggered JK ff is shown in Figure 5.8(b). Note that the logic symbol of an edge triggered flip-flop has a triangle at its clock input. The logic symbol of a pulse triggered flip-flop has no triangle in the front. There is a circle at the clock input because the trailing edge of a clock determines the timing of output change. In circuit design, if a flip-flop is edge triggered, it is simpler and faster. In logic design, both types of flip-flops provide the same function.

5.3.3 T FLIP-FLOP

The T (triggered) flip-flop is known as a *binary trigger*. The single input is T, and the two outputs are denoted Q and \Q. Usually, the T flip-flop is derived from another flip-flop, such as D, RS, or JK. If the T input is merged into the clock, the logic schematic of a binary trigger using a D ff is shown in Figure 5.9(a). Intuitively, we use the \Q output as the D (data) input in the next output state. As a consequence, the ff toggles back and forth after receiving an input pulse. The initial state of the T ff is assumed to be 0. When the first input pulse arrives, its trailing edge changes the output state of the flip-flop from 0 to 1. When the second pulse arrives, its trailing edge changes the output state of the flip-flop from 1 to 0. This device is called a binary trigger because the T ff serves as a one-bit counter.

The T flip-flop can be derived from an RS flip-flop whose logic schematic is shown in Figure 5.9(b). Intuitively, the S input is \Q and the R input is Q. We plot the truth table in Table 5.5. Then, from the Qn and $Qn+1$ outputs, we can figure out the excitation inputs for R and S.

From the excitation entries in Table 5.5, we obtain

$$S = T \setminus Q$$
$$R = T Q$$

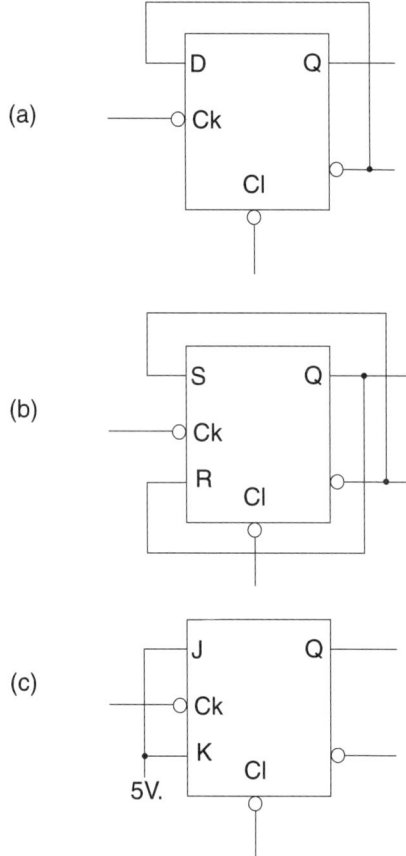

Figure 5.9. Binary triggers: (a) using a D flip-flop, (b) using an RS flip-flop, and (c) using a JK flip-flop.

Because the T signal is the same as the clock signal, it can be omitted from the equation. In practice, we often implement a T flip-flop from a JK ff whose logic schematic is shown in Figure 5.9(c). Intuitively, the J input and the K input are tied to 5 v. We plot the truth table in Table 5.6 to find the relationship between Qn and $Qn+1$. Then we decide on the J and K inputs for excitation.

From the excitation entries in Table 5.6, we use don't cares to simplify the excitation equations as follows:

$$J = T\ (\backslash Qn + Qn)$$
$$= T$$
$$K = T\ (Qn + \backslash Qn)$$
$$= T$$

Table 5.5. Truth table for a T flip-flop using RS.

Input		Output	Excitation	
T	Qn	Qn+1	R	S
0	0	0	—	0
0	1	1	0	—
1	0	1	0	1
1	1	0	1	0

Because the function of T is embedded in the clock signal, the J and K inputs are all 1s, say 5 v.

5.3.4 HAZARDS

In sequential circuit design, one potential hazard is the circuit delay problem. When the trailing edge of a clock arrives while the input data have not yet arrived, the flip-flop has a false trigger to generate the wrong output. In that regard, a logic designer often does a worst-case analysis by adding all the circuit delays in the longest path. It is safe if the total circuit delay is shorter than the clock period. That is, the input data must show up in time before the trailing edge of the clock signal.

5.4 Sequential Circuit Design Cases

Sequential circuits are designed to change the state of a set of flip-flops in response to an input sequence. Because the number of input states and output states is finite, such a circuit is also called a finite state machine (FSM). An FSM generates a sequence of output after receiving a sequence of input. Each output line may be used as a timing control signal to clock information from one device to another.

Table 5.6. Truth table for a T flip-flop using JK.

Input		Output	Excitation	
T	Qn	Qn+1	J	K
0	0	0	0	—
0	1	1	—	0
1	0	1	1	—
1	1	0	—	1

5.4.1 REGISTERS

A *register* is an ordered set of high-speed flip-flops; each ff is used to store one bit. The register size equals the number of bits it can store. A high-speed register can be used in a CPU, in memory, or in an I/O controller. In general, microcomputers use sixteen-bit registers, mainframes use 32-bit registers, and supercomputers use 64-bit registers. A simple finite state machine has many registers, and the output states of all the registers change with time, as controlled by a clock. The memory word can also be thought of as a register operating at a much slower speed.

Serial Data Vs. Parallel Data

The number of wires used to transfer data is defined as the *width* of the data path. If only one wire is used, we can transfer data in serial mode, and the voltage level on the wire varies as a function of time. If many wires are used, we can transfer data in parallel mode. That is, all the bits are placed on the wires at the same time. Therefore, a register may operate in four transfer modes:

1. Serial in, serial out
2. Serial in, parallel out
3. Parallel in, serial out
4. Parallel in, parallel out

5.4.2 CPU REGISTERS

There are many high-speed registers in a CPU. In particular, the PC (program counter) is used to store the memory address of the instruction in execution. The register is designed as a counter so the CPU can increment its value by the length of instruction. Before each instruction executes, it must be fetched from memory into IR (instruction register). A CPU also supports a set of working registers for storing address or data during executions.

In sum, a CPU register is designed to store an instruction, an instruction address, the address of data, a piece of data, or something similar. Each CPU register uses a clock signal to synchronously transfer bits of information in parallel. Note that both PC and IR are read only, but the working registers are for both reading and writing.

5.4.3 I/O REGISTERS

There are many IORs (I/O registers) in an I/O controller, and each IOR may be a data register, a control register, or a status register. If the IOR is used to receive data from an input device or to transmit data to an output device, then it is a hardware buffer in the I/O controller. An I/O buffer uses flip-flops to hold data bits that are different from buffer gates. During a transfer operation, the I/O buffer can change not only the speed, but also the transfer mode. As an example, an I/O buffer can receive parallel data from the CPU and transmit serial data to the printer. That is, the I/O controller changes the transfer mode from parallel to serial. In addition, the speed of the output transfer can be slowed by decreasing the clock frequency when the data are serially shifted out to the device. That is, the I/O buffer serves as the middleman between the CPU and the outside world. Some IORs provide the status information to the programmer, so their access right is read only. In other words, a program can read the bits in the register but not write into it. Other IORs may allow write only or both read and write. An IOR is very much like a memory word except that the device is hardwired with flip-flops.

It should be stressed that an I/O buffer is different from a software buffer, which is really a block of memory. A software buffer is used to store input data or output data. An input software buffer is used to read data from an input hardware buffer in a I/O controller. In contrast, an output software buffer is used to store output data before writing them into an output hardware buffer. It is called a *software buffer* because its memory address can be changed from time to time.

Shift Register

The logic schematic of an eight-bit I/O buffer designed as a shift register is shown in Figure 5.10(a). The clock input is drawn from left to right to cut it short, and the eight data flip-flops are leading edge triggered. The I/O buffer operates in serial mode, that is, serial in, serial out. The I/O buffer is designed as a shift register in that data bits flow from left to right at the leading edge of a clock. In other words, the eight flip-flops share one clock input in sync with the serial data input. The output of each flip-flop is fed as input to the next flip-flop on its right with one exception. The rightmost flip-flop has its output open-ended. In the schematic, each output bit of the D flip-flop is denoted Xn, where n indicates the bit position in the buffer. Assume that we have eight serial bits as input. After eight clock pulses, the eight serial bits reside in the buffer, denoted by X7, X6, . . . X1, X0 from left to right. The X0 bit arrives first, and the X7 bit arrives last. If this I/O buffer is used in a LAN (local area network) to receive a message on the line, the LAN circuit can decode the opcode in the buffer and decide which operation to act on next. Given that eight bits reside in the I/O buffer, eight more clock pulses can shift all the bits out, one by one, in sequence. If we keep the input data line low during shifting, the buffer is cleared to all 0s.

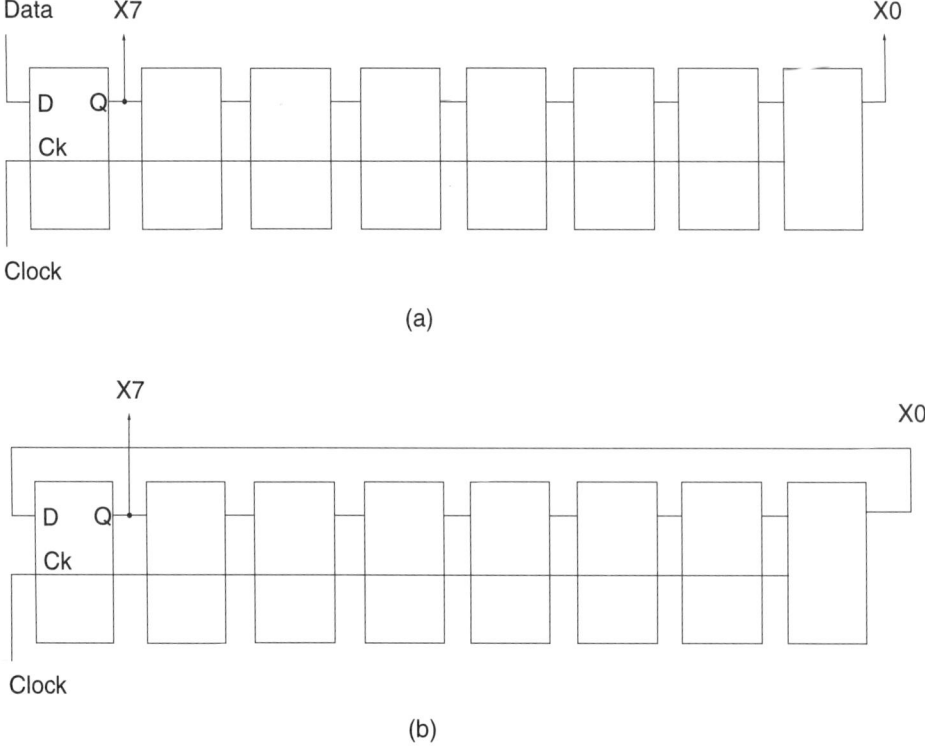

Figure 5.10. An eight-bit serial-in, serial-out hardware buffer: (a) a shift register and (b) a circular shift register.

Note that an I/O buffer may have the capability to reset all its flip-flops asynchronously through its dc clear pin. An I/O buffer may also be designed for parallel data inputs, so all the bits are clocked into the register at the same time. After that, the logic circuit may determine to transfer or route the bits from the register to another register in parallel or in serial.

Circular Shift Register

As a basic concept, we study a circular shift register design that has many applications. The logic schematic of such a register is shown in Figure 5.10(b). There are eight data flip-flops that are leading edge triggered. The circular shift register may set the input bits through its dc preset pin. The circular shift operation is also known as a *rotate shift*. It is similar to a shift register, except that the output of the rightmost flip-flop (X7) is routed back to the leftmost flip-flop as input. After a circular shift, all the bits retain in the register, but their respective bit positions change. For example, after a circular shift right operation by one bit, every bit is shifted to its right, and the rightmost bit is shifted into the leftmost bit in a circular fashion. Thus, the output X0 of the righmost flip-flop becomes the output X7 of the leftmost flip-flop.

5.4.4 Counters

A counter is a special register that can count the number of clocks received. With a running clock as input, the counter state also represents the time elapsed as each flip-flop changes its output state as a function of time. There are many types of counters, as discussed in the following.

Free-Running Counter

An n-bit free-running counter counts from 0 to $(2^n - 1)$, where n is the number of flip-flops used. Each flip-flop stores a bit, and if n equals 3, we have a mod 8 counter that counts from 0 to 7 repeatedly. The schematic of a three-bit ripple counter is shown in Figure 5.11(a).

In the design, each flip-flop is a trailing edge triggered JK and both J and K are tied to 5 v. Therefore, each ff acts like a binary trigger that changes state at the trailing edge of a clock. Each flip-flop is a one-bit counter and the least significant bit is the leftmost bit that receives the clock as input and generates X0 as output. The X0 output becomes the

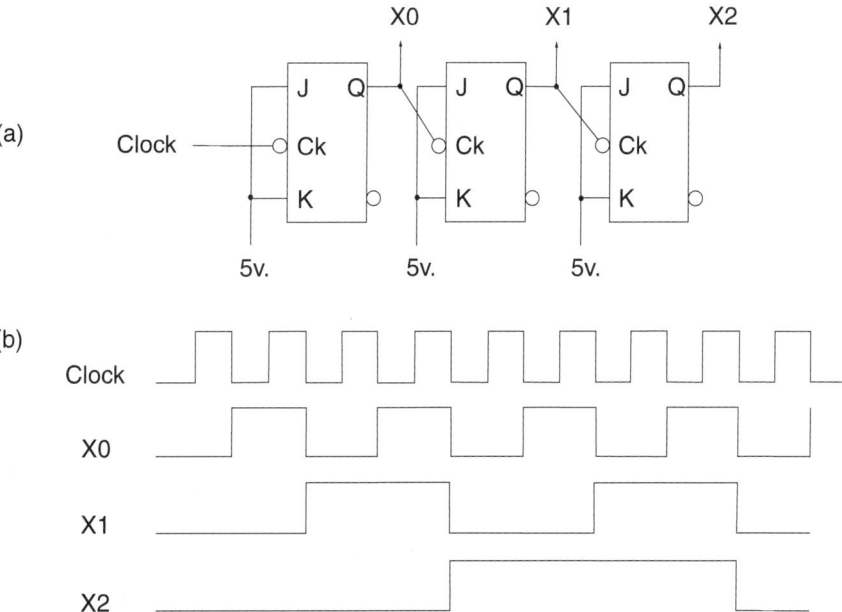

Figure 5.11. A three-bit ripple counter: (a) a logic schematic and (b) the waveforms of clock, X0, X1, and X2.

clock input to the flip-flop on its immediate right. In turn, the X1 output of the second flip-flop is the clock input to the third flip-flop. It has a rippled effect in that the next bit always changes its output state after the previous bit. For example, when the counter reaches 7, or 111 in binary, another clock input will change its state to 3 0s. However, each bit has a different circuit delay. The first flip-flop has one delay, the second has two, and the third has three. This is because the output of one flip-flop serves as input in order to trigger the next flip-flop on its immediate right. By neglecting the circuit delays, we plot the waveforms of the clock signal and the counter output in Figure 5.11(b).

Decade Counter

A *decade counter* counts from 0 to 9 repeatedly. Therefore, a total of four flip-flops are needed because the count goes beyond 7. The logic circuit counts the input pulse from 0 to 9, goes back to 0, and then repeats. That is, after reaching state 9, the next state is 0 instead of 10. Commercially, a synchronous decade counter uses the current output as input to its flip-flops, so the switching time for each ff is about the same within a couple circuit delays. The design of such a decade counter is left as an exercise.

Switch-Tail Counter

A switch-tail counter operates like a shift register, with one modification at the tail end. Many types of flip-flops can be used to design such a counter. If the number of ffs used is N, the number of states is $(2*N)$ where * is the multiply operator. As an example, we use three D flip-flops to support a total of six states. The state transition diagram of the counter is shown in Figure 5.12(a).

We use three bits to represent the state, and the initial state is assumed to be 000. The counter has the clock as the only input. After receiving a clock input, its state is changed to 100, as shown by the arrow in the transition. Subsequent clock inputs will change the counter state to 110, 111, 011, 001, and back to 000 repeatedly. The logic schematic of a switch-tail counter using three D flip-flops is depicted in Figure 5.12(b). In the design, we modify a three-bit circular shift register by connecting the complement output of the tail bit to the input of the first bit.

Let us trace the state transitions. From the initial state 000, the input to the first bit is 1, so X0 changes from 0 to 1 after the first clock pulse. Meanwhile, X1 and X2 remain 0s. The 1 signal of X0 sets the rest of the flip-flops as the next two clocks arrive in sequence. After the state becomes 111, the input to the first bit is switched to 0, so the next clock changes X0 to 0. Then the 0 signal of X0 resets the rest of the flip-flops, one by one, as each of the next two clocks arrives. After receiving the sixth clock, the counter goes back to the original state 000.

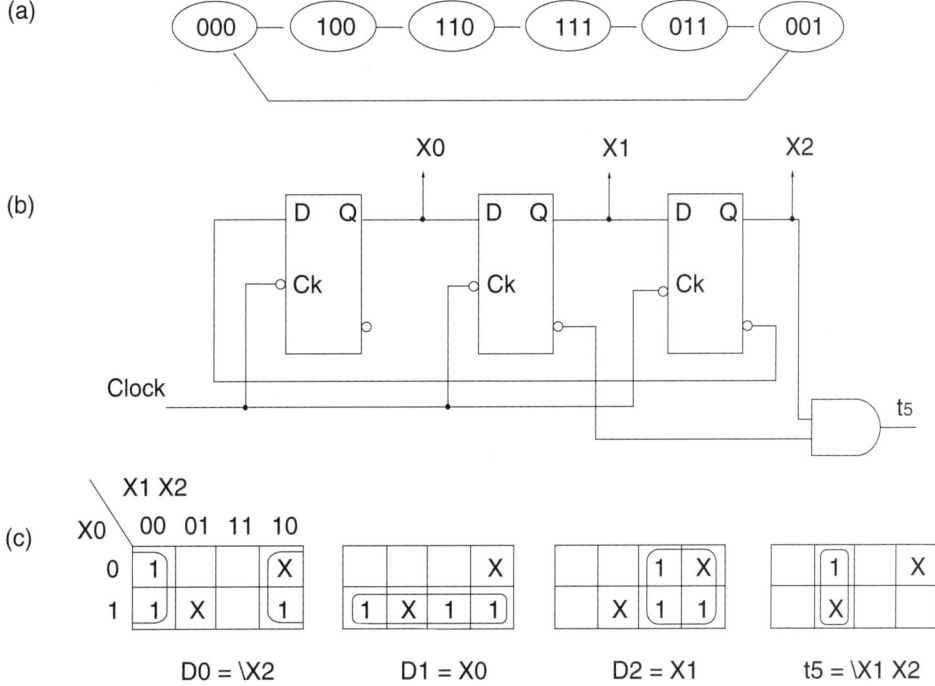

Figure 5.12. A three-bit switch-tail counter: (a) the state transition diagram, (b) a logic schematic, and (c) the Karnaugh maps for D0, D1, D2 and the timing state t5.

To decode any state, we need a two-input AND gate because of the don't cares.

Next, let us study the theory behind this clever design. Because the number of states is finite, we can list all the states in an excitation table, as shown in Table 5.7.

This is a simplified excitation table that has only two columns. For each row, the left-hand side represents a state and the right-hand side

Table 5.7. Excitation table for a switch-tail counter.

Output			Excitation			Output
X0	X1	X2	D0	D1	D2	t5
0	0	0	1	0	0	0
1	0	0	1	1	0	0
1	1	0	1	1	1	0
1	1	1	0	1	1	0
0	1	1	0	0	1	0
0	0	1	0	0	0	1

is the required excitation. The output of the leftmost flip-flop is denoted X0, so we name this D flip-flop X0. Each row on the left-hand side shows a three-bit state. For any two adjacent rows, the top row is the current state and the row beneath is the next state. As a result, the left-hand side really represents a state transition diagram in tabular form. The right-hand side is the excitation table that specifies the three inputs D0, D1, and D2 and the state transitions from top to bottom in sequence. The excitation table is arranged in a wrap around fashion. That means that the row on top is the next state of the row on the bottom. The entries in each row in the excitation table are strictly based on the following factors:

1. Two adjacent rows, the current state and the next state
2. The storage function of flip-flops used in the design

For each row, we decide on the excitation equation as input to the ff to generate the output based on the state transition. Note that in Table 5.7, the t5 (timing 5) is not part of the excitation, but rather is an output signal for decoding. There are six states all together; the two don't cares—(1 0 1) and (0 1 0)—are not shown in the table.

Let us explain the excitation table for the D flip-flops whose inputs coincide with the next row because of the one-bit delay property:

1. In the first row, the inputs for D0, D1, and D2 should be the same as X0, X1, and X2 in the second row. If X0 changes from 0 to 1, the D0 input in the first row must be a 1 in order to set X0.
2. Similarly, in the second row, the inputs for D0, D1, and D2 obey the outputs X0, X1, and X2 in the third row. In the third row, the D inputs obey the outputs in the fourth row. Because the D0, D1, and D2 inputs always obey the X outputs in the next state, we plot the D inputs for the fourth row and the fifth row. Finally, the D inputs in the last row obey the outputs in the first row.

Next, we use one don't care to reduce two variables in each equation so that each D input is one single variable as follows:

$$D0 = \backslash X0 \ \backslash X1 \ \backslash X2 + X0 \ \backslash X1 \ \backslash X2 + X0 \ X1 \ \backslash X2 + \{\backslash X0 \ X1 \ \backslash X2\}$$
$$= \backslash X2$$
$$D1 = X0 \ \backslash X1 \ \backslash X2 + X0 \ \backslash X1 \ \backslash X2 + X0 \ X1 \ \backslash X2 + \{X0 \ \backslash X1 \ X2\}$$
$$= X0$$
$$D2 = X0 \ X1 \ \backslash X2 + X0 \ X1 \ X2 + \backslash X0 \ X1 \ X2 + \{\backslash X0 \ X1 \ \backslash X2\}$$
$$= X1$$

In these equations, the chosen don't care is enclosed in a pair of braces for inspection. The three-variable Karnaugh maps are shown in Figure

5.12(c). In each map, one don't care is used to simplify the equation. The t5 signal is high if the counter reaches 001. After simplification, the t5 signal is high if X1 is low and X2 is high:

$$t5 = \backslash X0 \ \backslash X1 \ X2 + \{X0 \ \backslash X1 \ X2\}$$
$$= \backslash X1 \ X2$$

In the K-map, we obtain the same product as ($\backslash$X1 X2) by grouping the 1 entry with a don't care below it. The beauty of this counter design is its simplicity; all six timing states can be decoded using two-input AND gates.

5.5 *Sequencer*

A sequencer is a finite state machine that has many flip-flops and logic gates. The sequencer may accept external input signals and generate an output under the conditions determined by the current state and input. As an example, we use two JK flip-flops to design a sequencer that generates an output 1 after receiving three consecutive 1 as external input. In the following, we discuss the state transition diagram, excitation table, and logic implementation.

5.5.1 STATE TRANSITION DIAGRAM

The state transition diagram of a sequencer is plotted in Figure 5.13(a). The sequential circuit uses two JK flip-flops, identified as X1 and X0. The two-bit state represents a count output (X1 X0) of the flip-flops. The left output is X1 and the right output is X0. There are four states, denoted 00, 01, 10, and 11. In Figure 5.13, a state transition is shown by a line and an arrow. The arrow points to the direction of the transition. An I/O (input/output) condition is specified on top of each transition line. Each condition has two bits, with a slash in between. The first bit indicates an input for this transition to take place, and the second bit indicates an output.

From state 00 to 01, a condition is tagged as 1/0. That means that an external input 1 enables this transition and the circuit generates an output 0 at the same time. When the logic device is in initial state 00, there is an arrow pointing to itself with a condition specified as 0/0. Hence, if the input bit is 0, the state remains, and an output is generated as 0. Obviously, the device needs three consecutive 1s as external inputs to advance from state 00 to 11, the final state. After reaching the final state, any additional input 1 will generate an output with no state change. However, an input 0 will bring the device back to its initial state. When that

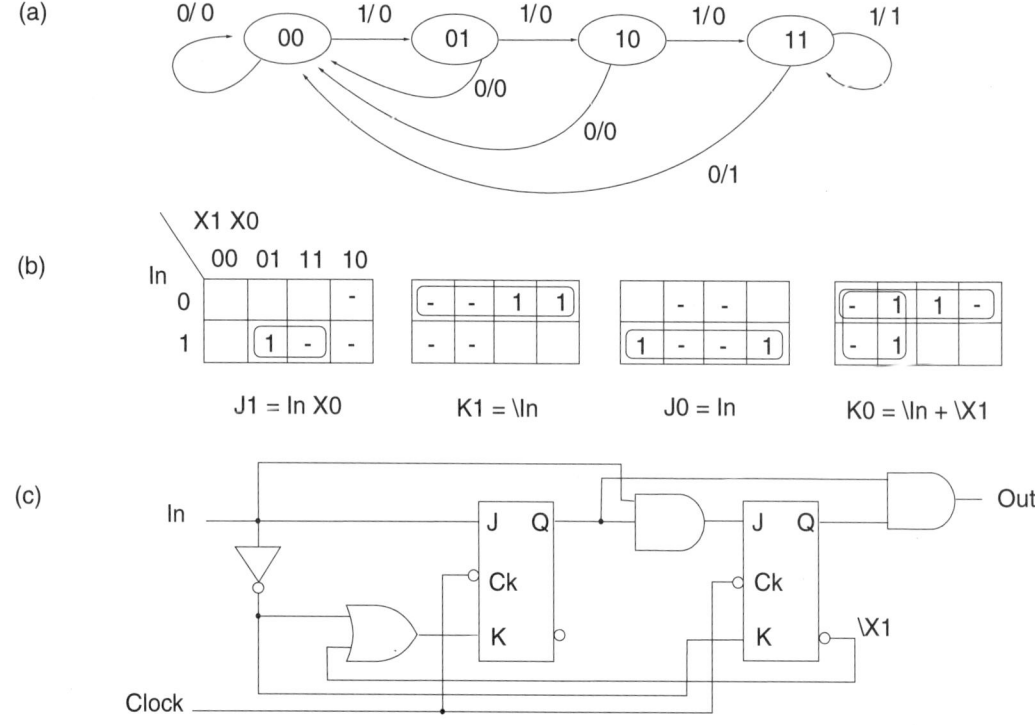

Figure 5.13. A sequencer design using JK flip-flops: (a) the state transition diagram, (b) Karnaugh maps for J1, K1, J0, and K0, and (c) a logic schematic.

happens, the circuit also generates 1 as output. While the device is in state 01 or 10, an input 0 will bring it back to 00 to start all over.

5.5.2 EXCITATION TABLE

Generally speaking, an excitation table has three columns, left, middle, and right. As an example, the excitation table for this sequencer is shown in Table 5.8.

In the left column, we specify the current state of three variables. The In (input) signal is in addition to the clock signal. The current output states are named X1 and X0. In the middle column, the next output states are also named X1 and X0. In the right column, we write down the excitation table and the Out (output) signal as follows.

In the left column, the three-bit current state pattern is arranged from top to bottom in ascending order. Each entry in the upper half has In specified as 0, and the lower half has specified the signal In as 1. The next output state obeys the state transition diagram, as shown in Figure 5.13(a). If the signal In is in sync with the clock, we can write down the excitation inputs for the two JK flip-flops in the right column.

Table 5.8. Excitation table for the sequencer.

Current			Next		Excitation				Output
In	X1	X0	X1	X0	J1	K1	J0	K0	Out
0	0	0	0	0	0	—	0	—	0
0	0	1	0	0	0	—	—	1	0
0	1	0	0	0	—	1	0	—	0
0	1	1	0	0	—	1	—	1	1
1	0	0	0	1	0	—	1	—	0
1	0	1	1	0	1	—	—	1	0
1	1	0	1	1	—	0	1	—	0
1	1	1	1	1	—	0	—	0	1

5.5.3   INPUT VS. OUTPUT

A sequential machine may receive an external input (In) signal that is
different from the clock or the excitation inputs. The machine may also
generate an external output (Out) signal under a certain condition. In
this design, the output condition is when the current state is (1 1), and
there is an external input. The two excitation inputs to the X1 flip-flop
are J1 and K1. The two excitation inputs to the X0 flip-flop are J0 and
K0. The current state and the next state will jointly decide the inputs
J1, K1, J0, and K0 for excitation. For each state transition, the J or K
input may be 0, 1, or don't care. To appreciate the logic behind the con-
struction of the excitation table, we discuss the excitation input entries,
row by row, as follows:

1. In the first row, the current state is (0 0) and the next state is (0 0),
   so J1 and J0 must stay 0s, but both K1 and K0 are don't cares. This
   is because the current state is 0, and another reset signal will not
   make any change.
2. In the second row, because X1 remains 0 like in row 1, the J1 input
   must be 0, but the K1 input is a don't care. However, X0 is changed
   from 1 to 0, so its K0 input must be 1, and J0 is a don't care. Recall
   that a JK changes state if both inputs are 1s.
3. In the third row, X1 changes from 1 to 0, so K1 is 1 and J1 is a don't
   care. Because X0 remains 0 like in row 1, J0 is 0, and K0 is a don't care.
4. In the fourth row, both X1 and X0 change from 1 to 0, so both K
   inputs are 0s and both J inputs are don't cares. Because the final
   state has been reached, it generates an output 1 even though the data
   input bit is a 0.
5. In row 5, the output X1 remains 0, so J1 must be 0 and K1 is a don't
   care. The output X0 changes from 0 to 1, so J0 is 1 and K0 is a don't
   care.

6. In row 6, the output X1 changes from 0 to 1, so J1 is 1 and K1 is a don't care. Because the output X0 changes from 1 to 0, K0 must be 1 and J0 is a don't care.
7. In row 7, the output X1 remains 1, so J1 is a don't care and K1 must be 0. Because the output X0 changes from 0 to 1, J0 is 1 and K0 is a don't care.
8. In row 8, an input data 1 will not change the state (11), so the J inputs are don't cares and the K inputs must be 0s. In addition, the Out signal should be a 1.

For excitation input to a JK flip-flop, we observe the following:

1. If the J input is 1, the K input is a don't care.
2. If the K input is 1, the J input is a don't care.
3. If the J input is 0, the K input is a don't care.
4. If the K input is 0, the J input is a don't care.

We plot the three-bit Karnaugh maps in Figure 5.13(b). In each K-map, the vertical variable is the In signal and the horizontal variables are the current state outputs (X1 X0). By selecting don't cares in each K-map for grouping, we obtain the simplified equations for excitation inputs to the JK flip-flops and the generated output:

$$J1 = In\ X0$$
$$K1 = \backslash In$$
$$J0 = In$$
$$K0 = \backslash X1 + \backslash In$$

$$Out = \backslash In\ X1\ X0 + In\ X1\ X0$$
$$= X1\ X0$$

The logic schematic of this sequencer using NAO (NOT-AND-OR) gates is shown in Figure 5.13(c). The X0 bit is positioned on the leftmost side to simplify wiring. The logic gates are used for controlling proper state transitions. If we use RS or D flip-flops in the design, more logic will be required, because fewer don't cares can be used.

5.5.4 COMPUTER PROGRAM EXECUTION

A digital computer operates like a complex sequential machine. A computer program consists of many instructions and data. Each instruction has an opcode that tells the CPU what to do. A computer program is stored in memory before it can be executed by the CPU. Let us trace the execution of a single instruction. Where instruction execution is concerned, the CPU keeps two important registers. One is the PC (program counter), or IAR (instruction address register), which is used to store the memory address of the current instruction in execution. The other is the IR (instruction register), which is used to store the instruction being fetched from memory. In regard to CPU execution, there are three phases: instruction fetch, instruction interpret, and instruction execute. The CPU uses logic circuits to execute instructions in memory in an infinite hardware loop, as described in the following.

Instruction Fetch

The CPU uses sequential logic circuits to generate many timing signals. The first set of signals are used to transfer the address of the current instruction from P-counter to memory. Where memory is concerned, it reads the address on the address bus, performs a read cycle, and places the instruction on the data bus. The CPU uses timing signals to transfer the instruction from the data bus to the IR.

Instruction Interpret

Each instruction has an opcode. After an instruction resides in IR, the CPU uses a combinational logic circuit to decode the opcode. Consequently, one or more enable signals are generated high to perform a sequence of operations.

Instruction Execute

The CPU executes the current instruction according to the decoded (i.e., enable) signals. A CPU usually has a set of working registers; each register is used to store a computation result during instruction execution. The enable signal generated by the decoder may open a logic gate to let information flow from a register to an adder. In a simple CPU, we can embed logical operation capabilities into the design of an adder, also called an arithmetic and logic unit (ALU). Using such an adder, the CPU can perform a variety of operations, including add, subtract, multiply, divide, NOT, AND, OR, and EOR.

While the CPU is busy executing the current instruction, it uses a combinational logic circuit to increment the PC by the length in bytes of the current instruction. After completing the execution of the current instruction, the CPU goes back to step 1 and the hardware instruction fetch/interpret/execute cycle is repeated again.

We should know two things. First, the instruction execution phase is usually done in one clock cycle, but there are some exceptions. For example, an instruction to move a block of bytes from one memory location to another takes more clocks. Second, a high-speed CPU can use parallel logic circuits to fetch instructions, interpret instructions, and execute more than one instruction at the same time.

5.6   Logic Simulations

If we have millions of transistors in a VLSI or ULSI design, we must find the design errors through software simulations before the chip is manufactured or built. In the following, we describe the ASIC (application-specific integrated circuit) and the software simulation tools that are needed to develop such circuits.

5.6.1   APPLICATION-SPECIFIC INTEGRATED CIRCUIT

An application-specific integrated circuit (ASIC) is a VLSI chip to support a specific control function. Henceforth, an ASIC chip contains more complex logic circuits that are usually application-dependent. Such a chip contains massive quantities of flip-flops and logic gates. As an example, each printed circuit board may have one CPU chip and several ASIC chips. More often than not, an ASIC chip is proprietary to a company. The disk controller chip may perform the control and transfer data functions between disk and memory. To design such an ASIC chip requires special software simulation tools. The trend is to replace logic schematics with logic equations written in HDL (Hardware Description Language). After the chip is tested through extensive simulations, it is given to a semiconductor company for mass production.

5.6.2   HARDWARE DESCRIPTION LANGUAGES

The following three reasons explain why HDL is often used to describe and simulate logic circuits:

1. An HDL description of a logic circuit can serve as a specification of the design. Each HDL statement is prepared by an editor, which is a software program running on a personal computer. The HDL statement is composed of ASCII characters, so it can be easily modified by the editor.
2. Simulating the design can uncover errors that would otherwise be detected only when the hardware chip is built.
3. Logic synthesis tools are provided to interpret an HDL description and to generate a gate-level netlist (network list) for implementation. The various component modules of circuits are stored in a library on disk. These synthesis tools often optimize the design with respect to speed, circuit size, or some other cost function.

One popular tool is Verilog, which has a syntax similar to the programming language C. The other tool is VHDL, which has a syntax similar to ADA, another high-level programming language. Our objective here is to study the basic design concept rather than the language constructs.

5.7 Verilog

The Verilog tool was created in 1985 by Gateway; it was later merged with Cadence Design Systems [Verilog, Paln96]. The simulation language allows four levels of design description as described here:

1. Algorithmic level: A module can be described at the algorithmic level without worrying about the hardware implementation details. Designing at this level is like C programming. As an example, we implement the Exclusive OR function to illustrate the concept as follows:

   ```
   /*----------------------------------------------------- comment block
         Scaler variables a, b are two input signals and scaler variable
         f is the output signal. A keyword symbol is a reserved symbol
         or name in a programming language. The keyword symbol != 
         means not equal, defined as a relational operator.
   ----------------------------------------------------- end of comment
   */
   if a != b, f = 1; else f = 0;
   ```

2. Dataflow level: The module is designed so that dataflow operations are specified in detail. The designer must know the logic equations of a function or dataflows between two registers. However, the details of gates and flip-flops do not need to be selected in the design. For example, the statement can be a logic equation to implement the Exclusive OR function:

$$f = a \wedge b$$

   The keyword symbol $\wedge$ is the bitwise Exclusive OR operator in Verilog; some other operators are listed in Table 5.9.

   In Table 5.9, the first set of symbols resembles C, and the second set provide mnemonic meanings.

3. Gate level: At this level, the module definition is written in terms of all the logic gates and the interconnect wires. Designing at this level is very much like drawing a logic schematic at the gate level. We try to implement the Exclusive OR function using NAO gates as follows:

   ```
   not (aBar, a);
   not (bBar, b);
   and (f1, aBar, b);
   and (f2, a, bBar);
   or (f, f1, f2);
   ```

Table 5.9. Bitwise logical operators in Verilog.

Symbol Set 1	Symbol Set 2	Description
~	'not	NOT function
&	'and	AND function
|	'or	OR function
^	'xor	Exclusive OR function
~^	'xnor	Exclusive NOR function

The logic circuit uses five primitive gates, and each gate has a name followed by a terminal list. Each terminal list consists of many output and input signals enclosed in parentheses. More design examples at the gate level will be provided, with Verilog language descriptions as discussed later.

4. Switch level: This is the circuit level, the lowest abstraction provided by Verilog. A module can be written in terms of transistor switches, storage nodes (i.e., elements), and the interconnect wires between them.

5.7.1   MODULE DEFINITION

The building block in Verilog is called a *module*. The module definition syntax is as follows:

```
/* ---------------------------------
    Verilog module definition
--------------------------------- */
module ⟨moduleName⟩ ((⟨terminalList⟩));
   . . .
<statement>
   . . .
endmodule
```

A module is the basic unit of logic design in Verilog. In a module definition, many statements are enclosed to describe the logic circuit. A comment statement starts with /* and ends with */. In the preceding definition, the first three lines constitute a header for comment and the fourth line is the declaration statement. Many keyword symbols are reserved in Verilog, and each has a special meaning. In the declaration statement, the keyword *module* is followed by a name, a terminal list, and a semicolon. A module name serves as the id (identity) of the logic circuit. Each module definition can be thought of as a design template. A module call may be placed in another module definition block to instantiate the circuit into the design. The purpose of a terminal list is to specify the output and inputs to the logic device. The variable names in the terminal list are equivalent to dummy arguments in a programming language. During a call, the terminal list contains the actual passing arguments. In the last statement, the keyword *endmodule* serves as a delimiter. A pair of angular brackets is used to enclose a metasymbol that is not part of the language. Rather, it describes the syntax and what information can be placed in a statement or a module definition. The metasymbol *moduleName* means a class of module names, and the metasymbol *terminalList* means a class of terminal list.

Each module definition contains many statements, and each statement is a string of ASCII characters ending with a semicolon (;). Note that a module definition cannot be nested in another definition. That is, all the module definitions must be placed at the same level. Each Verilog statement obeys a set of syntactic rules. Just like in C, the statement is case-sensitive. When a module is called, the Veriog software interprets each statement in the definition module (i.e., block), simulates, and implements its logic in the circuit. A typical design flow has many milestones, as shown in Figure 5.14.

As a first step, the project team prepares design specifications. Second, designers write Verilog HDL to describe the logic circuit. Third, the design block is fully tested through software simulations. It is important for the team to write a stimulus block that can be applied to the design block to generate results. After checking the results, if an error is found, the HDL design modules must be rewritten, so the design process is repeated. After extensive simulation and testing are successfully completed, a netlist is generated at the logic gate level. The netlist provides detailed information about gates, storage elements, and interconnect wires. Software tools are also available to take the netlist as input, lay out the physical circuits, and generate tape out. If difficulty is encountered, the team may need to change the HDL and try again. A final process, tape out, generates a magnetic tape that is sent to the semiconductor manufacturer for making the mask.

5.7.2 MODULE CALL

Verilog supports many logic gates as predefined modules. Such a module is called a *primitive* and is stored in the library on disk. Because a primitive is already written, no module definition is required. Each primitive gate is assigned a name, such as NOT, buf, AND, OR, NAND, NOR, XOR (Exclusive OR), or XNOR (Exclusive NOR). The logic gate name represents the primitive. We observe the following points:

1. The NOT and buf gates have one output and one input. However, each gate may have an enable input that can be asserted high or low.

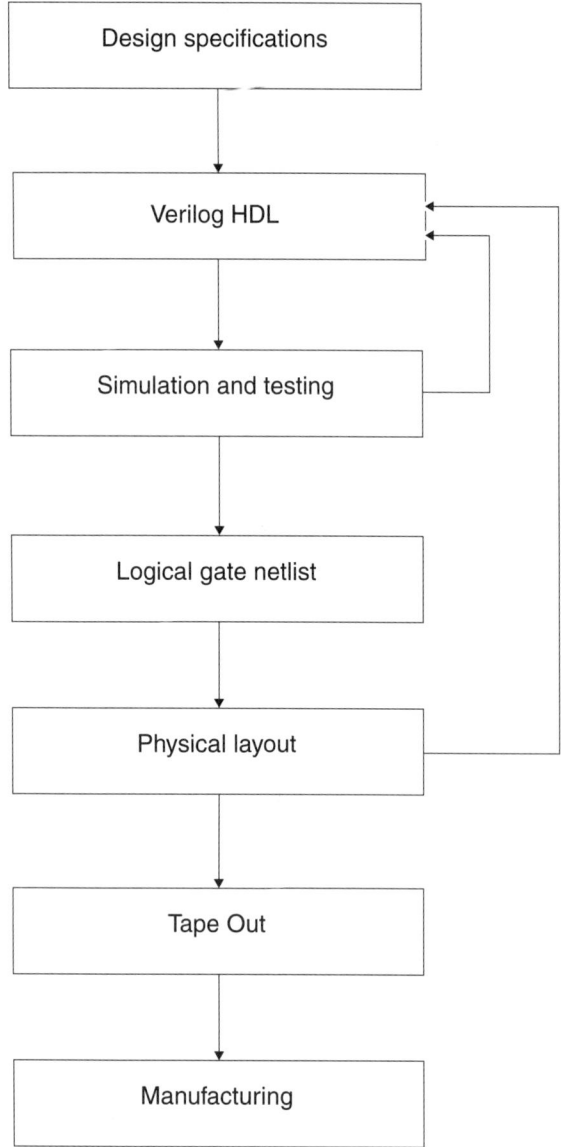

Figure 5.14. Verilog design flow.

The four different gate names are chosen as notif0 (not if enable is 0), notif1 (not if enable is 1), bufif0 (buf if enable is 0), and bufif1 (buf if enable is 1).

2. Each of the AND, OR, NAND, and NOR gates has one output with two or more inputs.

3. Each of the XOR and XNOR gates has one output with two or more

inputs. If three XOR inputs are specified, then it becomes an even parity bit generation circuit. In the following, the two primitives

```
xor(p, a, b);
xor(sum, p, cin);
```

can be replaced by

```
xor(sum, a, b, cin);
```

A primitive call may be issued in another module definition. If it is, the logic gate is instantiated into the design. In order to write modules, let us establish a naming convention as described here:

1. A logic gate, circuit, or signal name starts with a lowercase letter. Any subsequent term starts with an uppercase letter.
2. A module name is written in all uppercase letters.

At the gate design level, we attempt to define a module named OBFADDER (one-bit full adder) that issues six primitive calls:

```
/* -----------------------------------------------------------------
   Module definition of OBFADDER (ONE_BIT_FULL_ADDER)
   The three inputs are: a, b, cin (carry in).
   The two outputs are: sum, cout (carry out).
   ----------------------------------------------------------------- */
module OBFADDER (sum, cout, a, b, cin);
    /* I/O port declaration */
input a, b, cin;
output sum, cout;
    /* Declare internal net or wire connection */
wire a1, a2, a3;
    /* The xor primitive takes a, b cin as inputs and
       generates sum (even parity) as output. */
xor(sum, a, b, cin);
    /* ----------------------------------------------------
       Three 2-input AND gates and one 3-input OR
       gate are called to generate Cout.
       ---------------------------------------------------- */
and(a1, a, b);
and(a2, a, cin);
and(a3, b, cin);
or(cout, a1, a2, a3);
endmodule
```

The terminal list has a total of five dummy signal names separated by commas. The first two signals are sum and cout (carry out) for output. The next three signals are a, b, and cin for input. Four arguments are passed in the call. The first passing argument is sum for output, and the next three passing arguments are for input. There are six primitive calls, and each call means that the logic device is instantiated into the design. In a primitive call, a logic device id may be placed between the primitive name and the terminal list as an option. After the module OBFADDER is defined, a call of the module can be issued in another module definition:

OBFADDER obfa0(c1, s0, a0, b0, c0);

The logic device id is chosen as obfa0 (one-bit full adder 0), and the passing arguments are c1 (carry 1), s0 (sum 0), a0, b0, and c0 (carry 0). The two basic signals are wire and reg, as explained in the following.

5.7.3   BASIC DESIGN ELEMENTS

A wire signal represents an internal connection line between two gates. A reg (register) signal represents the output of a storage element, such as a flip-flop, or another storage device. Each type of signal can be used as an input or output port to a gate or flip-flop. If several output signals belong to an ordered set of flip-flops, they may be grouped as a vector (i.e., an array):

output [3:0] x;

The keyword *output* specifies a vector of four output port signals. A pair of square brackets is used to enclose its dimension. The upper-bound subscript is 3 and the lower-bound subscript is 0. Thus, the output vector x consists of x[0], x[1], x[2], and x[3].

5.7.4   DESIGN EXAMPLE

At the gate level, we attempt to design a four-bit carry rippled counter with D flip-flops. Assume that a D ff has three inputs: d (data), Ck (clock), and Cl (clear). The lone output is q, because \q is not available. The ff output changes state at the trailing edge of the clock. In addition, if the dc clear signal is high, the ff is reset to 0. The module definition of a D ff is:

```
/* ----------------------------------------------------------------
   Module definition of a D_FF
   1. The ff is triggered by the trailing edge of ck (clock).
```

2. The ff is cleared by the leading edge of an asynchronous cl (clear) signal.
```
----------------------------------------------------------- */
module D_FF (q, d, ck, cl);
output q;
input d, ck, cl;
reg q;
    /* ----------------------------------------------------------------
```
The D_FF always changes state at the posedge (positive edge) of a clear signal or at the negedge (negative edge) of a clock. The bit string 1'b0 is explained as follows:

1. The digit 1 is a length specifier.
2. The apostrophe is a delimiter.
3. The letter b means bit string.
4. The last digit 0 means bit 0.
```
    ----------------------------------------------------------- */
always @ (posedge cl or negedge ck)
if (cl)
    q = 1'b0;
else
    q = d;
endmodule
```

First, we build a T flip-flop out of the D flip-flop; the module definition of a T_FF (T Flip-Flop) is shown here:

```
/* --------------------------------
    Module definition of a T_FF
    -------------------------- */
module T_FF (q, ck, cl);
output q;
input ck, cl;
wire d;
D_FF dFF0 (q, d, ck, cl);
    /* ------------------------------------
```
An inverter named n0 is used to generate \q as the d input.
```
    ------------------------------------ */
not n0 (d, q);
endmodule
```

In the module definition of a four-bit carry rippled counter, four T_FF calls are issued as shown here:

```
/* ------------------------------------------------------------
        Module definition of CARRY_RIPPLED_COUNTER
   ------------------------------------------------------- */
module CARRY_RIPPLED_COUNTER (x, clk, clear);
output [3:0] x;
input clk, clear;
T_FF tFF0 (x[0], clk, clear);
T_FF tFF1 (x[1], x[0], clear);
T_FF tFF2 (x[2], x[1], clear);
T_FF tFF3 (x[3], x[2], clear);
endmodule
```

In the module definition, the T_FF tFF0 call has two meanings. The device id is tFF0 and the circuit type is T_FF. After the call is interpreted, Verilog brings an instance of the logic circuit of T_FF into the design. The logic device id is tFF0; its logic schematic is shown in Figure 5.15(a).

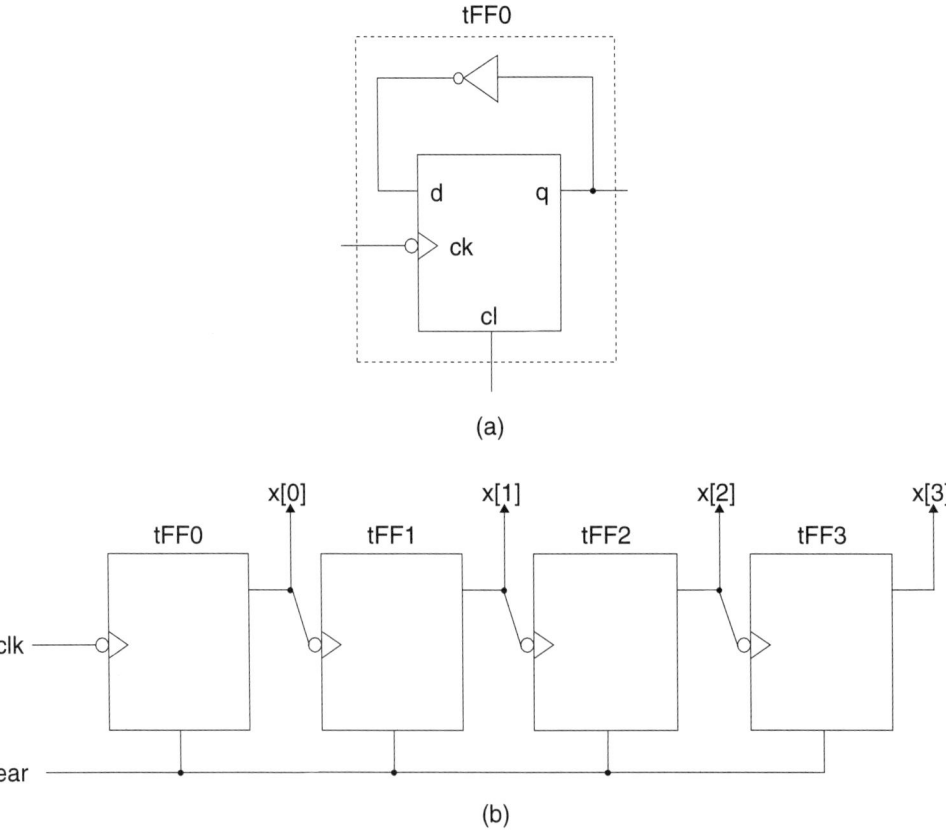

(a)

(b)

Figure 5.15. Instantiation of modules: (a) a T flip-flop and (b) a four-bit carry rippled counter.

If a CARRY_RIPPLED_COUNTER call is issued in another module, then Verilog brings the entire circuit of the four-bit carry rippled counter into the design. We further assume that passing arguments are the same as the dummy arguments in the definition block. The logic schematic of instantiation is shown in Figure 5.15(b). The counter output is declared the x vector that has four bits. Interestingly, during the second T_FF call, the passing argument is x[0], which serves as the clock input to the T flip-flop on its right. Similarly, x[1] is the clock input to the third ff, and x[2] is the clock input to the last ff, whose output is x[3]. In the counter output, x[0] is the least significant bit and x[3] is the most significant bit.

5.8 Summary Points

1. Each flip-flop may have one or two data inputs, and its output changes state based on the data input signals.
2. An asynchronous flip-flop has no clock input, so its output changes as soon as the input signal arrives.
3. In contrast, a synchronous flip-flop always has a clock input. Depending on the design, either the leading edge or the trailing edge of a clock determines the timing when its output voltage should change.
4. The characteristic equation of a flip-flop represents its storage function that specifies data input, the current state, and the next state.
5. By using one extra inverter, we can design a D flip-flop from an RS flip-flop.
6. We can make a JK flip-flop from an RS flip-flop.
7. We can make a T flip-flop from a D flip-flop, an RS flip-flop, or a JK flip-flop.
8. A register is an ordered set of flip-flops.
9. Each CPU register has high speed because data are transferred parallel in, parallel out.
10. A sequential circuit still uses combinational logic to generate excitation inputs to the flip-flops so that the state of a register changes by the next clock.
11. Each sequential circuit, also called a finite state machine, uses many flip-flops and logic gates.
12. In sequencer design, the inputs to flip-flops are specified in its excitation table.
13. An excitation table has three columns: the current state, the next state, and the excitation input.
14. The CPU executes an instruction in three phases: instruction fetch, instruction interpret, and instruction execute.

15. Logic simulation software tools are used to develop ASIC chips.
16. Verilog is a popular logic simulation language whose syntax closely follows the programming language C.
17. A system design flow chart includes logic design, software simulation, physical circuit layout, tape out, and manufacturing.
18. A module call brings an instance of the logic circuit in the module definition into the design.

Problems

5.1 Explain the function of an RS flip-flop.

5.2 What is the characteristic equation of an RS flip-flop?

5.3 Explain the timing difference between an asynchronous RS flip-flop and a synchronous RS flip-flop?

5.4 What does it mean that a flip-flop is trailing edge triggered?

5.5 In Figure 5.5(c), the schematic of a synchronous D flip-flop is made of a synchronous RS flip-flop and an inverter. Plot the truth table and find the excitation equations for input S and R. After simplifications, verify the results as follows:

1. $S = D$ 2. $R = \backslash D$

5.6 Use four RS flip-flops to design a switch-tail counter, mod 8. Find the logical equation of the sixth timing state and verify that a two-input gate should be adequate to decode the signal out.

5.7 Use four D flip-flops to design a circular shift register. Assume that its initial state is 0001, and after each clock cycle the bit 1 is shifting from left to right in a circular fashion. That is, the state changes from 0001 to 1000, 0100, 0010, and back to 0001. Plot the excitation table and simplify the D inputs, and the circuit should be fairly simple. The output of each flip-flop also signals the timing state without decoding.

5.8 When a group of D flip-flops is used to construct an I/O buffer, what kind of electric attributes can be changed during a register transfer operation?

5.9 If the T flip-flop is derived from an RS flip-flop, plot the truth table and find the excitation equations for the S input and the R input.

5.10 Why does a high-speed CPU register use the parallel-in, parallel-out transfer mode?

5.11 Five RS flip-flops are denoted T0, T1, T2, T3, and T4. Design a five-bit circular shift register whose state transition table is shown in Table 5.10.

5.12 As shown in Figure 5.1(a), the logic schematic uses two OR gates

Table 5.10. Five-bit circular shift register.

T0	T1	T2	T3	T4
1	0	0	0	0
0	1	0	0	0
0	0	1	0	0
0	0	0	1	0
0	0	0	0	1

to implement an RS flip-flop, but in Figure 5.2(c), the logic schematic uses two NAND gates instead. Verify that either design is correct because its characteristic equation is $(S + \backslash R\ Qn)$.

5.13 Show the different logic schematics of a binary trigger:

1. using a JK flip-flop.
2. using an RS flip-flop.
3. using a D flip-flop.

5.14 A synchronous counter means that all the flip-flops switch states at the same time. Use four JK flip-flops to design a synchronous decade counter that counts from 0 to 9. Based on the two adjacent counter states (X3 X2 X1 X0), plot the excitation table for all the J and K inputs. Use a four-bit K-map to simplify and draw the logic schematic.

5.15 Use two D flip-flops to design a sequencer that can generate an output 1 after receiving three consecutive 1s as input.

5.16 What is the difference between a shift register and a circular shift register?

5.17 What is the difference between a shift register and a switch-tail counter?

5.18 What are the three phases of instruction execution?

5.19 What are the four levels of design descriptions in Verilog?

5.20 Briefly describe the syntax of a module definition block in Verilog.

5.21 The following C program verifies the results from bitwise logical operations between two 32-bit integers.

```
/* ---------------------------------------------------------------
Description:
```
In the C program, we declare two 32-bit integer variables. We assign the two variables A and B with integers written in hex. A bitwise logical operator performs the logical operation on two bits at the same position in two given variables. The logical operation is performed, bit by bit, through the entire variable.

Bitwise logical operator	Description
~	NOT
&	AND
		OR
^	Exclusive OR

The two variables and the three results are printed out and the format control field %8X specifies eight hex characters with leading 0 digits suppressed. Note that the uppercase X requests an output written in uppercase, and a lowercase x requests an output written in lowercase. With some minor changes in the program, you can request interactive input from the keyboard and then output:

```
------------------------------------------------------------------------- */
#include ⟨stdio.h⟩
void main( void)
{
int a, b;
a = 0x80808080;
b = 0xf000000f;
printf( "Given: a = %8X, b = %8X in hex. \n", a, b);
printf( "The three results are: %8X %8X %8X in hex. \n", a & b,
a | b, a ^ b);
}
/* ------------ Output
Given: a = 80808080, b = F000000F in hex.
The three results are: 80000000 F080808F 7080808F in hex. */
```

Acronyms and Abbreviations

\	NOT function
.	AND function
+	OR function
⊕	Exclusive OR function
⊙	Exclusive NOR function
^	exponential; concatenate
ACM	Association of Computing Machinery
ALU	arithmetic and logic unit
ANSI	American National Standards Institute
ASCII	American Standard Code for Information Interchange
b	bit; binary digit
B	byte; billion
BCD	Binary coded decimal
bit	binary digit
BL	bit line
bps	bits per second
Bps	bytes per second
C	carry
CACM	*Communications of the ACM*
CC, cc	condition code
CD	compact disc
Cin	carry in
CMOS	complementary MOS
com	communication; commercial
Cout	carry out
CPA	carry propagated adder
CPI	clocks per instruction
CPU	central processing unit
CSA	carry save adder
D	data; drain; delay; decimal; D flip-flop

dc	define constant; direct current
DRAM	dynamic random access memory
EBCDIC	extended binary coded decimal for information inter-change
ECL	emitter coupled logic
EEPROM	electrically erasable programmable read-only memory
email	electronic mail
ENOR	Exclusive NOR function
EOR	Exclusive OR function
EPROM	erasable programmable read-only memory
exp	exponent; exponential
ff	flip-flop
fixed	fixed point
float	floating point
g, G	giga: 10^9 to measure speed or 2^{30} to measure memory size
GB	gigabyte
gbps	gigabits per second
gHz	gigaHertz
hex	hexadecimal
Hz	Hertz (cycles per second)
IC	integrated circuit
ID	instruction decoder; identifier
IEEE	Institute of Electrical and Electronic Engineers
Internet	internetworking
I/O	input/output
IOR	I/O register
IR	instruction register
JK	JK flip-flop
k, K	kilo: 10^3 to measure speed or 2^{10} (1024) to measure memory size
KB	kilobyte
km	kilometer
LAN	local area network
lsb	least significant bit
LSI	large-scale integration
m, M	meter; memory; mega: 10^6 to measure speed or 2^{20} (1,048,576) to measure memory size
MB	megabyte
μ	micro
micron	one-millionth of a meter
MOS	metal oxide semiconductor
MOSFET	MOS field effect transistor
ms	millisecond (10^{-3})
msb	most significant bit
MSI	medium-scale integration

μs	microsecond (10^{-6})
NAND	NOT AND function
NMOS	N-channel MOS
NOR	NOT OR function
ns	nanosecond (10^{-9})
O	octal; overflow
Op	opcode; operation code; operator
org	origin; organization
OS	operating system
P	peta: 2^{15} to measure memory size; parity; program
PB	petabyte
PC	program counter; printed circuit
PLA	programmable logic array
PMOS	P-channel MOS
POS	product of sum
Proc	procedure; proceedings
PROM	programmable ROM
ps	picosecond (10^{-12})
R	register; reset; resistor
RAM	random access memory
ROM	read-only memory
RS	RS flip-flop; recommended standard
RTL	Register Transfer Language
S	sign; source; set
Si	Silicon
SL	source line
SOC	system on chip
SOP	sum of product
SRAM	static random access memory
SSI	small-scale integration
T	trigger; T flip-flop; trillion; tera: 2^{12} to measure memory size
TB	terabyte
Thz	trillion Hertz
Trans	transactions
TTL	transistor-transistor logic
UART	universal asynchronous receiver/transmitter
ULSI	ultralarge-scale integration
v.	volt
Vcc	voltage collector
Vdd	voltage drain
Vss	voltage source
VLSI	very large-scale integration
WORM	write once read-only memory
WWW	World Wide Web
Z	zero

APPENDIX B

Logic Symbols and Equations

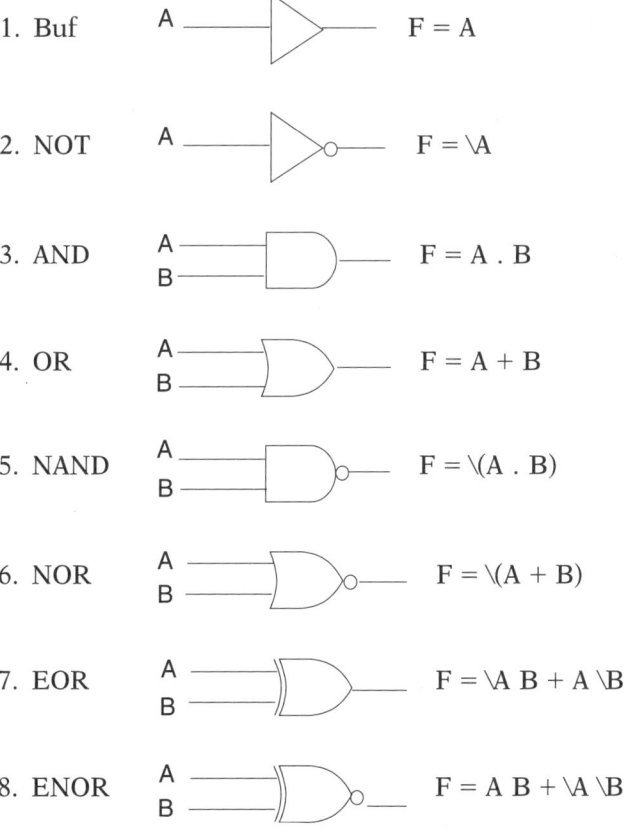

1. Buf   A ⟶ ▷   F = A

2. NOT   A ⟶ ▷○   F = \A

3. AND   A, B ⟶   F = A . B

4. OR   A, B ⟶   F = A + B

5. NAND   A, B ⟶   F = \(A . B)

6. NOR   A, B ⟶   F = \(A + B)

7. EOR   A, B ⟶   F = \A B + A \B

8. ENOR   A, B ⟶   F = A B + \A \B

References

[Brau99] Braun, A. E. Copper moves CMP to center stage, *Semiconductor International*, Vol. 22, No. 14, Dec. 1999, pp. 54–62.

[Broc00] Brock, D. E., et al. Superconductor ICs: The 100 Ghz generation, *IEEE Spectrum*, Dec. 2000, pp. 40–46.

[Burk46] Burks, A., von Neumann, J., and Goldstine, H. Preliminary discussion of the logical design of an electronic computing instrument, Institute for Advanced Study, Princeton, NJ, 1946.

[Comp96] *Computer*, Special issue on 50 years of computing, IEEE, Oct. 1996.

[Dace55] Dacey, G. C., and Ross, I. M. The field effect transistor, *Bell System Technical Journal*, Vol. 37, 1955, pp. 1149–89.

[Hsu01] Hsu, J. Y. *Computer Architecture: Software Aspects, Coding, and Hardware*, CRC Press, 2001.

[Hsu96] Hsu, J. Y. *Computer Networks: Architecture, Protocols, and Software*, Artech House, 1996.

[IEEE91] IEEE Standard 91, Graphic Symbols for Logic Functions, Institute of Electrical and Electronics Engineers, Inc., New York, NY 10017, 1991.

[Karn53] The map method for synthesis of combination logic circuits, *Trans. AIEE Comm. Electronics*, Vol. 72, 1953, pp. 593–9.

[Lenk97] Lenk, J. D. *Simplified Design of Data Converters*, Newnes, Boston, MA, 1997.

[Paln96] Palnitkar, S. *Verilog HDL: A Guide to Digital Design and Synthesis*, Prentice Hall, 1996.

[Pawl84] Pawloski, M. B., et al. Inside CMOS technology, reprinted in *Microcontroller Handbook*, Intel Corp., Santa Clara, CA 95051, 1984.

[Sher01] Sherwin, R. M. Memory on the move, *IEEE Spectrum*, Vol. 38, No. 5, May 2001, pp. 55–9.

[Tred96] Tredennick, N. Microprocessor-based computers, *Computer*, Oct. 1996. pp. 27–37.

[Unicode] The Unicode Standard 3.0, Addison Wesley, 1992.

[wwwa] http://www.unicode.org

[Verilog] Verilog Language Reference Manual, Cadence Design Systems, San Jose, CA 95134.

Index